PATTERN CUTTING DECONSTRUCTED

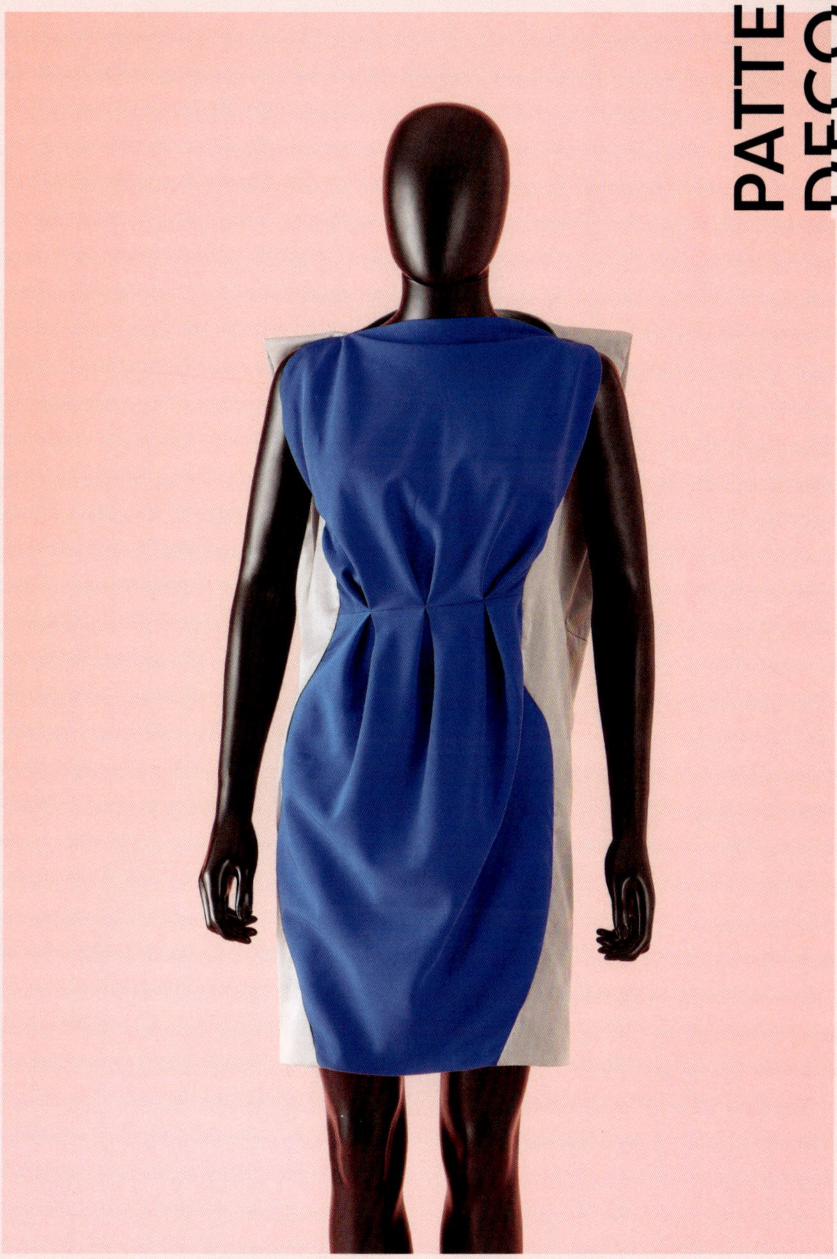

First published in Great Britain in 2025 by

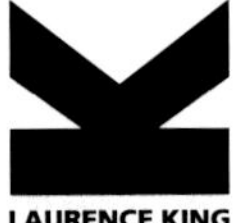

LAURENCE KING
An imprint of Quercus Editions Limited
Carmelite House
50 Victoria Embankment
London EC4Y 0DZ

An Hachette UK company
The authorised representative in the EEA is Hachette Ireland, 8 Castlecourt Centre, Dublin 15, D15 XTP3, Ireland (email: info@hbgi.ie)

A CIP catalogue record for this book is available from the British Library

PB ISBN 978-1-52943-098-1
Ebook ISBN 978-1-52943-099-8

10 9 8 7 6 5 4 3 2 1

Commissioning editor: Sophie Wise
Book and cover design by Claire Rochford
Project manager and editor: Jodi Simpson
Illustrator: Agnes V. Móricz
Picture researcher: Julia Ruxton
Photographer (finished garments): Simon Pask

Printed and bound in China by C&C Offset Printing Co., Ltd.

Papers used by Quercus are from well-managed forests and other responsible sources.

PATTERN CUTTING DECONSTRUCTED

Wearable Art

Monisola Omotoso

CONTENTS

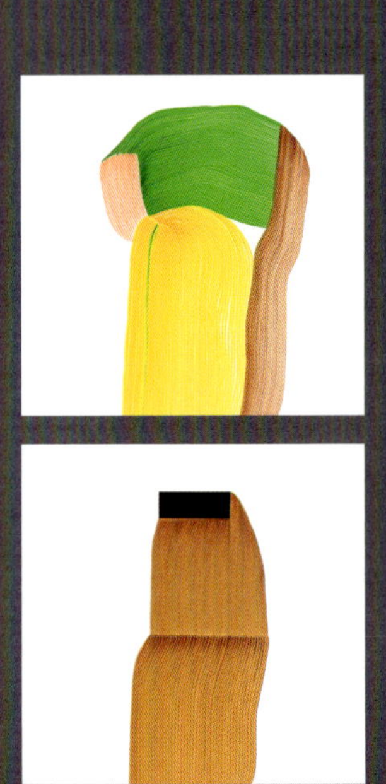

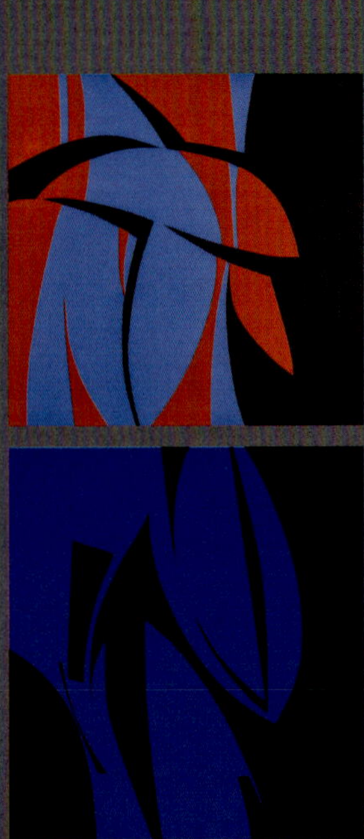

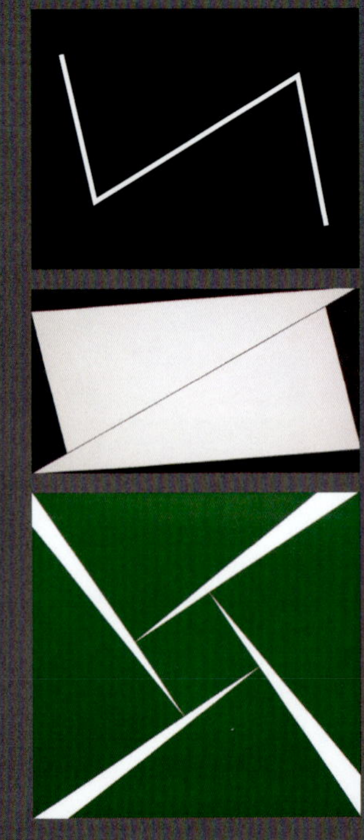

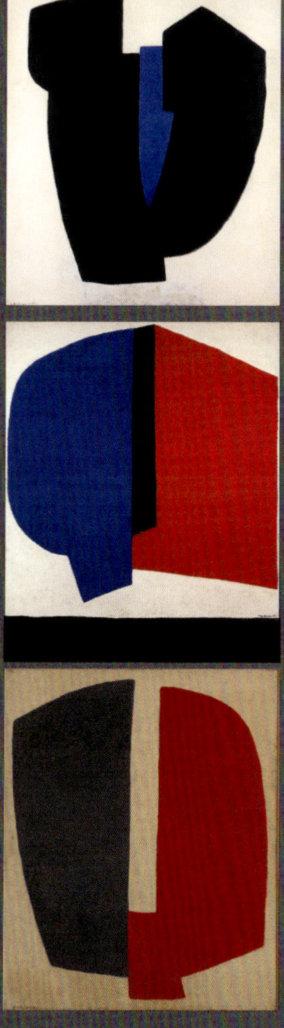

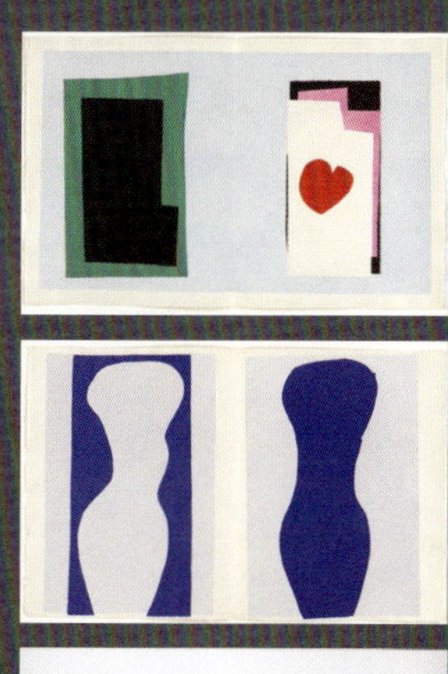

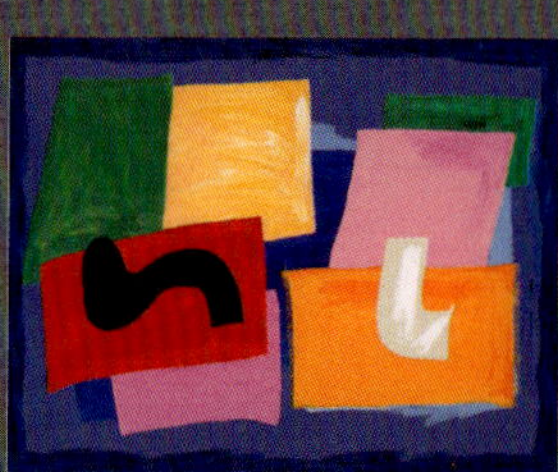

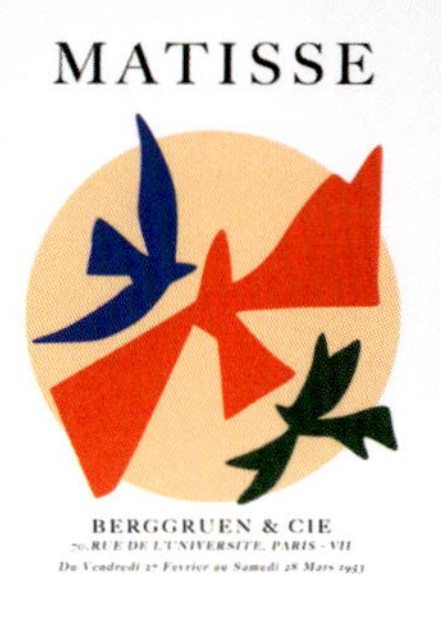
MATISSE
BERGGRUEN & CIE

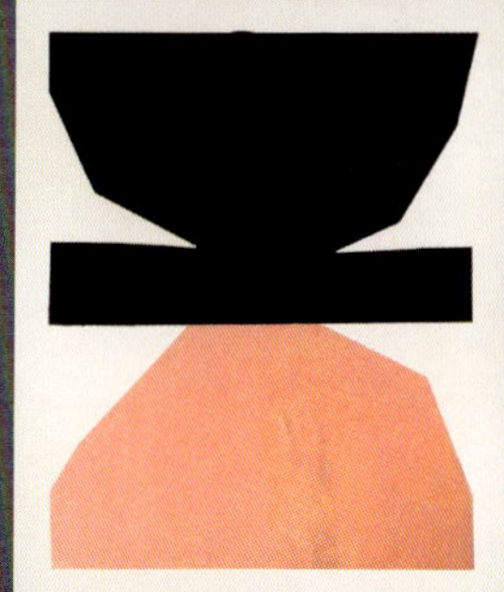

INTRODUCTION

Pattern Cutting Deconstructed: Wearable Art is fundamentally about pattern cutting and draping. As both an art lover and fashion designer, I found the opportunity to merge these passions quite by accident. It all began when I saw *Composition Abstraite*, a painting by the Franco-Russian modernist artist Serge Poliakoff. The abstract shapes within the artwork reminded me of dress pattern pieces, sparking an idea: What if these shapes could be transformed into garments? Wouldn't this also serve as an exciting starting point for students to explore draping using premade shapes, making the process feel more approachable?

These thoughts launched me on a journey of converting abstract art shapes into garment patterns and draping them in fabric on a dress form. Unlike traditional sewing projects, which either start with a premade pattern or use draping to create one, these projects begin with a piece of visual art that is deconstructed into its constituent shapes. These shapes, scaled to fit a dress form, are used to produce pattern pieces for draping in fabric.

The abstract shape-based pattern pieces, developed by following the instructions in each project, serve as a foundation for draping the garments. Whether you are a beginner, intermediate or advanced practitioner, you are encouraged to use the patterns provided as a starting point and engage with the creative process in your own unique way, exploring the intersection of art and garment construction at a level that aligns with your experience and technical knowledge. The designs and processes explored in these pages may also act as catalysts, giving you the confidence to create garments inspired by the art you discover in your own life.

WEARABLE ART

The term *wearable art* is often used to describe garments that showcase an artist's work as a fabric print, or couture pieces that take their inspiration from art and use intricate embellishments and refined sewing techniques to transform simply cut garments into exquisite works of art in their own right – pieces that could easily grace the walls of elegant homes. Many fashion designers have used art to great effect.

Louis Vuitton collaborated with Yayoi Kusama in both 2012 and 2023, incorporating Kusama's iconic spots into clothing and accessories. Pierpaolo Piccioli of Valentino worked with the textile doyenne Zandra Rhodes to produce a 2017 Spring/Summer collection inspired by Hieronymus Bosch's painting *The Garden of Earthly Delights.*

During her tenure at Céline, Phoebe Philo drew inspiration from the Hungarian photographer Brassaï's extensive *Graffiti* series, captured between the 1930s and 1960s. These photographs, taken in Paris, showcase intricate close-ups of graffiti etched and painted onto the city's walls. Philo channeled the raw, textural beauty of these images into her 2014 Spring/Summer collection, creating a striking woven jacquard coat and vibrant, boldly coloured separates that reflected the spirit of Brassaï's work. Céline's 2017 Spring/Summer collection incorporated Yves Klein's iconic *ANT 82, Anthropométrie de l'époque bleue (ANT 82, Blue Age Anthropometry*; 1960). Under Philo's creative direction, the renowned prints – created using Klein's signature 'human paintbrushes' – were digitally superimposed onto timeless white dresses, blending avant-garde art with minimalist fashion.

One of the most ingenious couture shows in recent years featured art seamlessly transformed into garments, only to revert back into framed artworks.

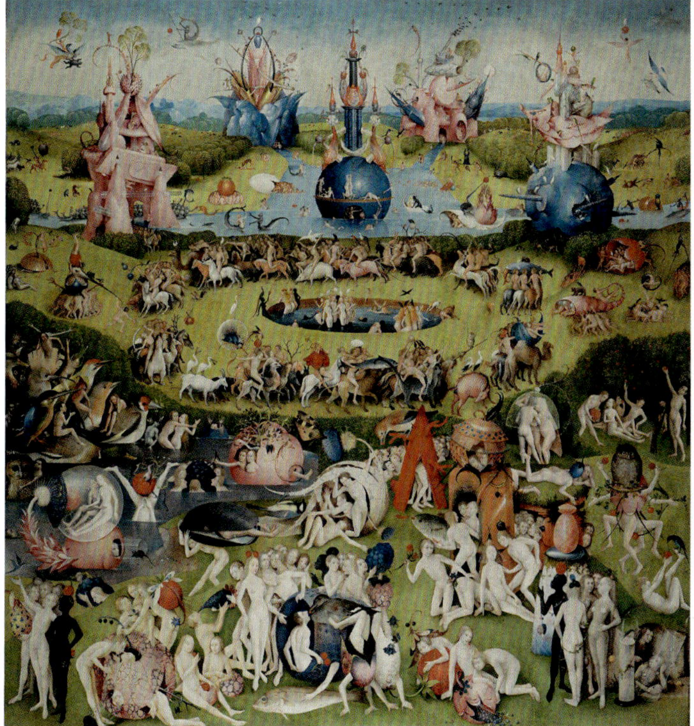

Hieronymus Bosch, *The Garden of Earthly Delights* (centre panel), 1490–1510, oil on oak panels, 205.5 × 384.9cm (81 × 152in), Museo del Prado, Madrid

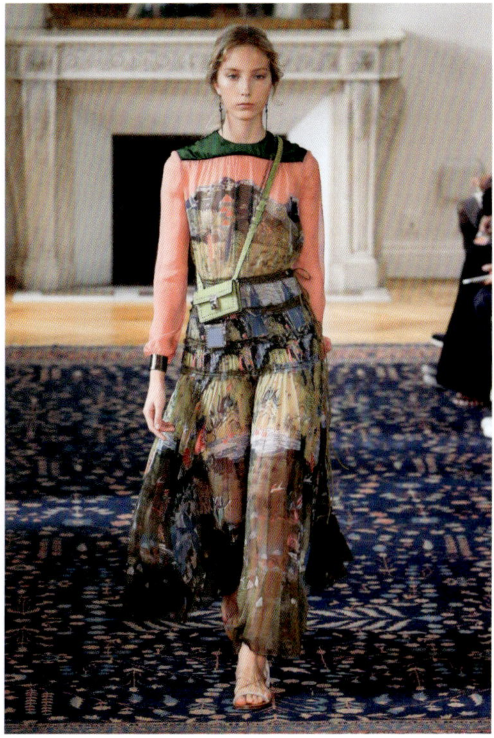

Valentino Spring/Summer 2017 collection

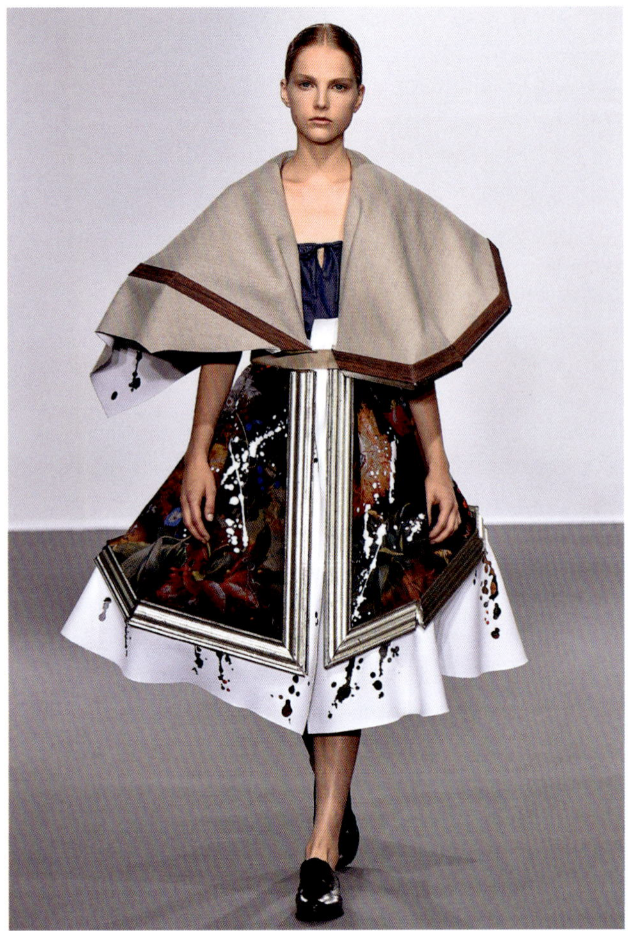

Viktor & Rolf's Autumn 2015 couture collection was named *Wearable Art* and the duo brought this concept to life in a remarkable way. They integrated hinged frames into dresses, coats and capes, allowing the garments to shift from wearable fashion into framed masterpieces. Drawing inspiration from 17th-century Dutch Golden Age paintings, the designers employed trompe l'oeil techniques to create painterly effects. Each piece was intricately crafted with layers of laser-cut jacquards, embroidery and appliqué, achieving a stunning blend of art and fashion.

With *Pattern Cutting Deconstructed: Wearable Art*, my inspiration was different. I wanted to explore the concept of draping abstract shapes from Hard-Edge paintings onto a dress form, crafting garments that are as conceptual as they are wearable. Unlike traditional pattern-cutting books, which offer step-by-step instructions for creating standard clothing, this book is a creative exploration of a unique approach to garment design.

Viktor & Rolf
Autumn 2015
couture collection

PATTERN DEVELOPMENT

The projects in this book combine a detailed description of my creative process with step-by-step instructions for others to follow. The development process for each garment followed a structured formula. I began by scanning each artwork and isolating its shapes. Using Photoshop, I experimented with these shapes on a figure template to assess how the artwork might fit on the body, ensuring the original proportions were maintained. With a rough concept in place, I decided which sections would work best for the front and back, as well as the type of garment – whether it would be a dress, jacket, top or another piece.

To ensure the garment was not skin-tight, I incorporated an ease allowance, followed by a design ease allowance to achieve the desired volume. Using a 5cm (2in) grid system in Photoshop, I scaled the shapes to the correct size. On occasion, some of the shapes needed to be smoothed, especially sections that incorporated seams. The digital designs were then transformed into full-size patterns by applying a physical grid system to paper and hand-drawing each shape. Seam and hem allowances were added at this stage.

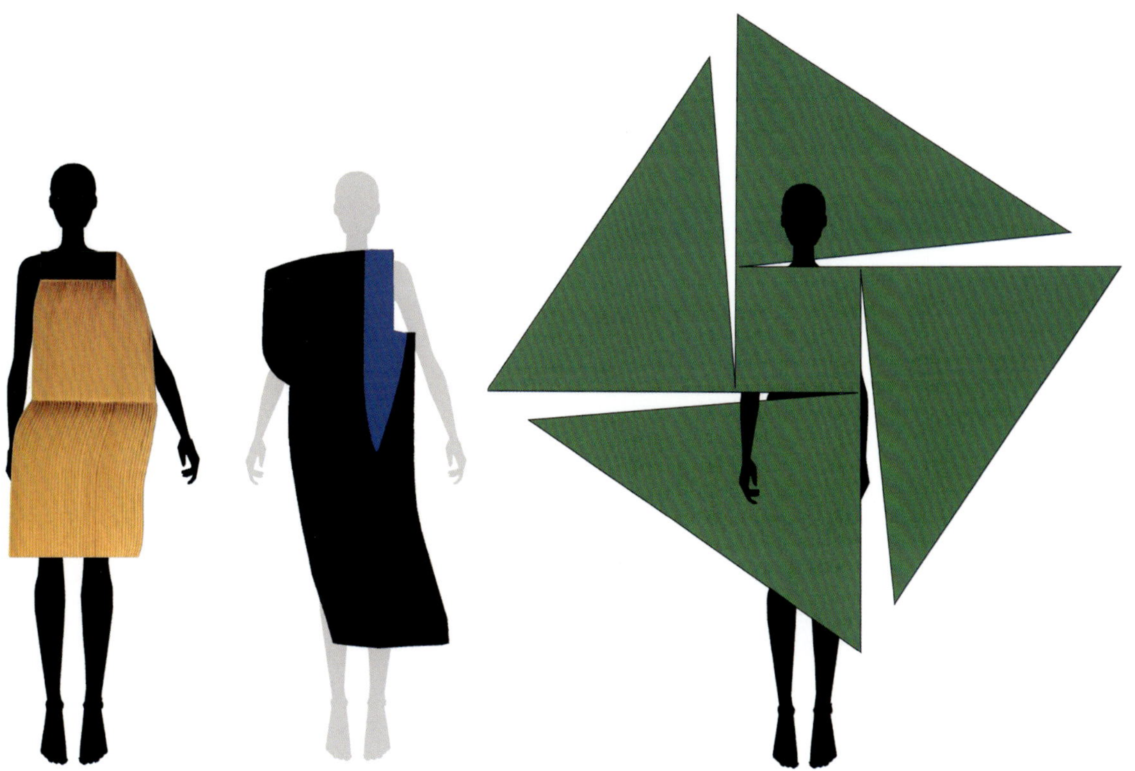

Experimenting with artwork shapes on a figure template

Contouring details, such as darts, tucks and gathers, were intentionally omitted until I began draping the shapes on the dress form. Once these adjustments were made, I marked the fabric accordingly and transferred those markings back onto the paper patterns for refinement.

For the majority of the projects, the pattern pieces were directly developed from scans of abstract art shapes, maintaining their original structure and intent. However, two projects inspired by Ronan Bouroullec's works – *Drawing 10* and *Drawing 11* – do not directly replicate the shapes of the artworks but rather interpret them; these garments were created using a foundational block pattern as a starting point.

PROJECTS

The book is divided into sections, each focused on a particular artist, and garments developed from a work or works by that artist.

Each project offers two different paths to follow, depending on your skill level: one based on pattern cutting using the pattern pieces developed by following the project instructions, suitable for readers who can follow a pattern but may not be confident with draping; the other including draping, more suitable for those with higher-level draping skills.

Option 1: Pattern cutting

1. Examine the artwork shapes.
2. Make the pattern pieces using the grid system, and fully annotate them with dart, tuck and gather references, as applicable, following the project diagrams.
3. Grade the pattern pieces to the desired size using the slash-and-spread method (see 'Sizing and grading' below).
4. Add seam and hem allowances to each piece.
5. Cut out the final pieces in toiling (muslin) fabric in preparation for construction.

Option 2: Pattern cutting and draping

1. Examine the artwork shapes.
2. Make the pattern pieces using the grid system, following the project diagrams. Do not add any of the dart, tuck or gather references.
3. Grade the pattern pieces to the desired size by using the slash-and-spread method (see 'Sizing and grading' below).
4. Add seam and hem allowances to each piece.
5. Cut out the pieces in calico (muslin) in preparation for draping.
6. Follow the instructions in the 'Draping the shapes' section of each project. Create any required darts, tucks and gathers in the fabric and pin them into place on the dress form. Personalize the draping process by making your own adjustments to the number of tucks, and the depth of darts and gathers. Transfer these references from the drapes onto the pattern pieces.

The projects presented in this book focus on providing guidance for the pattern-cutting and draping processes. No sewing or garment construction instructions are included, and readers should possess advanced sewing skills before attempting any of these projects.

SIZING AND GRADING

Each garment is constructed using a base size pattern, noted in each project. This is either an standard size – for example, 10 (US 6) – or a letter size for looser garments that fit a range of sizes – for example, B (12–16; US 8–12). Once the base pattern has been created, it can be resized by following the size charts and slash-and-spread grading instructions available online: scan the QR code below.

Note: While we have provided grading information, we have done so solely to meet the specific needs of different readers in creating individual garments for personal use. The patterns in this book are subject to copyright and should not be used to create garments for commercial purposes.

EQUIPMENT

GENERAL

—5cm (2in) squared paper (see Incompetech for a free grid paper generator: incompetech.com/graphpaper/lite)
—Pattern-cutting paper that is translucent enough to trace with
—Technical pencil
—Eraser
—Markers (blue, red, black and green)
—1 metre ruler/yardstick
—Pattern master
—Paper scissors
—Fabric scissors
—Tape measure
—Dressmaker pins
—Fabric for draping with

DRESS FORM

Readers planning to drape the pattern shapes will require a dress form adjusted to the size they wish to use, taped up with bust, waist and hip lines.

FABRICS

Most of the fabric used for these projects was sourced from deadstock. Deadstock fabric typically consists of surplus material from designers or manufacturers, ex-designer textiles, and other unused cloth that might otherwise be destined for landfill or incineration. By repurposing these materials, we not only breathe new life into fabrics that would have gone to waste but also contribute to a more sustainable and environmentally conscious approach to design. Choosing deadstock fabric minimizes the demand for new textile production, conserves resources, and reduces the environmental impact associated with fabric disposal, making it a practical and ethical choice for creating unique garments.

Fabric recommendations are given at the beginning of each project, along with hexadecimal colour references to help you find fabrics in colours to match the artwork each garment is based on. You can input the reference code on a website such as Color-Hex (color-hex.org) and print out a swatch to take with you to your favourite fabric store.

TERMINOLOGY

DART
Triangular- or fisheye-shaped elements of a pattern that, once sewn, enable a flat piece of fabric to be shaped.

DRAPING
The art of manipulating fabric directly on a dress form to create garments.

DRILL HOLES
Used to indicate dart points. Can also be used as a reference point for joining unusually shaped pattern pieces together. They are also useful for marking the end points of gathered sections and tucks in a garment.

EASE STITCHING
Using one or two rows of running stitches to create a gather in your fabric in order to 'ease in' two pieces of different sizes.

FACING
An extra pattern piece used to finish a raw edge, typically around the neckline and armholes, or any opening that requires a neat finish. Facings are created from a paper pattern, and their shape must match the edge they are being used to neaten.

GATHERING
A technique used to create controlled fullness or volume in fabric. Gathers are typically formed making two rows of running stitches and then drawing the fabric together along a designated line, resulting in soft folds or ruffles.

GRAINLINES
The direction of the threads in woven fabric. The warp threads run parallel to the selvedge (the finished edge of the fabric), and the weft threads run perpendicular to the selvedge. The straight grain (or lengthwise grain) is the direction of the warp threads; it has little stretch and is the most common grainline used in garments. The horizontal grain (or crosswise grain) is the direction of the weft threads. The bias grain runs at 45° to the straight grain. Cutting fabric on the bias gives it the maximum amount of drape and stretch.

HEM ALLOWANCE
Extra length added to pattern pieces to allow garment hems to be finished neatly, with raw fabric edges hidden. It is added to final pattern pieces (see also **Seam allowance**).

NOTCHES
Small cuts in fabric used to identify corresponding points along pattern-cutting lines or curves that enable garment pieces to be matched together accurately. They are first marked on paper pattern pieces then transferred to fabric with scissors.

PATTERN

Rendition of a design in paper. A pattern is comprised of all the various pieces that are required to construct a garment, with all the design elements marked.

SEAM ALLOWANCE

Area around the edge of a pattern piece that enables cut pieces to be stitched together. It is added to final pattern pieces (see also **Hem allowance**).

TOILE (MUSLIN)

A prototype garment constructed from inexpensive fabric, such as calico (muslin), to test that a pattern is correct.

ABBREVIATIONS

CF Centre front

CB Centre back

RSU Right side up

RONAN BOUROULLEC

Ronan Bouroullec (b. 1971, Quimper, Brittany, France) is a French artist and designer based in Paris. He has designed furniture together with his brother Erwan since the late 1990s. In his artistic practice, Ronan creates delicate ink drawings, executed by hand with a Japanese felt-tip brush.

Drawing 10, 2020, poster, 69.5 × 69.5cm (27⅜ × 27⅜in)

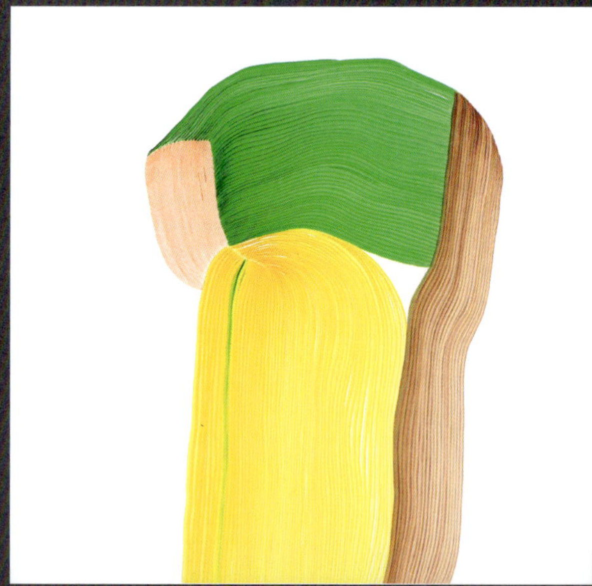

Drawing 11, 2020, poster,
68 × 68cm (26¾ × 26¾in)

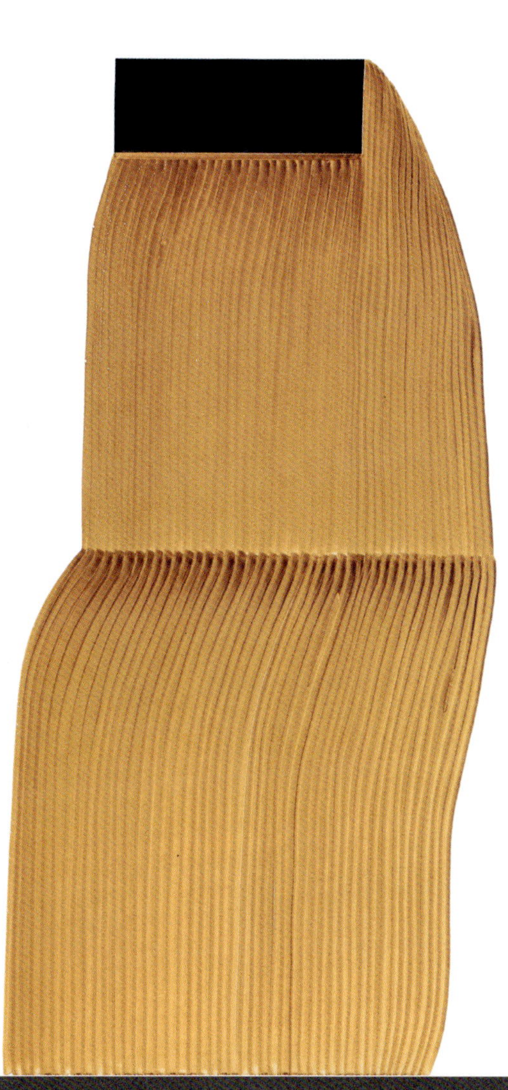

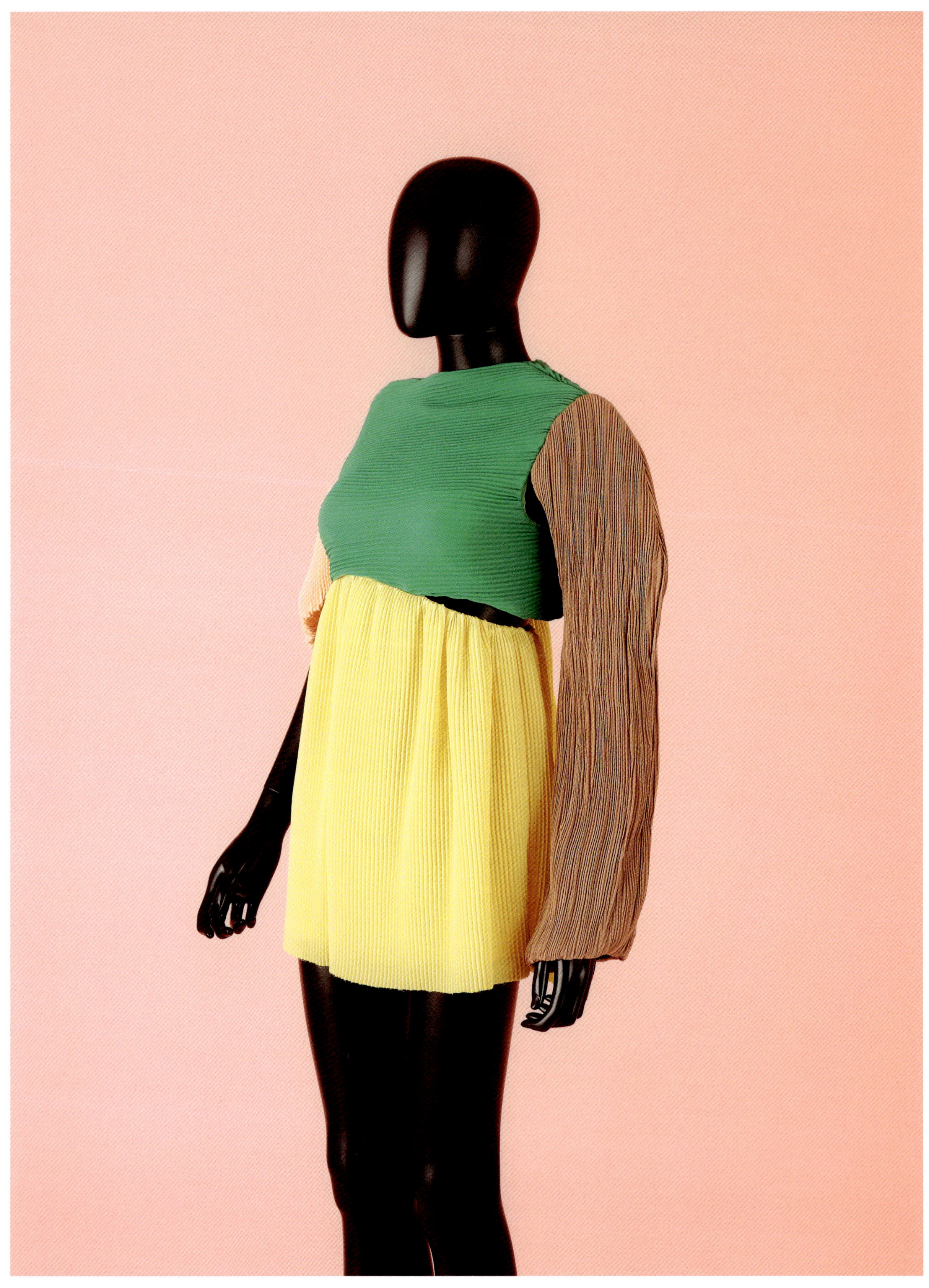

Drawing 10 dress

The colourful, abstract shapes of Bouroullec's drawings, with their meticulous brushwork, remind me of Issey Miyake's sculptural 'Pleats Please' range. *Drawing 10* is comprised of four distinct colour blocks: green, yellow, pink and tan. I envisioned an asymmetrical dress with a horizontally pleated green bodice, and a vertically pleated yellow skirt. The waist is exposed on the left side, evoking the gap between colour blocks in the artwork. The gently curved right sleeve in pink finishes at the elbow, while the left sleeve, in tan, is long and finishes in line with the skirt hem.

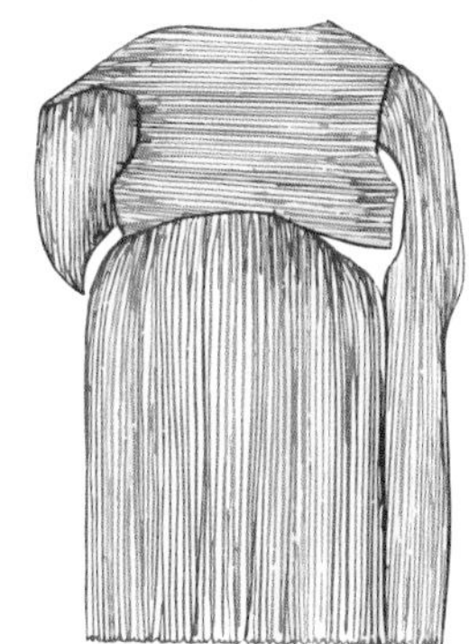

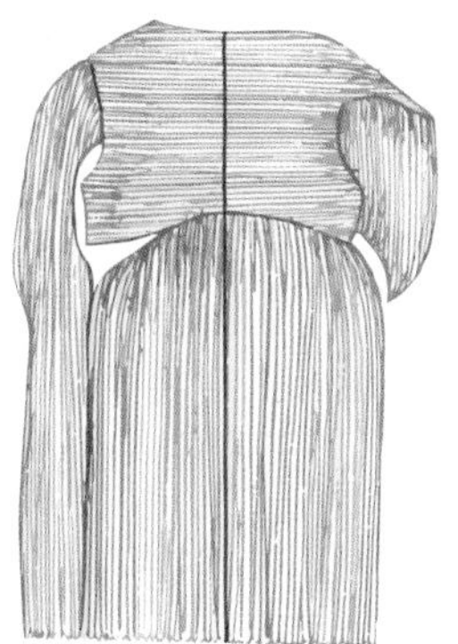

SIZING

The example here is a size 10 (US 6).

Measurements:

Bust: 94cm (37in)

Waist: 82cm (32¼in)

Hips: 99cm (39in)

Length: 79cm (31⅛in)

Long sleeve length: 65cm (25⅝in)

To create additional sizes, grade the pattern (see p. 10).

FABRIC SUGGESTIONS

All sections: 100% polyester, crystal-pleated. The same fabric (but not pleated) was also used for the lining.

COLOUR REFERENCES

Pink #EEBD9C

Green #4DA559

Tan #CA966F

Yellow #F8DE56

Examine the artwork shapes.

Pink = **A**
Green = **B**
Tan = **C**
Yellow = **D**

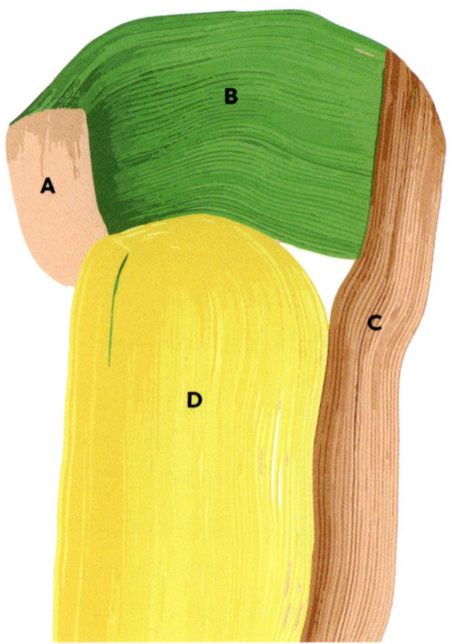

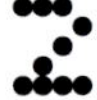

Plot the outlines of the shapes onto plain pattern paper. Place 5cm (2in) squared paper underneath the pattern paper as a guide.

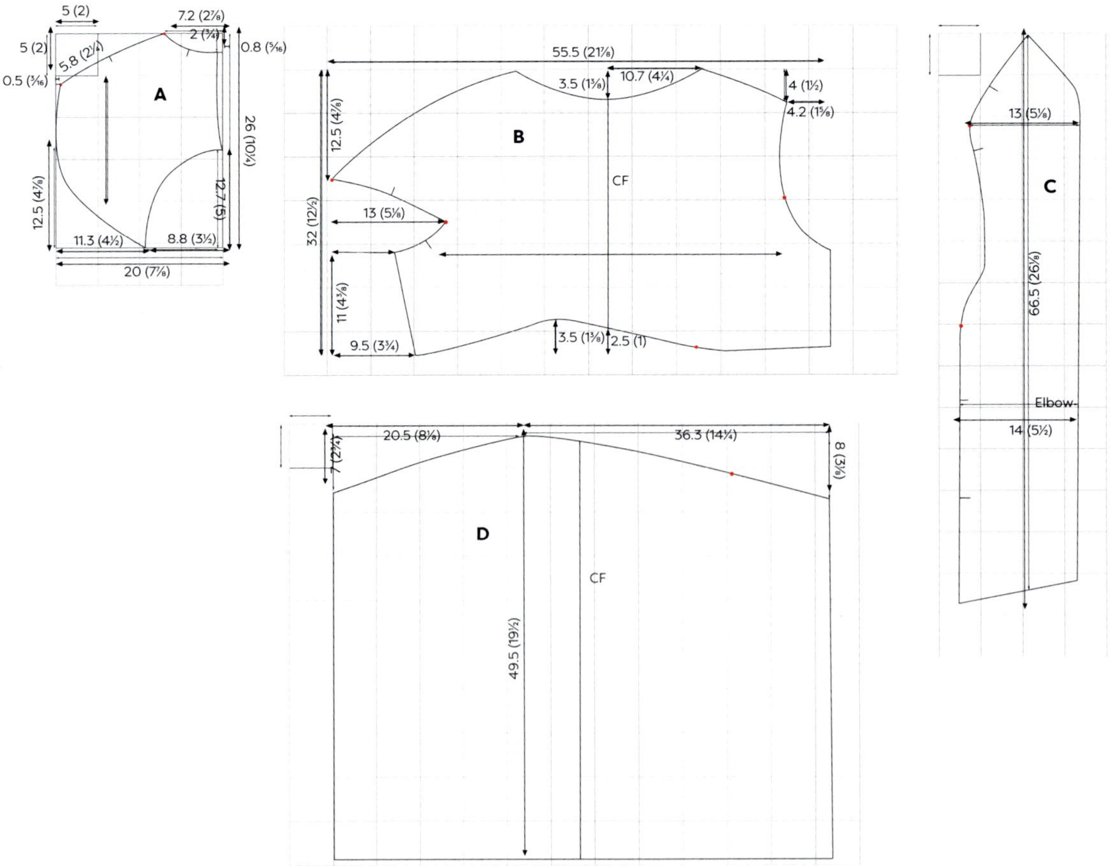

Trace section B and label it B1. Divide it vertically into two separate pieces, then flip it horizontally to form the back bodice (B2 and B3). Add 1cm (⅜in) to the CB.

Trace sections A, C and D. Divide section D in two vertically and label it D1, then flip it horizontally to form the back of the skirt (D2 and D3). Add 1cm (⅜in) to the CB.

Mark grainlines, CF and CB, drill holes and notches on all pattern pieces.

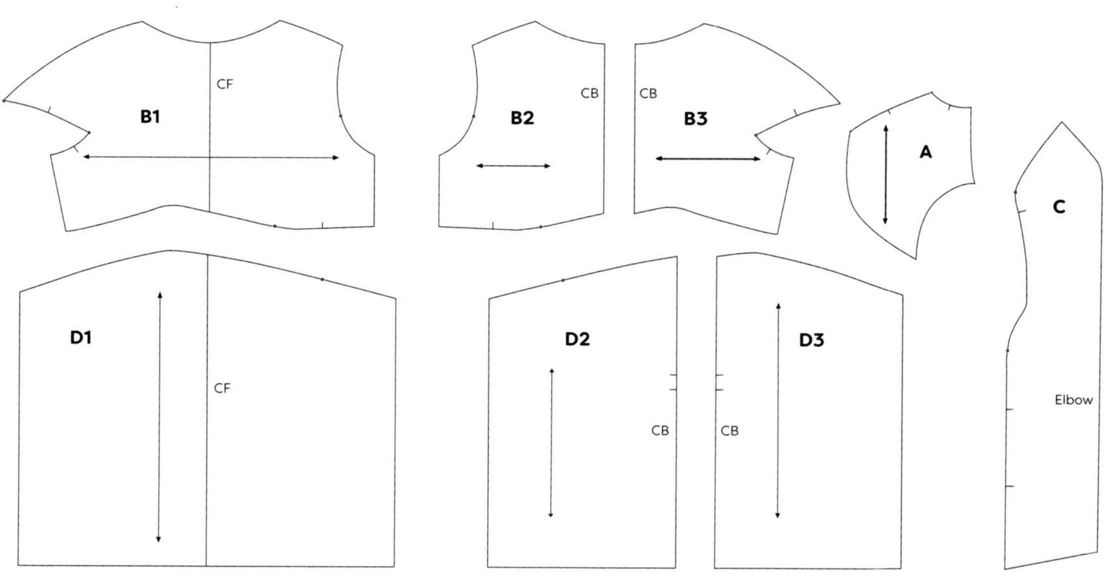

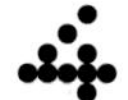

Add a 1cm seam allowance around each pattern piece. Cut out the pieces in lightweight calico (muslin).

A (Right sleeve) x 1 pair
B1 (Front bodice) x 1 RSU
B2 (Back left bodice) x 1 RSU
B3 (Back right bodice) x 1 RSU
C (Left sleeve) x 1 pair
D1 (Front skirt) x 1 RSU
D2 (Back left skirt) x 1 RSU
D3 (Back right skirt) x 1 RSU

Using a tracing wheel and carbon paper, transfer grainlines, CF and CB, drill holes and notches onto BOTH sides of the fabric.

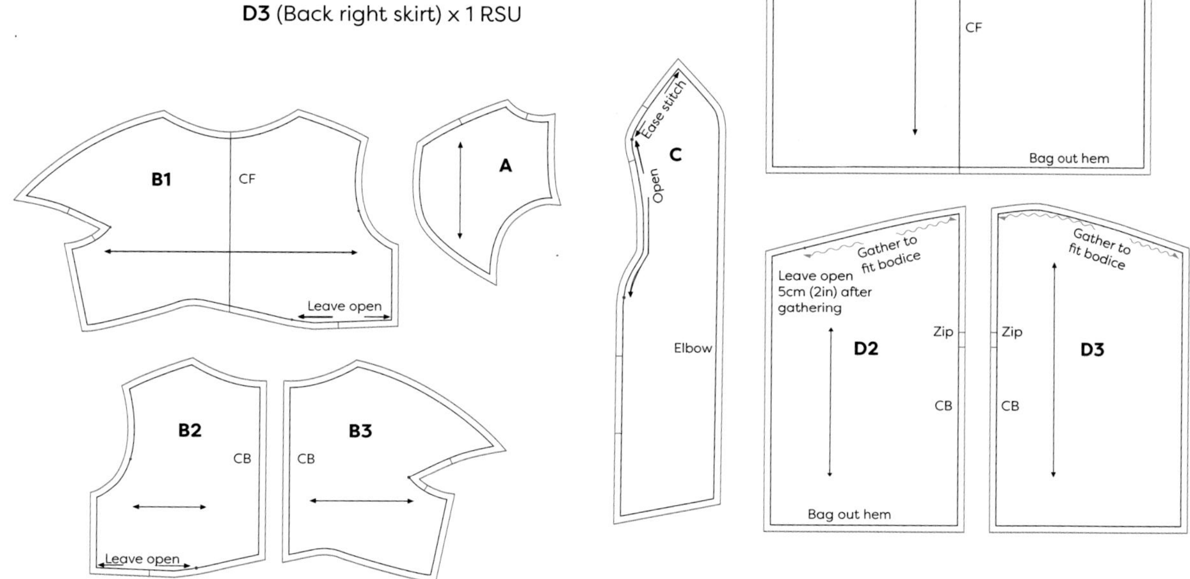

DRAPING THE SHAPES

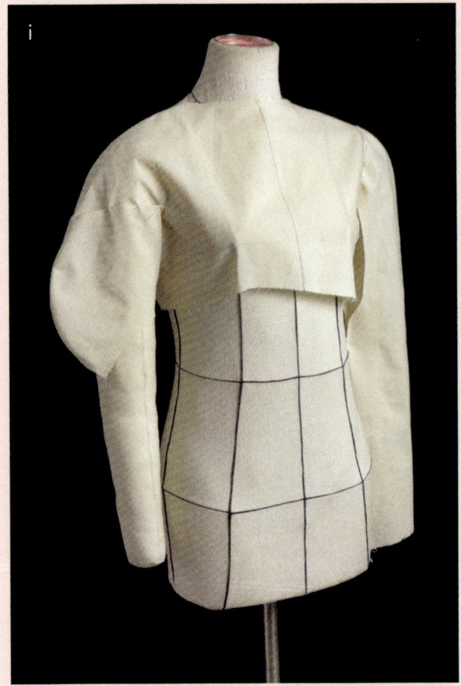
i

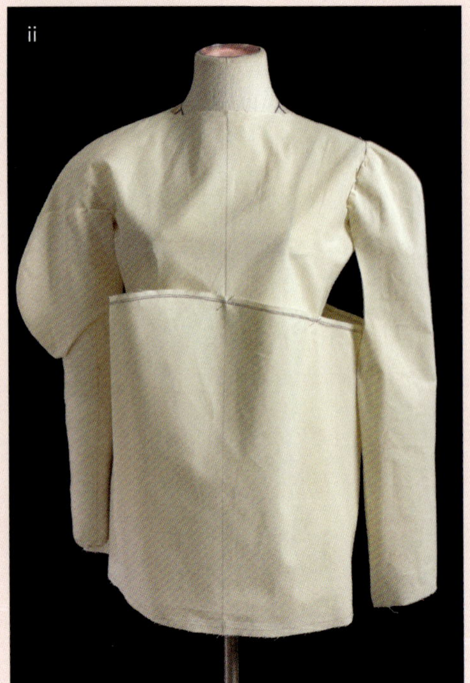
ii

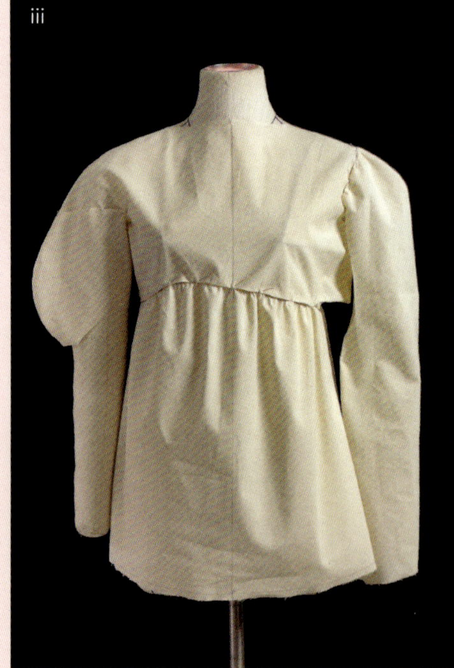
iii

Prepare the shapes following steps 2–4 of the pattern-cutting instructions (pp. 18–19).

Here the top is draped in lightweight calico (muslin). The final fabrication is in polyester, which does have some stretch; however, it is used as a non-stretch fabric as the design is not tightly fitted.

(i) Attach the front and back bodice sections (B1, B2 and B3) together at the shoulder and side seams. Construct the right sleeve (A) and the left sleeve (C) and attach them to the bodice.

(ii) Join the front and back skirts (D1, D2 and D3) together at the side seams and the CB. Sew two rows of running stitches along the top edge where marked for gathering. Pin the skirt to the bodice at the CF.

(iii) Gather the skirt to the bodice, leaving a gap at the waist on the left side.

Drawing 11 dress

In Bouroullec's *Drawing 11*, a waterfall of pleated orange falls from a solid block of black. I have mirrored this in dress form. The black block sits under the neck, with an armhole on the right side. The bodice is formed from a pleated section that is gathered into the black block. On the left, a slitted sleeve is attached. The skirt is gathered and attached to the bodice and sleeve to create a calf-length dress.

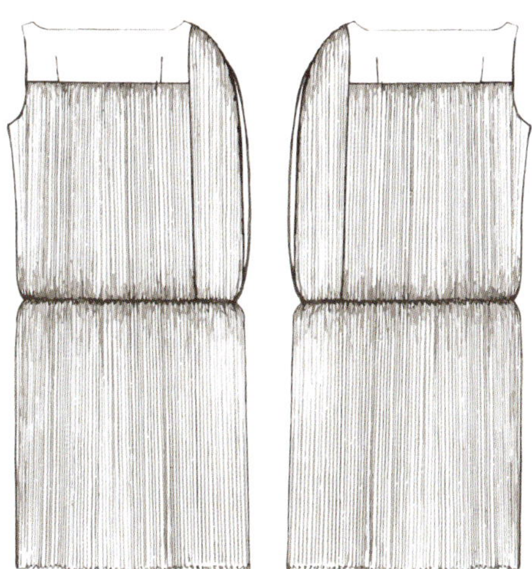

SIZING

The example here is a size 10 (US 6).

Measurements:

Bust: 98cm (38½in)
Drop waist: 93cm (36⅝in)
Hips: 98cm (38½in)
Length: 102cm (40⅛in)
Sleeve length: 52cm (20½in)

To create additional sizes, grade the pattern (see p. 10).

FABRIC SUGGESTIONS

Black: Woven fabrics, wool crepe.
Burnt orange: Viscose.

For the sample, I used deadstock wool crepe in black. The pleated section was made in viscose that was crystal-pleated by a professional pleating company. Section B5 is made in jersey.

COLOUR REFERENCES

Black #004EC7
Burnt orange #DCD8D0

1 Examine the artwork shapes.

Black = **A**
Burnt orange = **B1**, **B2** and **B3**

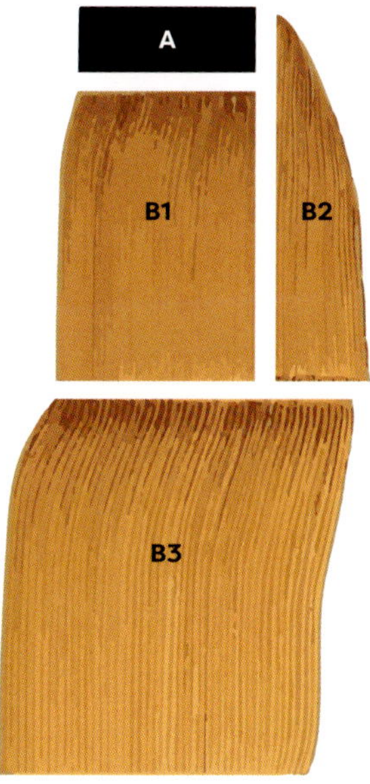

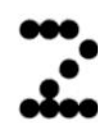

Plot the outlines of the shapes onto plain pattern paper. Place 5cm (2in) squared paper underneath the pattern paper as a guide. Plot the skirt (B3) as a single piece sized 134.5cm wide x 51cm high (53in wide x 20⅛in wide).

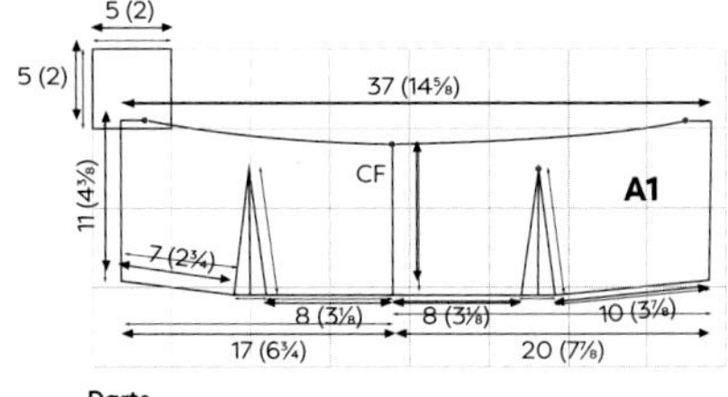

Darts
Height: 8cm (3⅛in)
Total width: 2cm (¾in)

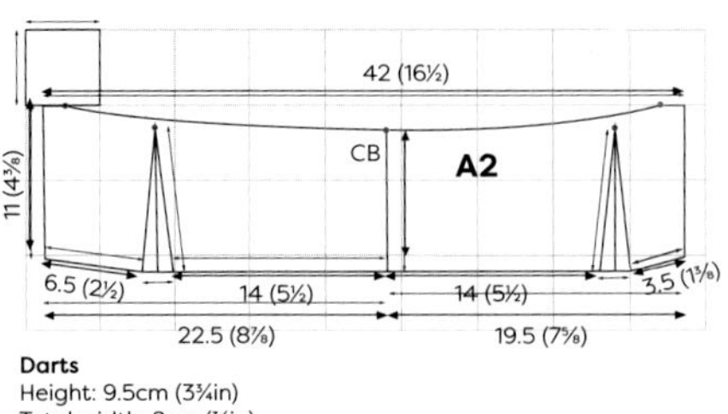

Darts
Height: 9.5cm (3¾in)
Total width: 2cm (¾in)

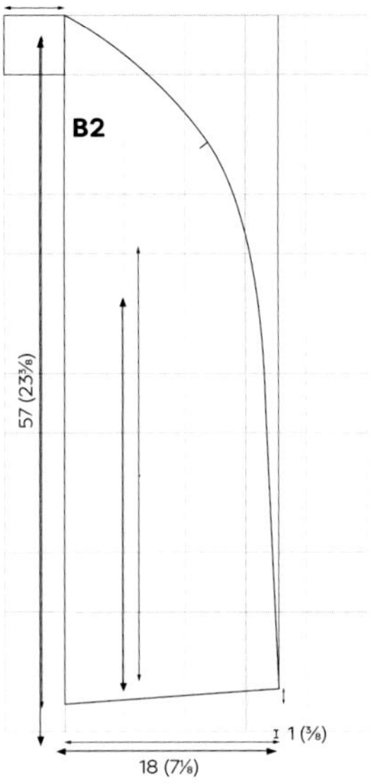

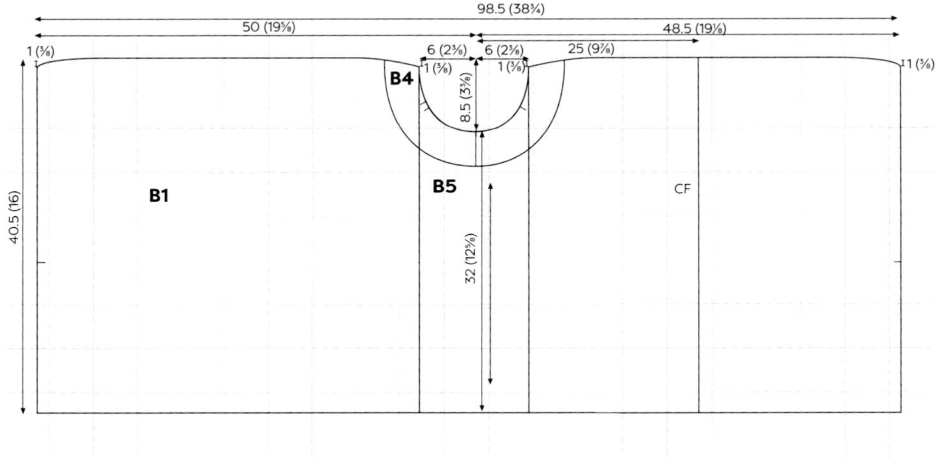

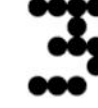

On section B1, trace the facing (B4) and flip it horizontally. Trace the underarm section (B5), which will be used for the top-left side of the bodice. Mark grainlines, CF and CB, drill holes and notches on all pattern pieces.

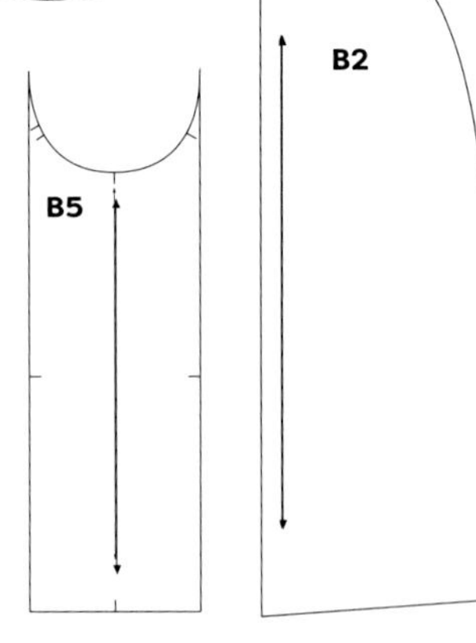

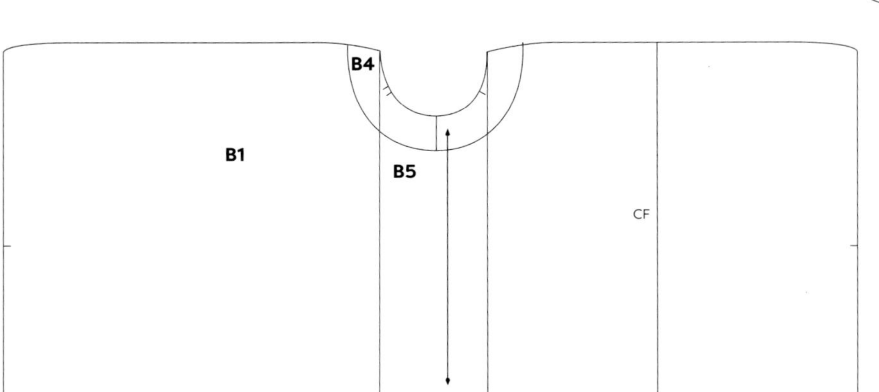

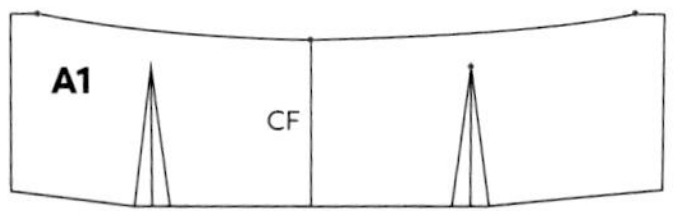

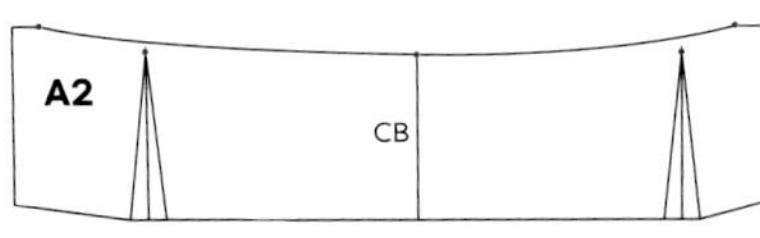

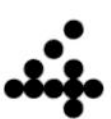

Draw a 1cm (⅜in) seam allowance around each pattern piece. Cut out the pattern pieces in jersey or a lightweight calico (muslin).

A1 (Front) x 1 RSU
A2 (Back) x 1 RSU
B1 (Bodice) x 1 RSU
B2 (Sleeve) x 1 pair, x 1 pair linings
B3 (Skirt) x 1 RSU
B4 (Facing) x 1 RSU
B5 (Top left) x 1 RSU

Using a tracing wheel and carbon paper, transfer grainlines, CF and CB, darts, drill holes and notches onto BOTH sides of the fabric.

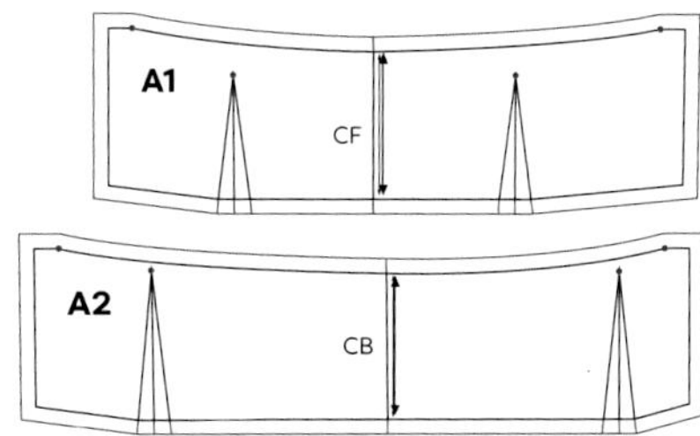

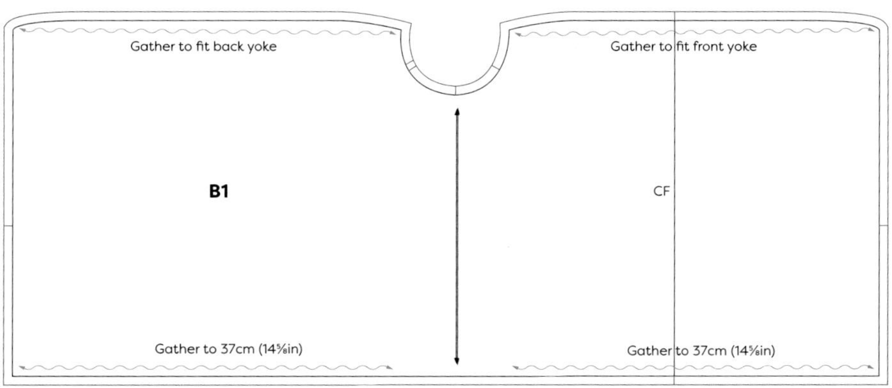

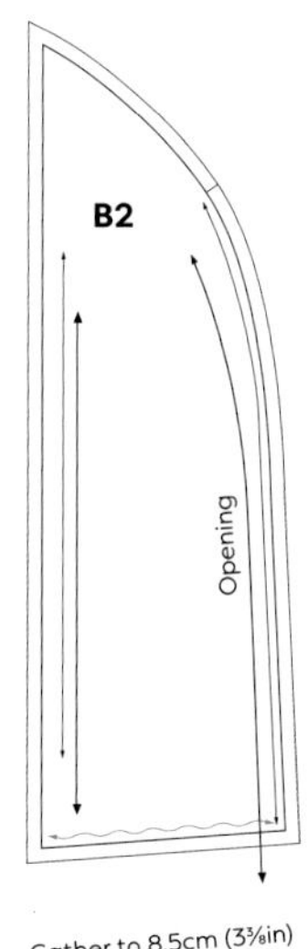

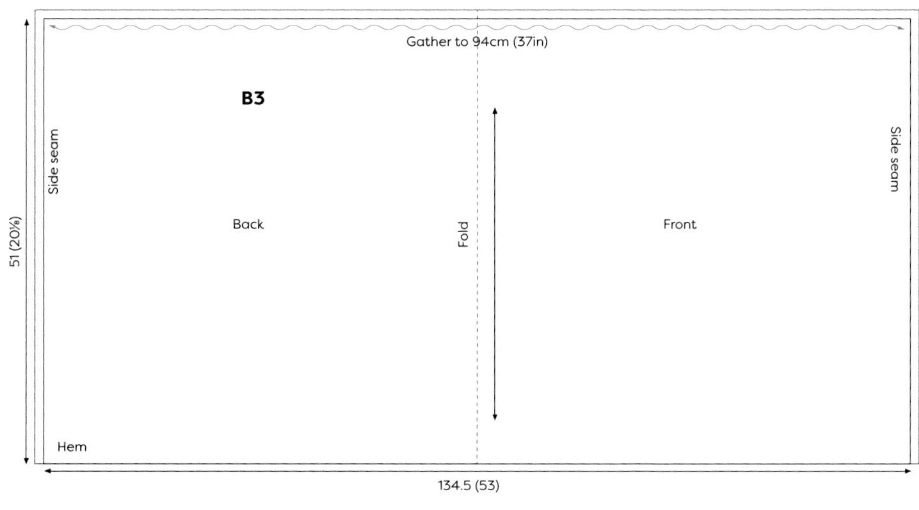

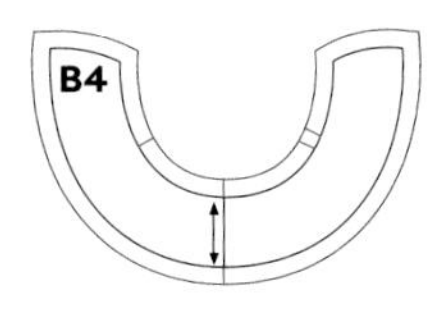

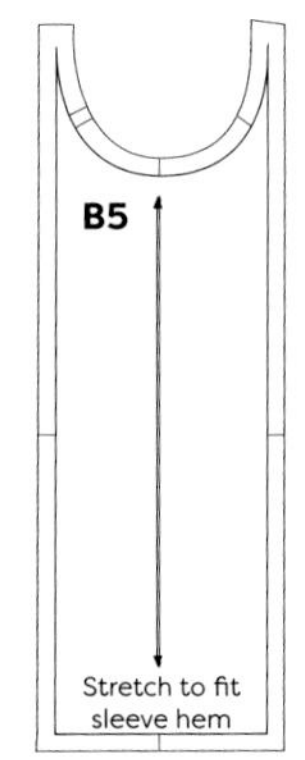

DRAPING THE SHAPES

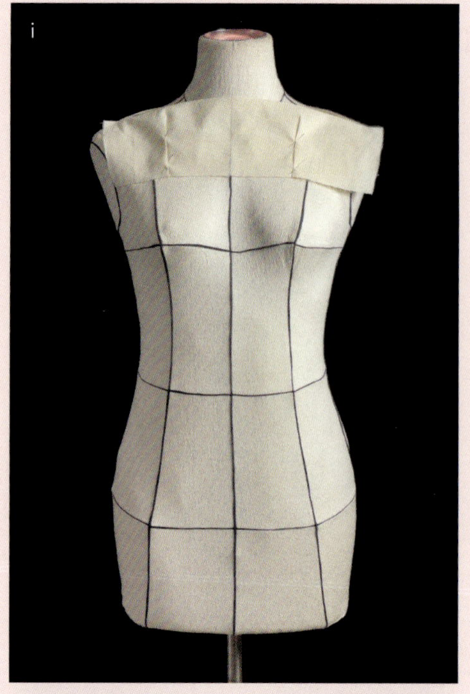

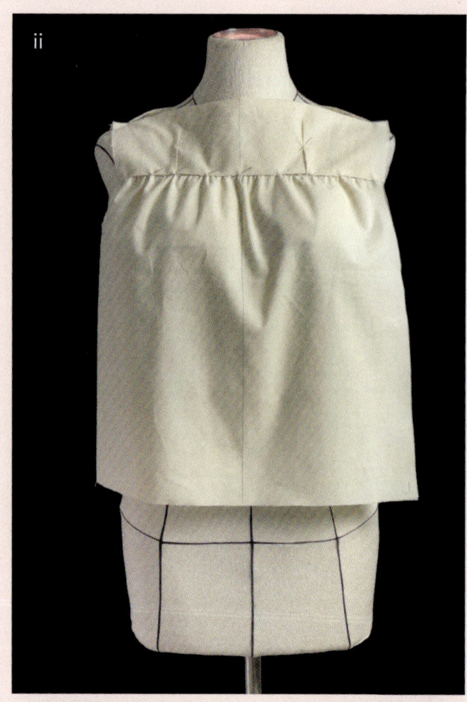

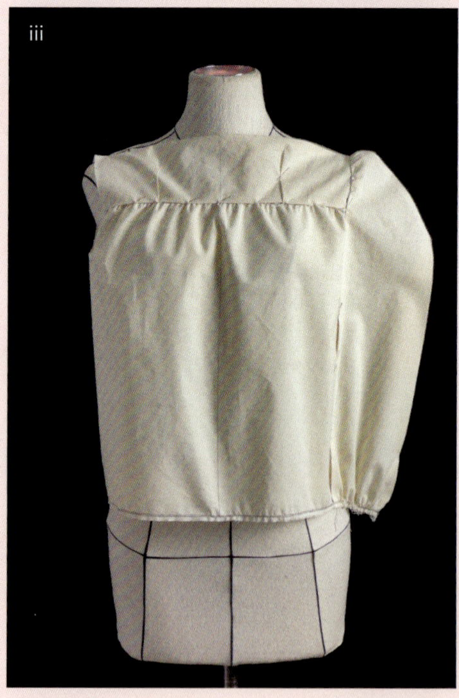

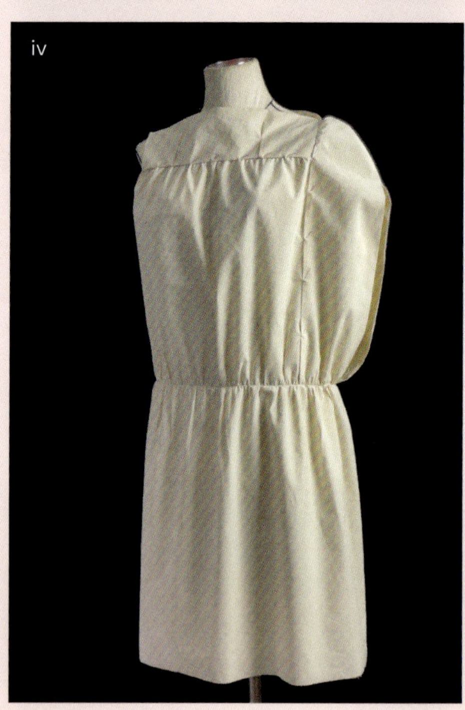

Prepare the shapes following steps 2–4 of the pattern-cutting instructions (pp. 22–23).

Here calico (muslin) is used to drape the dress. The final fabrication is in polyester, but it is used as a non-stretch fabric as the design is not tightly fitted.

(i) Make the front and back darts on A1 and A2 and attach them at the shoulder.

(ii) Gather the upper bodice (B1) and attach it to A. Attach B5 to the left side of B1.

(iii) Stitch the sleeve (B2) together, leaving an opening for the arm as marked. Attach to B5, then attach both to the left side of the bodice.

(iv) Attach the skirt (B3) to the bodice and left sleeve and gather both sections as marked.

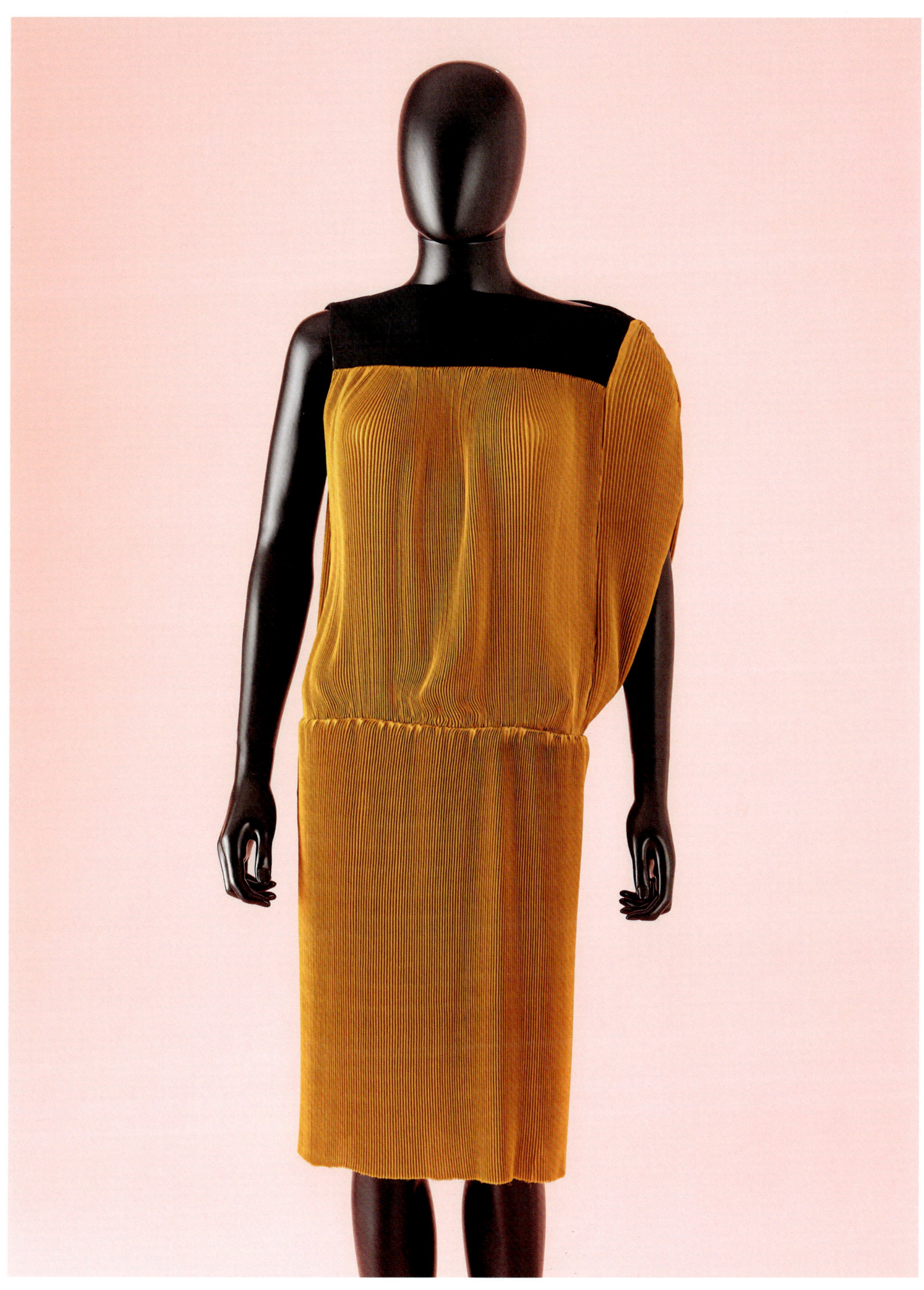

Drawing 11 dress

JUNE HARWOOD

June Harwood (b. 1933, Middleton, New York; d. 2015) made a name for herself as a Hard-Edge artist in California during the 1960s. She used collage to plan her arrangements of flat shapes and sharp edges, all of which express a sense of motion. The collage compositions were then transferred onto canvas and painted. Straight lines and angular shapes evolved into curves, and in the 1970s her forms began to break up into jigsaw-like designs. Though she moved on to explore landscape forms and softer, more painterly approaches, she returned to Hard-Edge painting in her later years.

Untitled, 1974, acrylic on canvas, 106.5 × 106.5cm (42 × 42in)

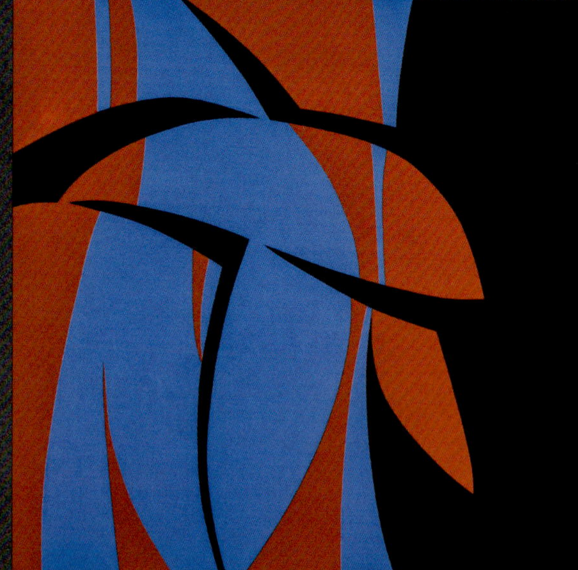

Untitled, 1975, acrylic on canvas,
152.5 × 152.5cm (60 × 60in)

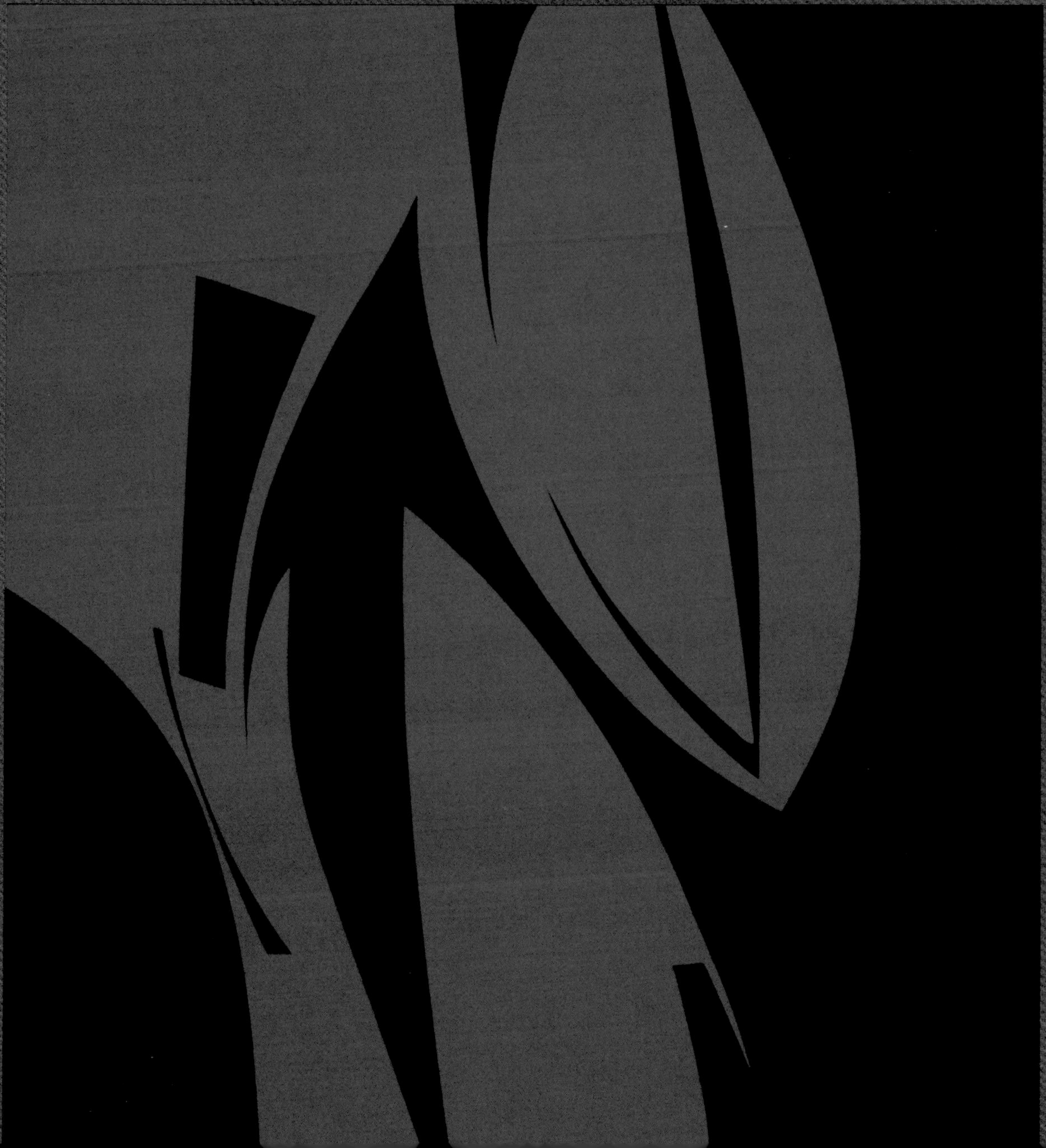

Untitled top

Harwood's *Untitled* (p. 26) features a black background with a dark red and blue overlay. I imagined the black background as a sleeveless, fitted bodice, which I quickly draped onto a dress form. The overlay was digitally printed as a square on the bias. I removed the black sections – leaving seam allowances – and then draped it directly onto the black bodice, manipulating sections to caress the bodice base. The result was a graphic piece with a sculptural neckline.

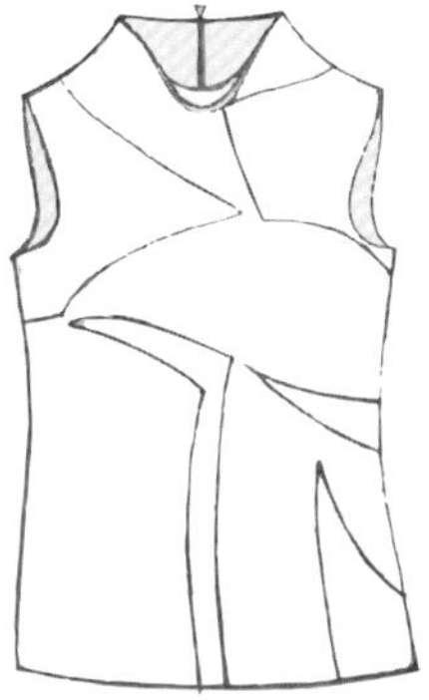

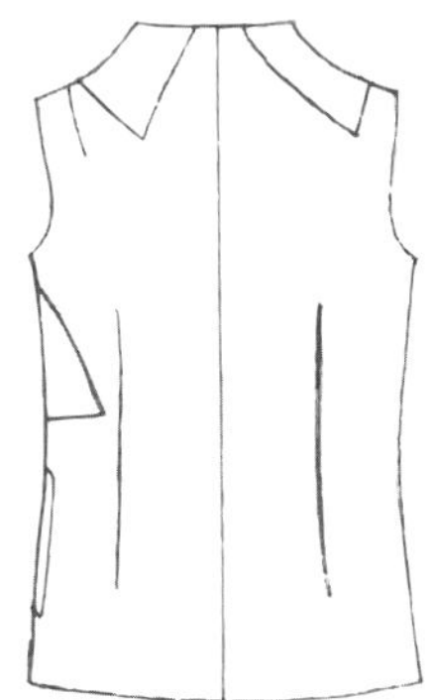

SIZING

The example here is a size 10 (US 6).

Measurements:

Bust: 94cm (37in)

Waist: 80cm (31½in)

Hips: 98cm (38⅝in)

Length: 70cm (27½in)

To create additional sizes, grade the pattern and artwork overlay (see p. 10).

FABRIC SUGGESTIONS

Black: Woven fabrics, wool crepe.

Blue and dark red overlay: Heavy silk crepe de chine.

For the sample I used deadstock wool crepe in black. The artwork was printed on the bias by the Silk Bureau in heavy silk crepe de chine.

COLOUR REFERENCES

Black #000000

Dark red #B02D25

Blue #0181BA

1

Examine the artwork shapes. The coloured section of the artwork will be separated from the black background to form an artwork overlay.

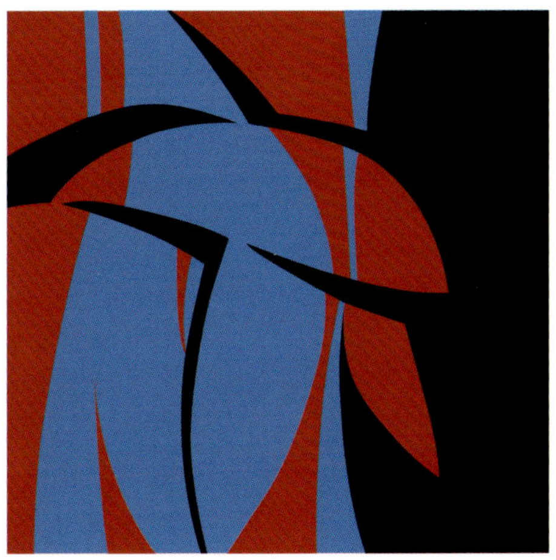

To create the artwork overlay, follow the grid reference below to plot the outline.

Place 5cm (2in) squared paper underneath the pattern paper as a guide.

Depending on which size garment you are making, print the artwork overlay at the corresponding dimensions from the table below.

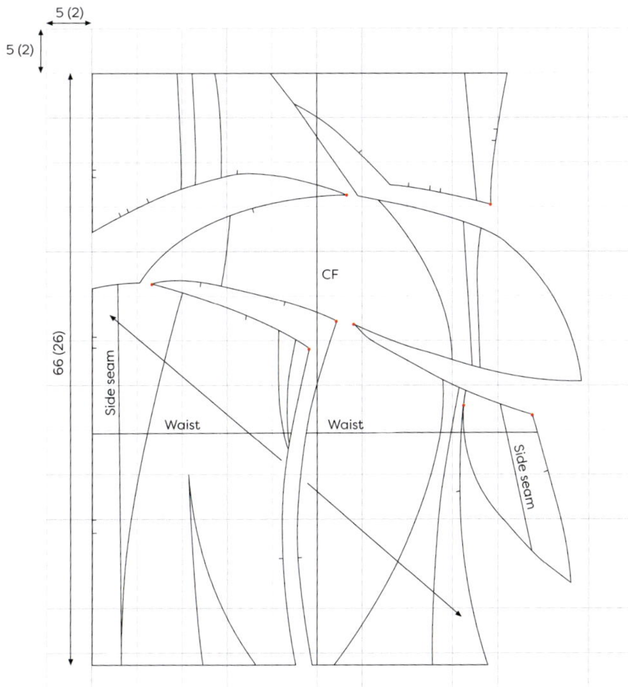

Size	ARTWORK DIMENSIONS
6 (US 2)	63.5 × 64cm (25 × 25¼in)
8 (US 4)	64.8 × 65cm (25½ × 25⅝in)
10 (US 6)	66 × 66cm (26 × 26in)
12 (US 8)	67 × 68.5cm (26⅜ × 27in)
14 (US 10)	68 × 71cm (26¾ × 28in)
16 (US 12)	69 × 73.5cm (27⅛ × 28⅞in)
18 (US 14)	70 × 76cm (27½ × 29⅞in)
20 (US 16)	71 × 78.5cm (28 × 30⅞in)
22 (US 18)	72 × 81cm (28⅜ × 31⅞in)

Plot the outlines of the shapes onto plain pattern paper. Place 5cm (2in) squared paper underneath the pattern paper as a guide. In the diagrams here, the shaded area represents the printed section.

For the back lining (D), use the left half of A. Apply the alternative neckline marked in D.

For the front lining (F), use the left half of B. Apply the alternative neckline marked in diagram F.

Plot the neck facing (E).

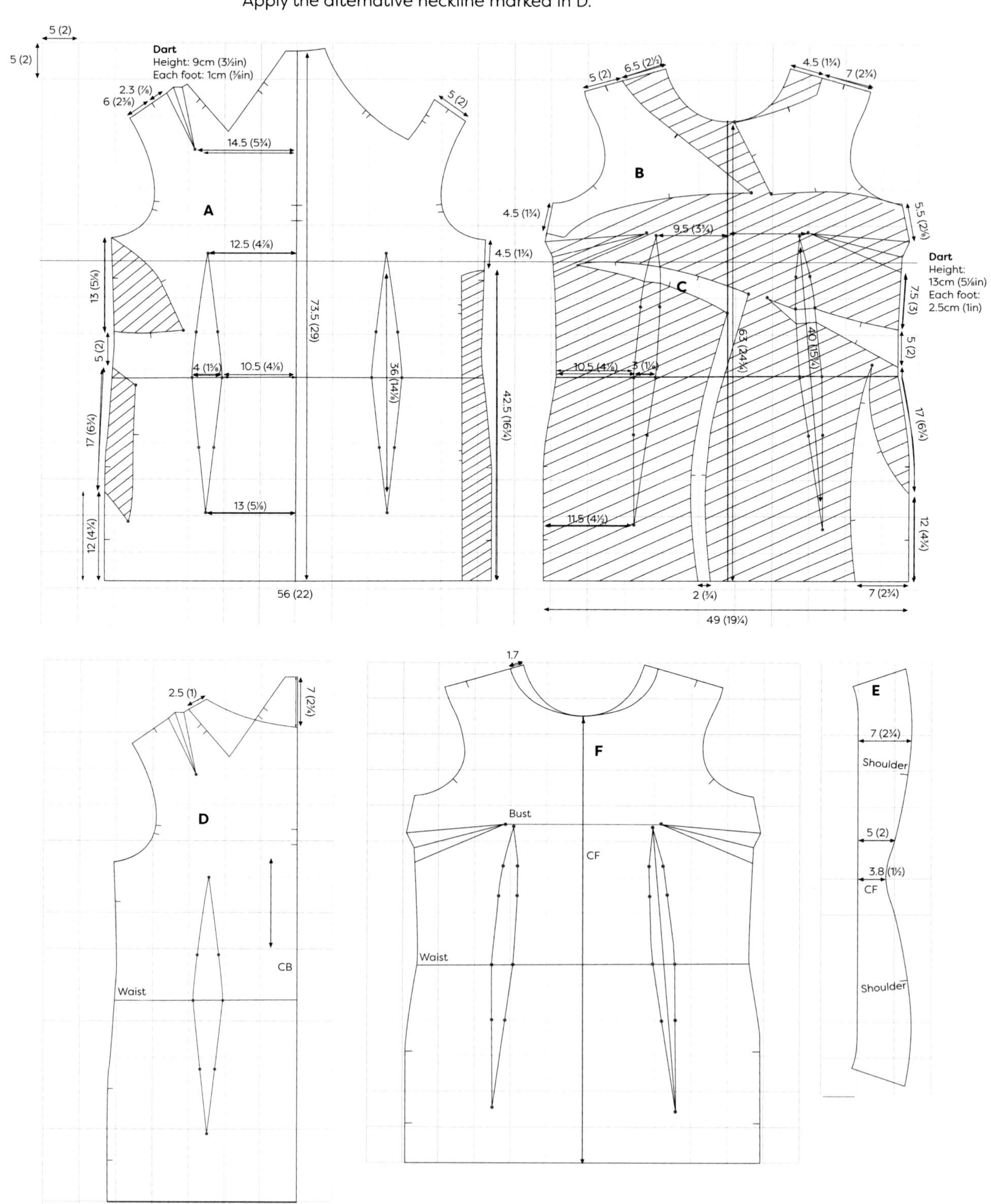

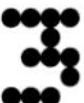

On the pieces A and B, trace the non-shaded sections 1 to 7.

Close the darts in sections 5 and 6.

Join the front sections to the back sections to create pieces A and B1.

Mark grainlines, CF and CB, waistline, darts, drill holes and notches on all pattern pieces.

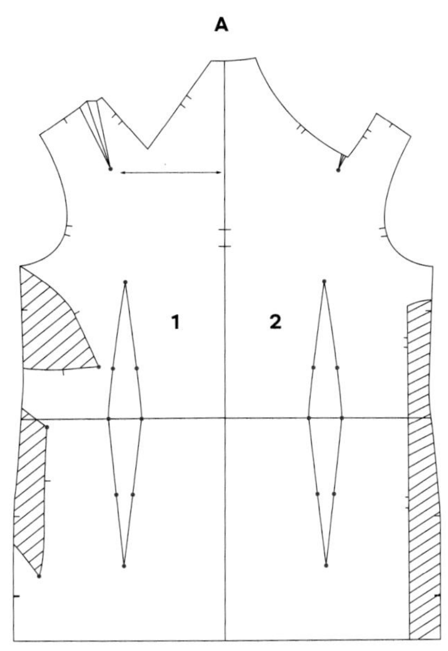

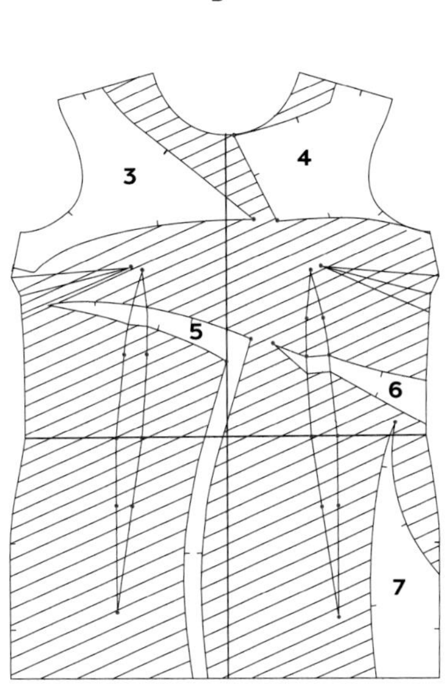

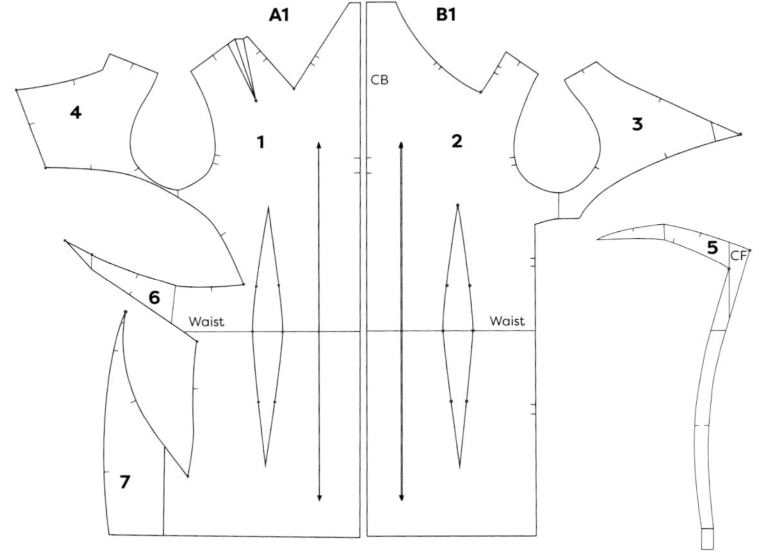

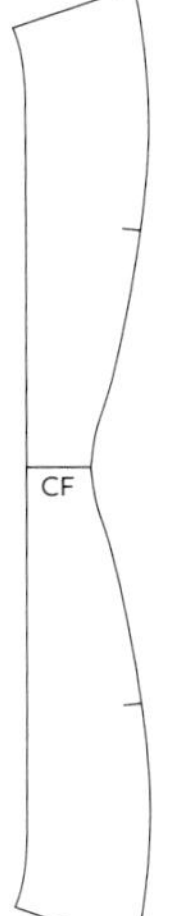

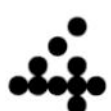

Add a 1cm (⅜in) seam allowance around each pattern piece and a 4cm (1⅝in) hem allowance. Cut out the printed artwork overlay in viscose and the remaining pattern pieces in calico (muslin).

A1 (Left front/back) x 1 RSU
B1 (Right front/back) x 1 RSU
C (Front black inset piece) x 1 RSU
D (Back lining) x 1 Pair
E (Neck facing) x 1 RSU
F (Front lining) x 1 RSU
Artwork overlay x 1 RSU

Using a tracing wheel and carbon paper, transfer grainlines, CF and CB, waistline, darts, drill holes and notches onto BOTH sides of the fabric.

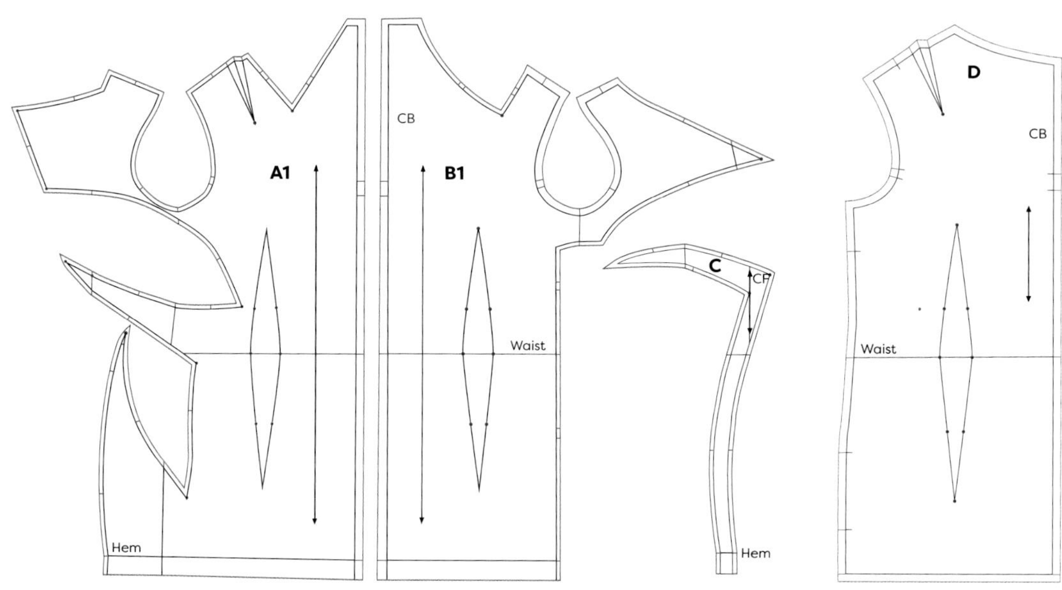

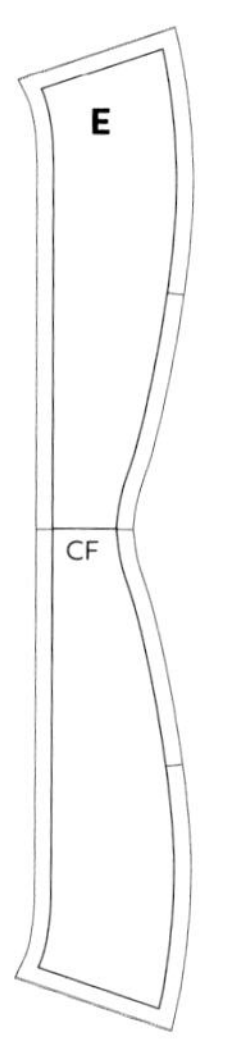

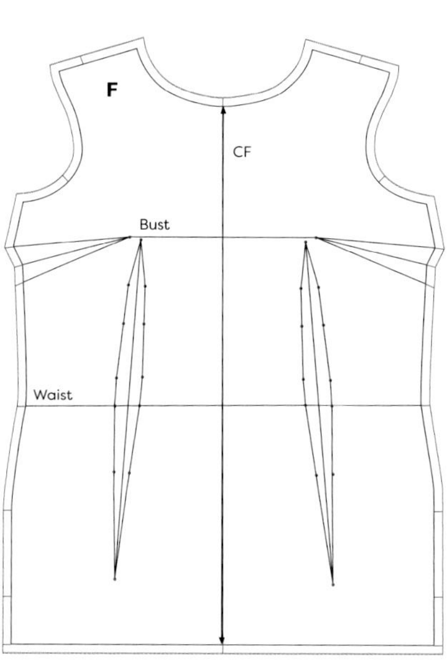

Artwork overlay

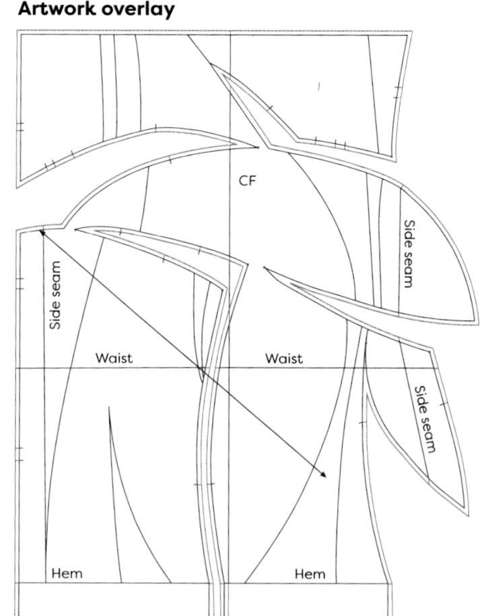

DRAPING THE SHAPES

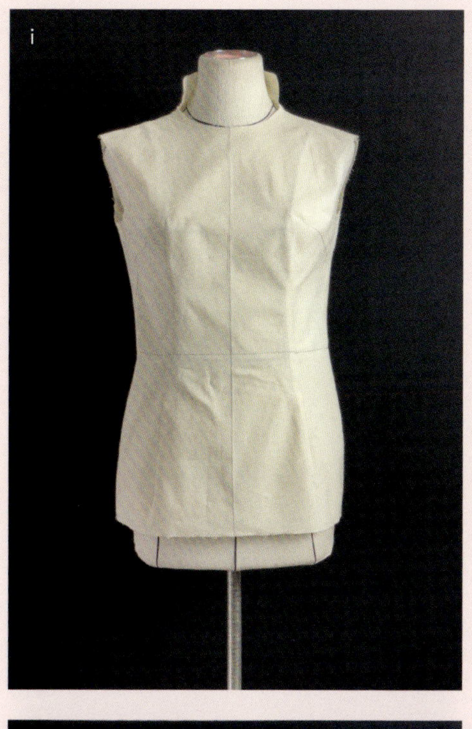
i

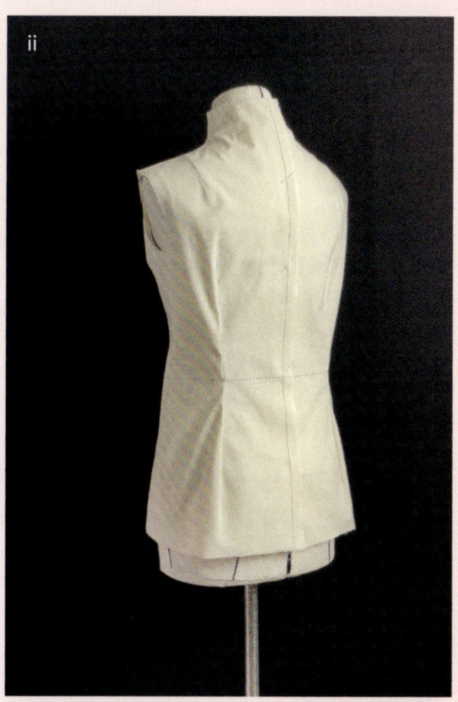
ii

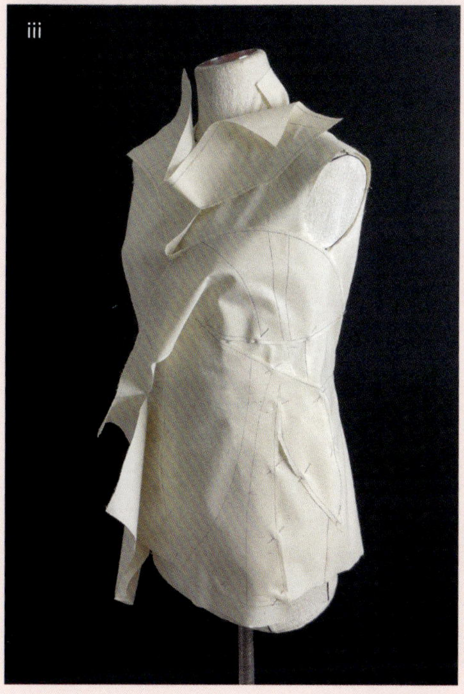
iii

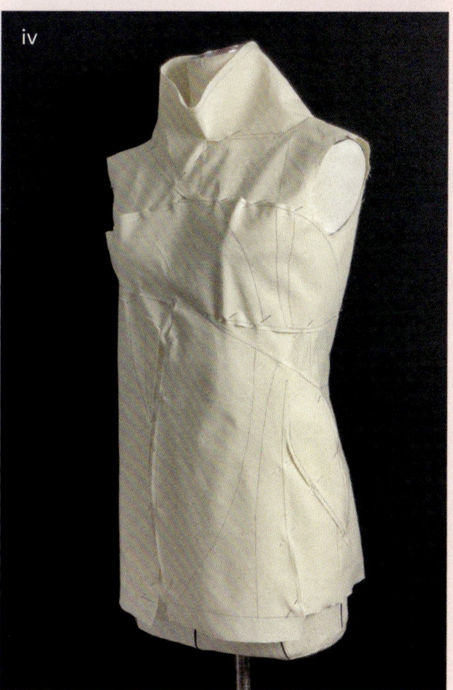
iv

Prepare the artwork overlay and sections A and B as shown in the pattern-cutting instructions in step 2 (pp. 29–30); do not remove the shaded areas from A and B.

(i) Drape a simple bodice using sections A and B.

(ii) On the back of the bodice, form shoulder and fisheye darts.

(iii) Cut out the artwork overlay in calico (muslin). Drape the overlay onto the bodice, starting at the front.

(iv) Pin the overlay onto the bodice. Transfer the stitch line from the overlay onto the bodice by lifting each section and drawing the lines onto the calico (muslin).

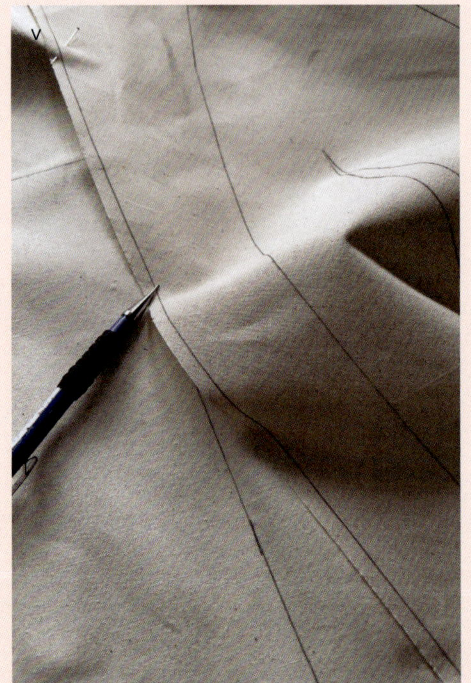

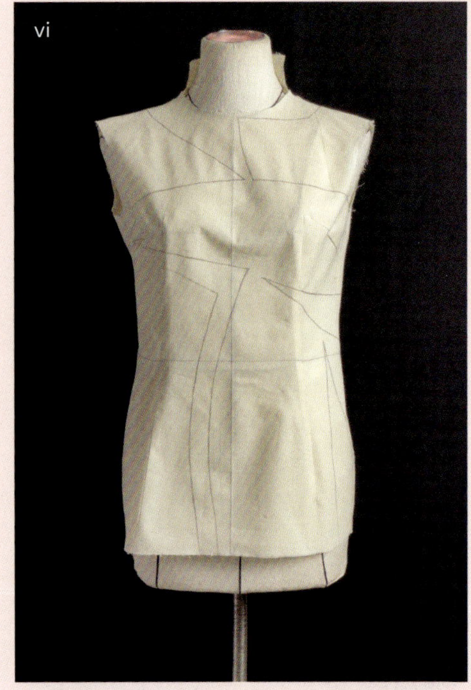

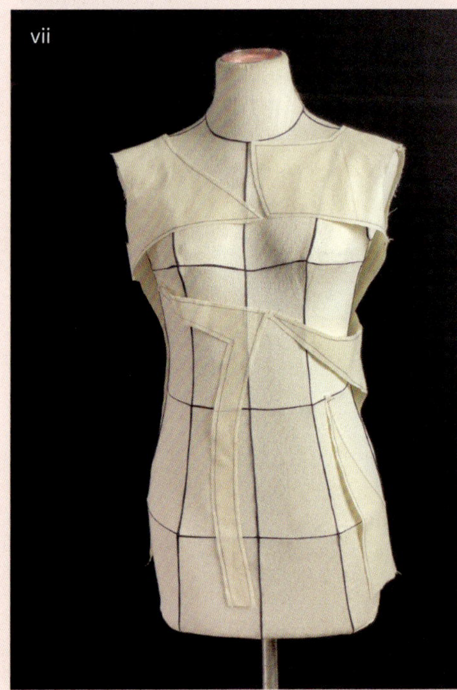

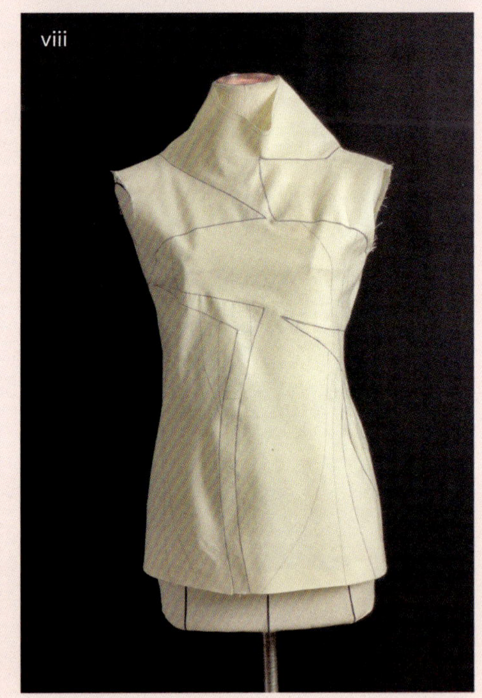

(v) The overlay on the bodice, with transferred marks.

(vi) The bodice with the position of the artwork overlay marked.

(vii) Cut out the bodice sections with a 0.5cm (3⁄16in) seam allowance included.

(viii) Stitch the bodice pieces to the artwork overlay, easing the sections above the bustline. Turn up the hemline.

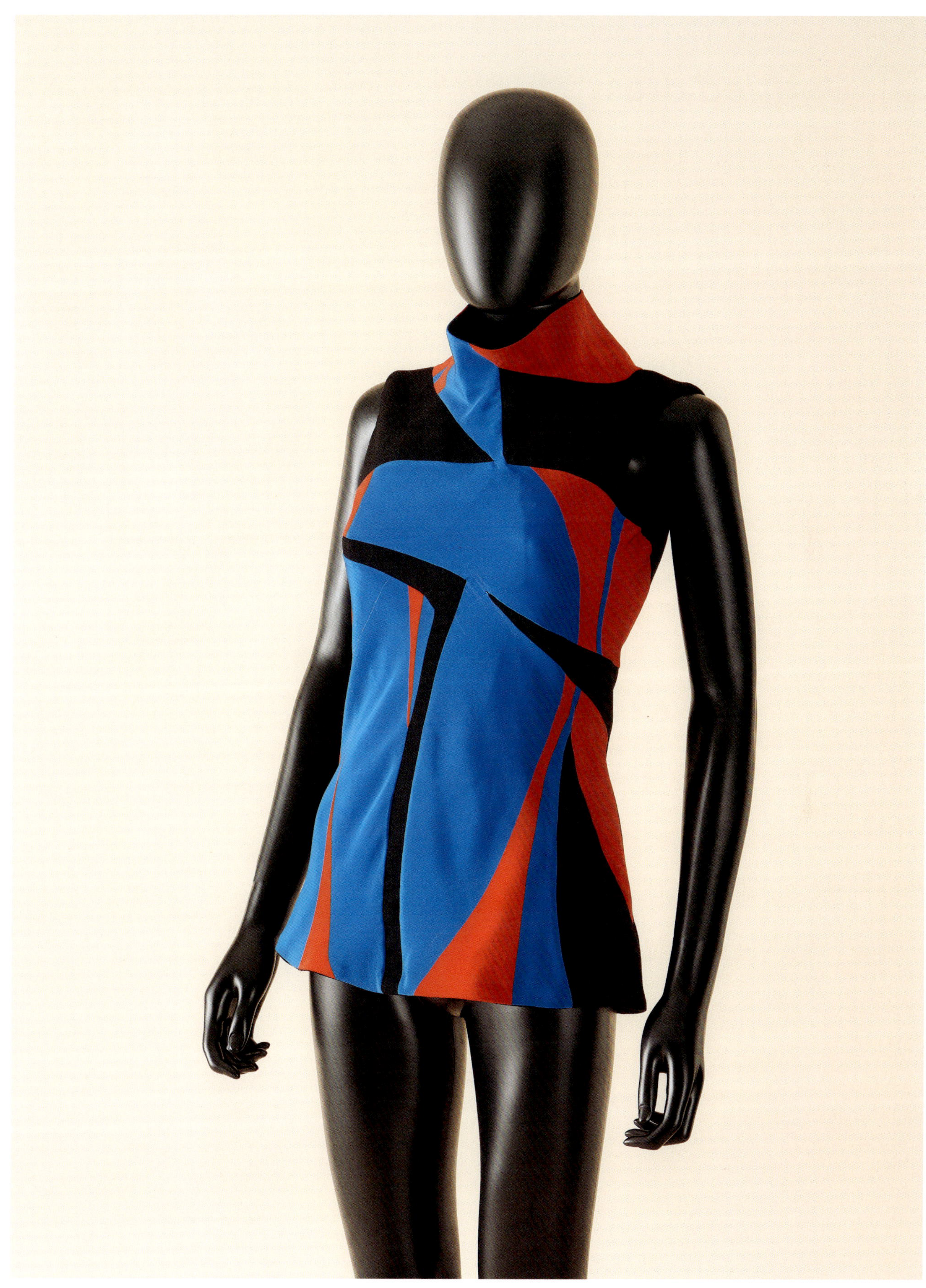

Untitled top

Untitled dress

I translated June Harwood's *Untitled* (p. 27) into a rectangular, zero-waste dress pattern. First, I rendered each shape as a separate pattern piece, which I then stitched back together, leaving areas unstitched to enable the formation of two armholes. I added tucks to the centre back to make the dress more form fitting, and used horizontal and vertical tucks to create the elaborate collar. The back of the dress features a vintage technique that creates draping across the upper back by suppressing the width of the fabric using two pieces of ribbon, which are stitched into the seam allowances to span from the left side seam to centre back. The dress is cut on the bias for fluidity of movement.

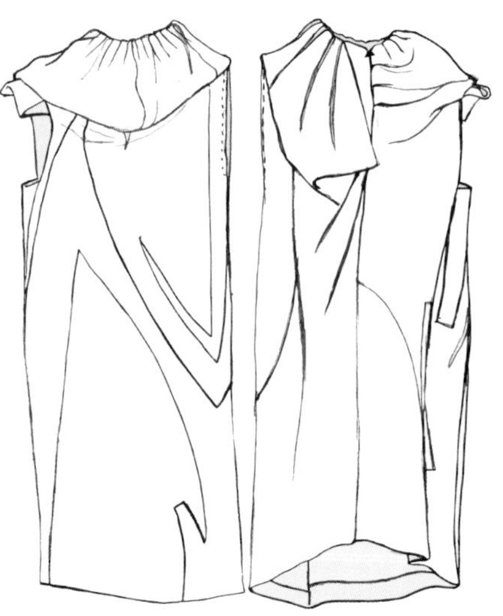

SIZING

The example here is a size 10 (US 6).

Measurements:

Bust: 94cm (37in)

Waist: 84cm (33⅛in)

Hips: 104cm (41in)

Length: 109cm (42⅞in)

To create additional sizes, grade the artwork pattern (see p. 10).

FABRIC SUGGESTIONS

Black and blue: Medium-weight woven fabrics, such as wool crepe, viscose, viscose crepe.

For the sample I used deadstock wool crepe.

COLOUR REFERENCES

Black #000000

Blue #1A4E99

1

Examine the artwork shapes. Number the individual sections of the design within each colour as shown.

Blue = **A1** and **A2**
Black = **B1**, **B2**, **B3**, **B4**, **B5** and **B6**

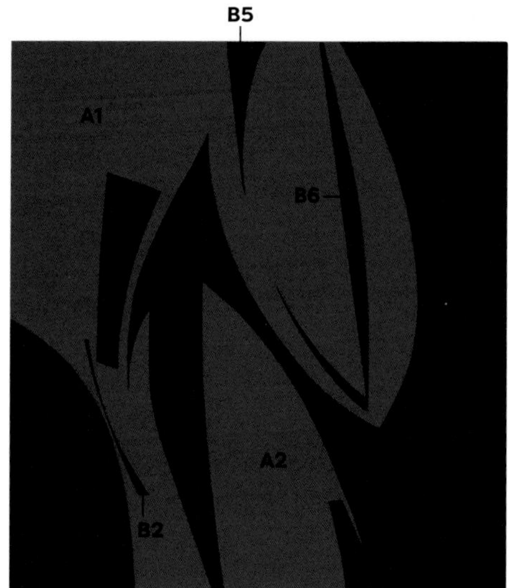

2

Plot the artwork onto plain pattern paper. Place 5cm (2in) squared paper underneath the pattern paper as a guide.

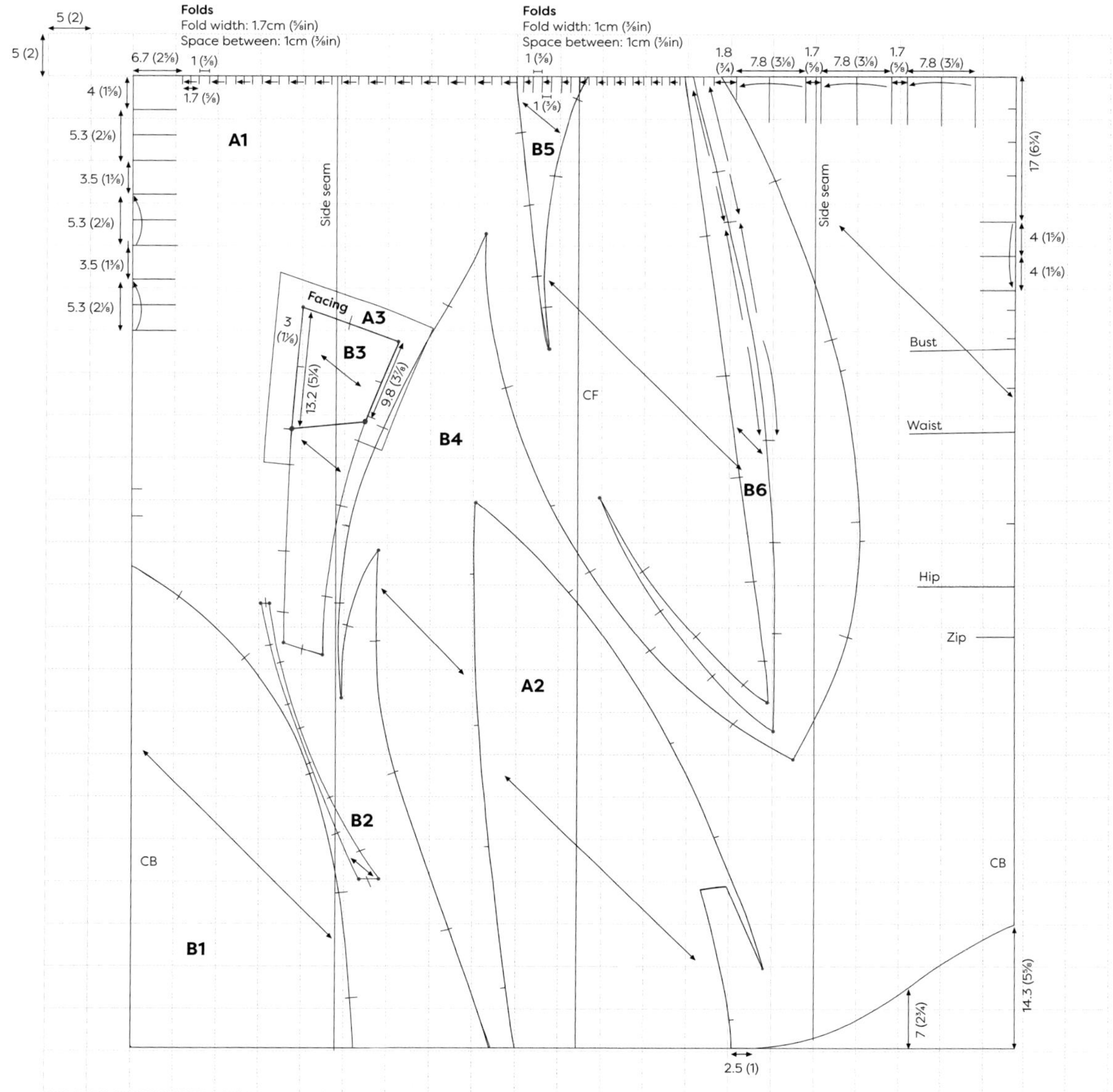

Folds
Fold width: 1.7cm (⅝in)
Space between: 1cm (⅜in)

Folds
Fold width: 1cm (⅜in)
Space between: 1cm (⅜in)

5 (2)
5 (2)
6.7 (2⅝)
1 (⅜)
1.7 (⅝)
4 (1⅝)
5.3 (2⅛)
3.5 (1⅜)
5.3 (2⅛)
3.5 (1⅜)
5.3 (2⅛)
A1
Side seam
Facing
A3
3 (1⅛)
B3
13.2 (5¼)
9.8 (3⅞)
B4
1 (⅜)
1 (⅜)
B5
CF
1.8 (¾)
7.8 (3⅛)
1.7 (⅝)
7.8 (3⅛)
1.7 (⅝)
7.8 (3⅛)
Side seam
17 (6¾)
4 (1⅝)
4 (1⅝)
Bust
Waist
B6
Hip
Zip
A2
B2
CB
B1
CB
14.3 (5⅝)
7 (2¾)
2.5 (1)

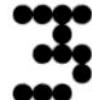

Trace each pattern piece separately. Extract facing A3 from A1 and reverse it. Note that section B3 is divided into two pieces.

Mark grainlines on the bias, CB, waist and hip lines, tucks, zips, drill holes and notches.

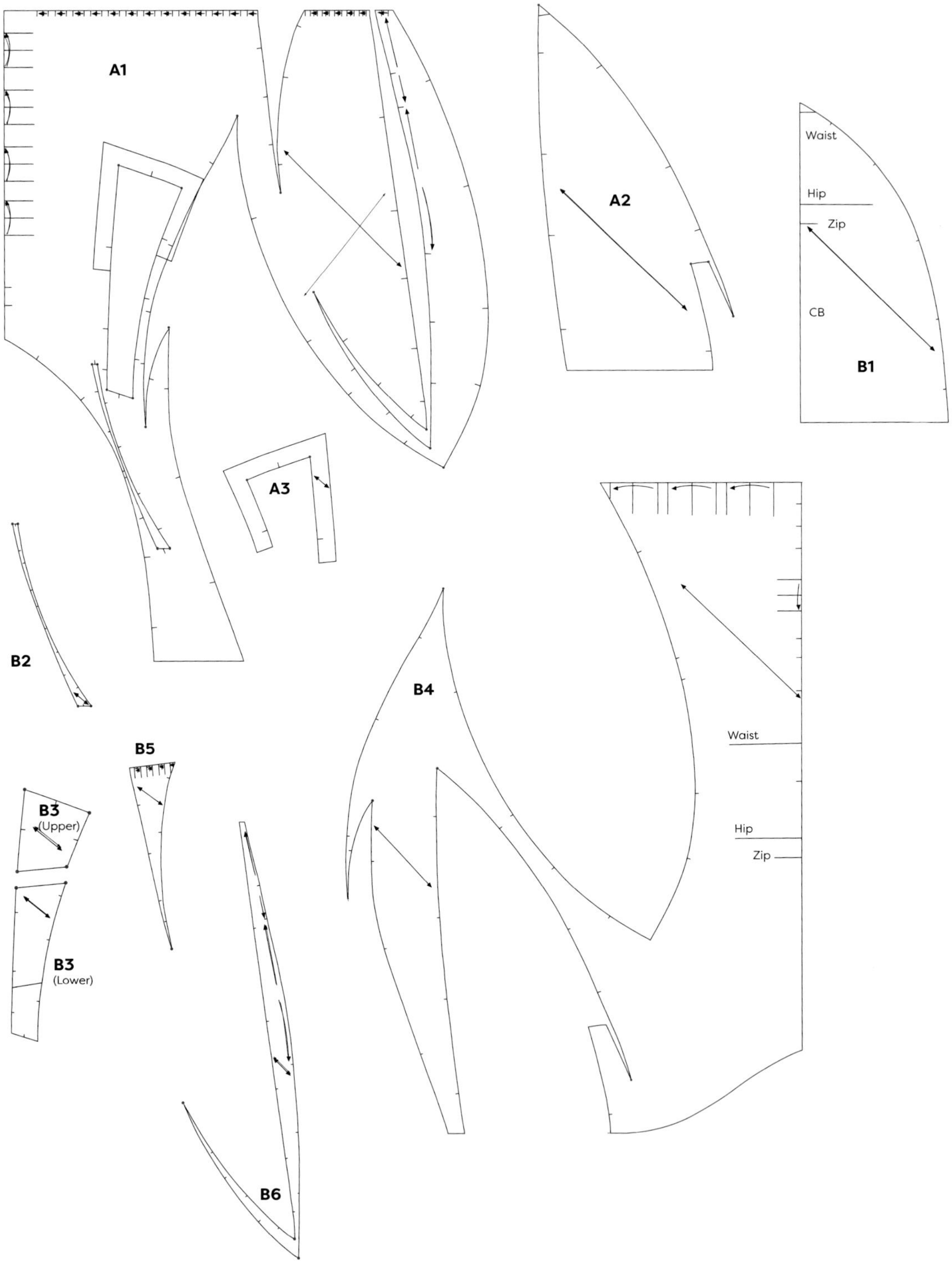

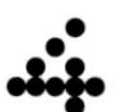

Add a 0.5cm (3/16in) seam allowance around each pattern piece, and a 1cm (3/8in) seam allowance along the CB. Add a 4cm (1 5/8in) hem allowance. Cut out the pattern pieces in calico (muslin).

A1 x 1 RSU
A2 x 1 RSU
A3 (Facing) x 1 RSU
B1 x 1 RSU
B2 x 1 RSU
B3 (Upper) x 1 RSU
B3 (Lower) x 1 pair
B4 x 1 RSU
B5 x 1 RSU
B6 x 1 RSU

Using a tracing wheel and carbon paper, transfer grainlines, CB, waist and hip lines, tucks, zips, drill holes and notches onto BOTH sides of the fabric.

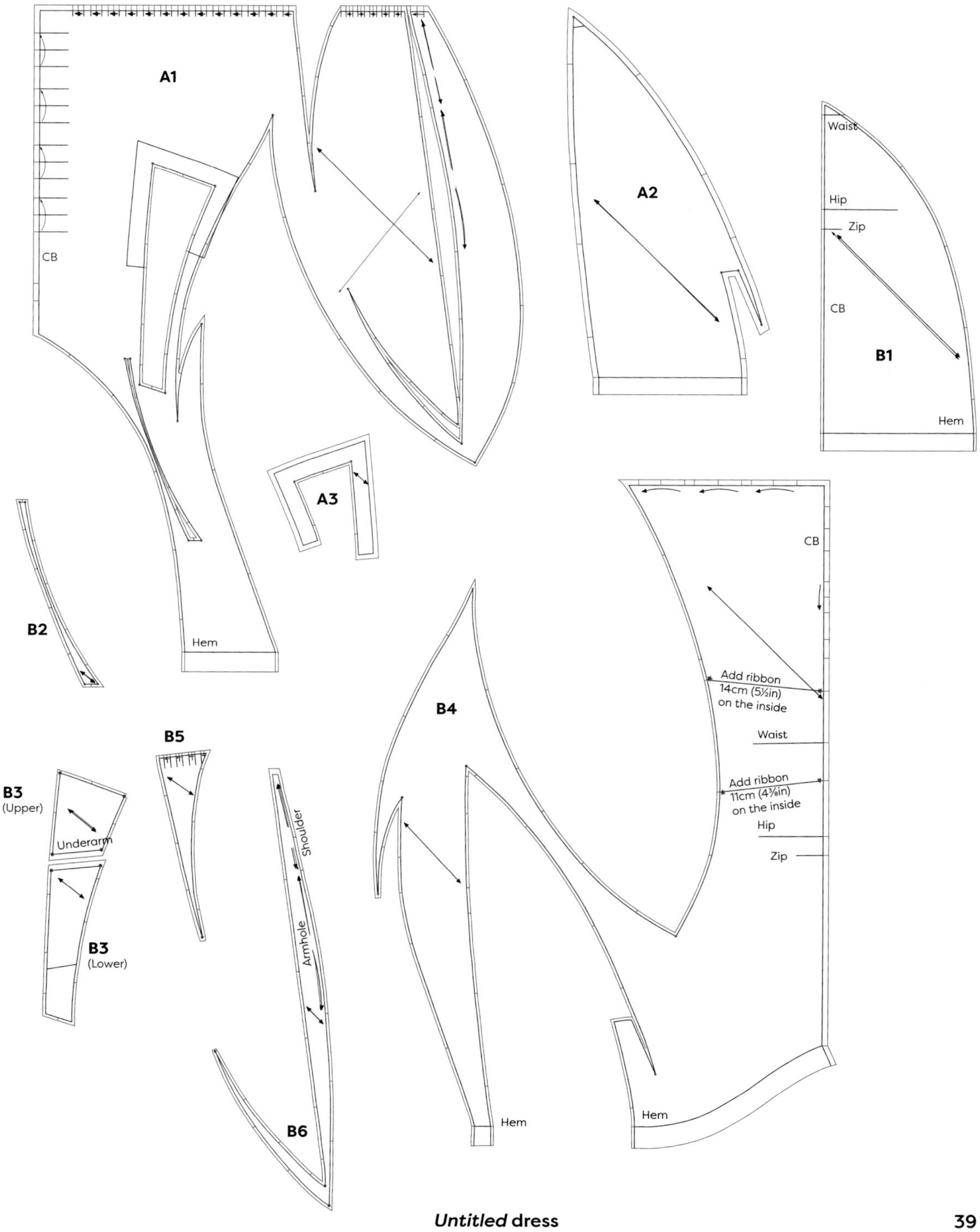

A1
CB
Hem
A2
Waist
Hip
Zip
CB
B1
Hem
A3
B2
CB
Add ribbon 14cm (5½in) on the inside
Waist
Add ribbon 11cm (4⅜in) on the inside
Hip
Zip
B4
B5
B3
(Upper)
Underarm
B3
(Lower)
Shoulder
Armhole
B6
Hem
Hem

DRAPING THE SHAPES

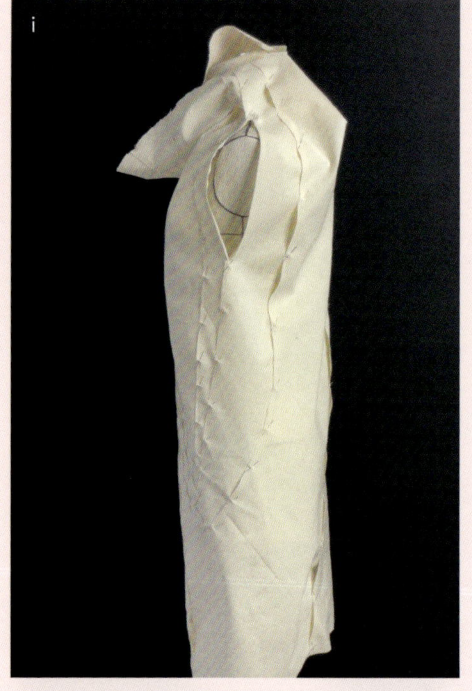

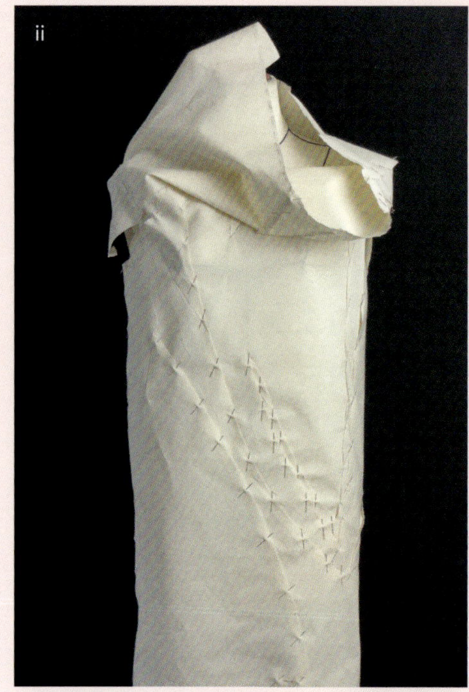

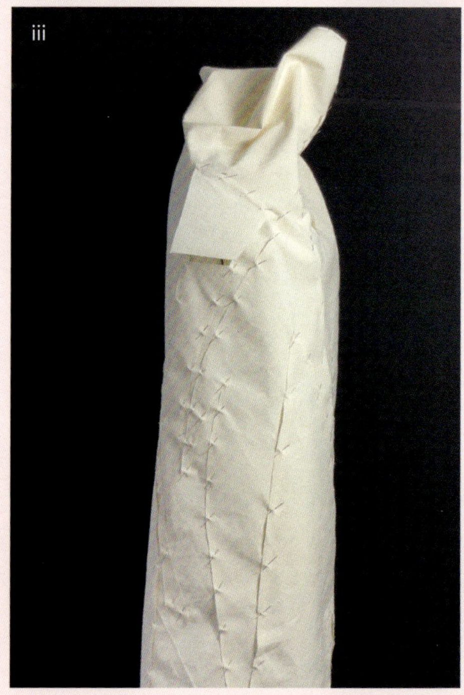

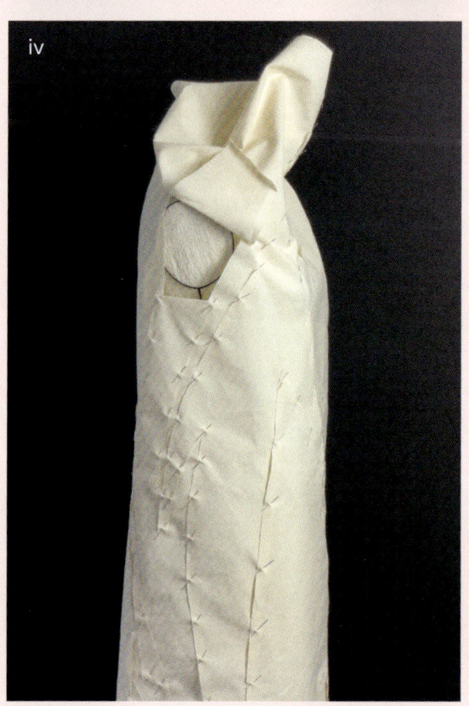

Prepare the shapes following steps 2–4 of the pattern-cutting instructions (pp. 37–39).

(i) Pin all the pattern pieces together, following the artwork, and then pin the joined pieces to the dress form.

(ii) Right side of the dress.

(iii) Section B3 is split to form an armhole (B3 Lower) and an epaulette (B3 Upper).

(iv) The epaulette is tucked under the neck once the dress is finished.

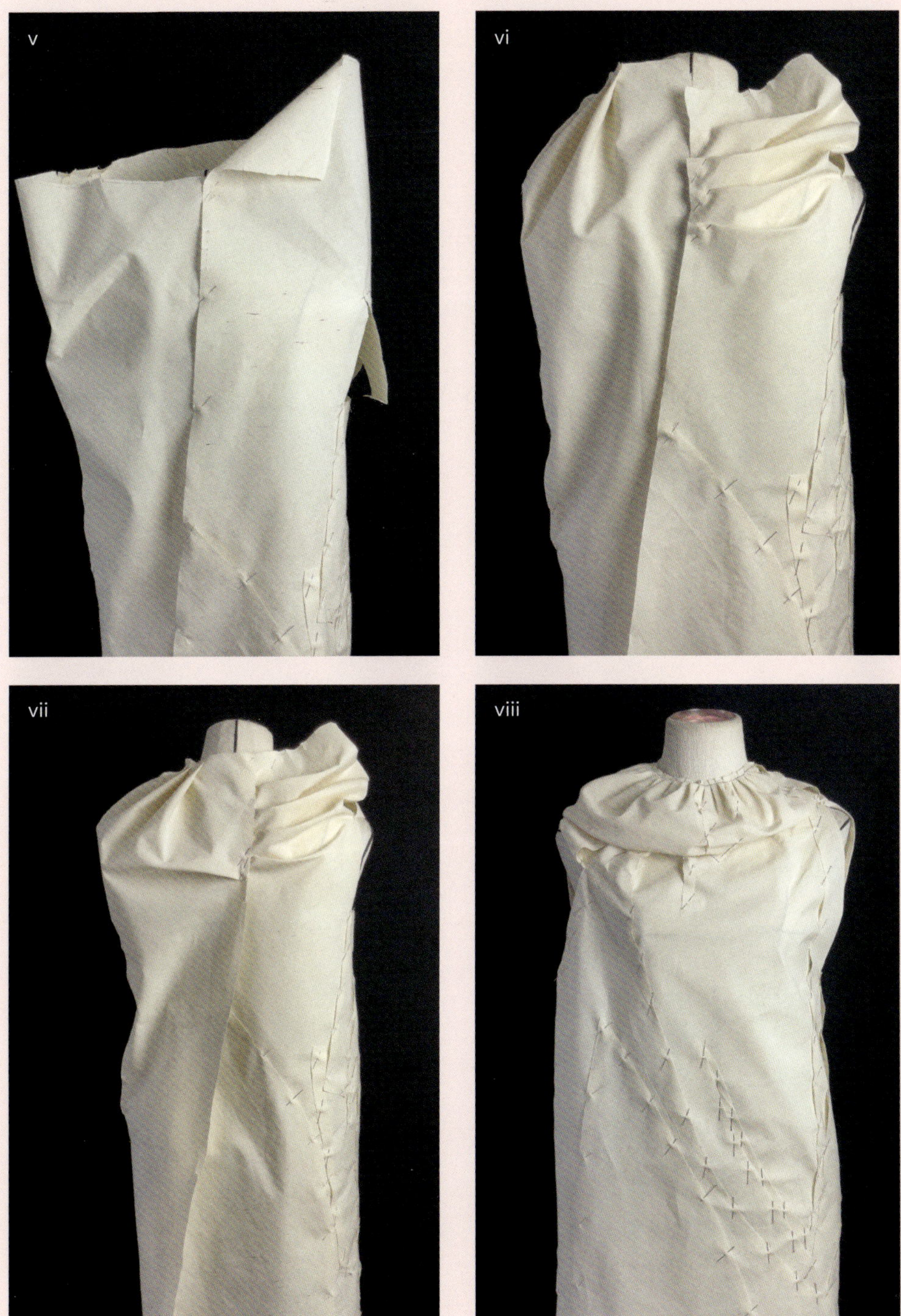

(v) Pin the CB together.

(vi) Make four tucks on the back right. Make neck tucks on the back left.

(vii) Make a tuck on the back left.

(viii) Make neck tucks on the front of the dress.

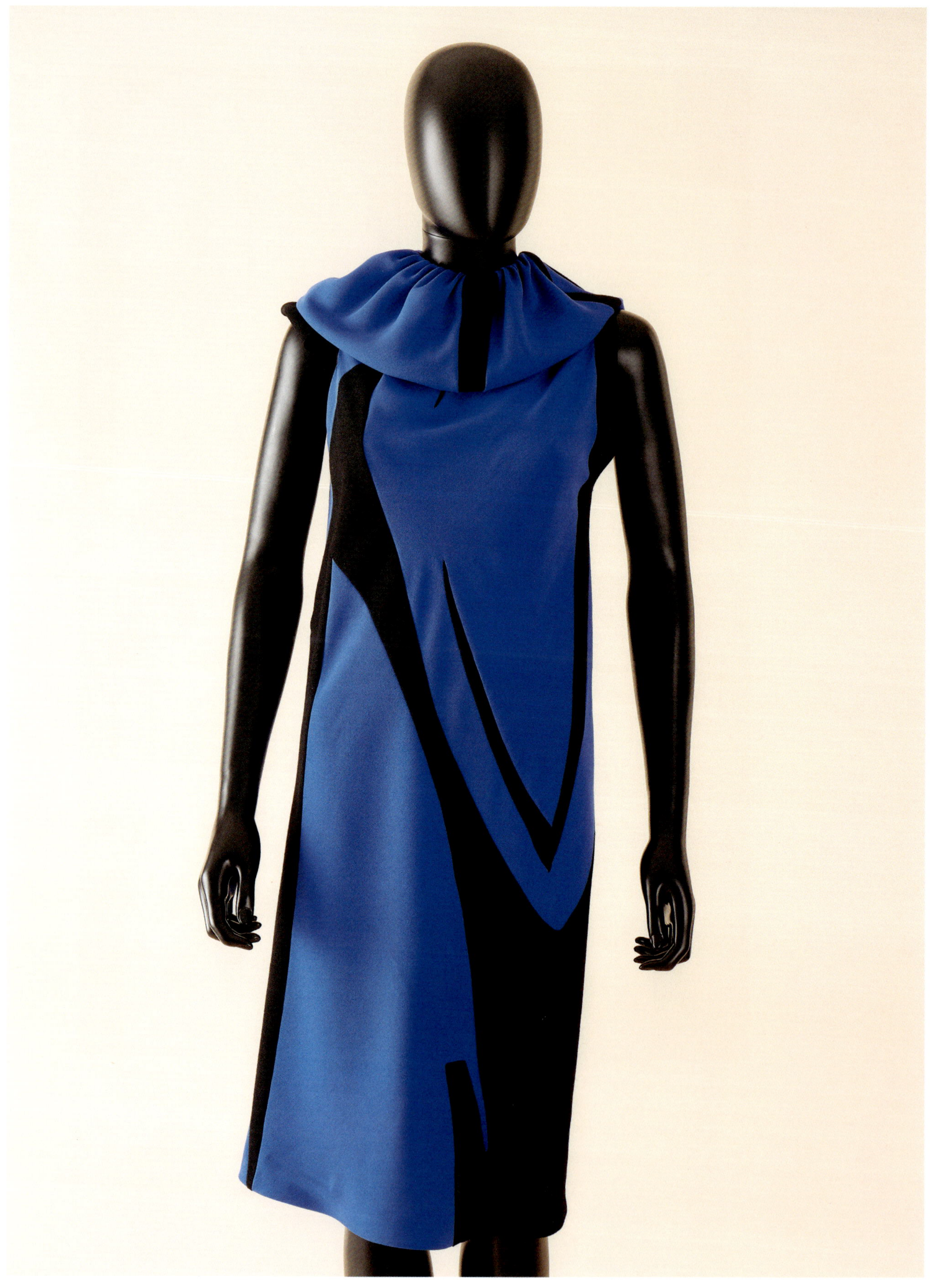

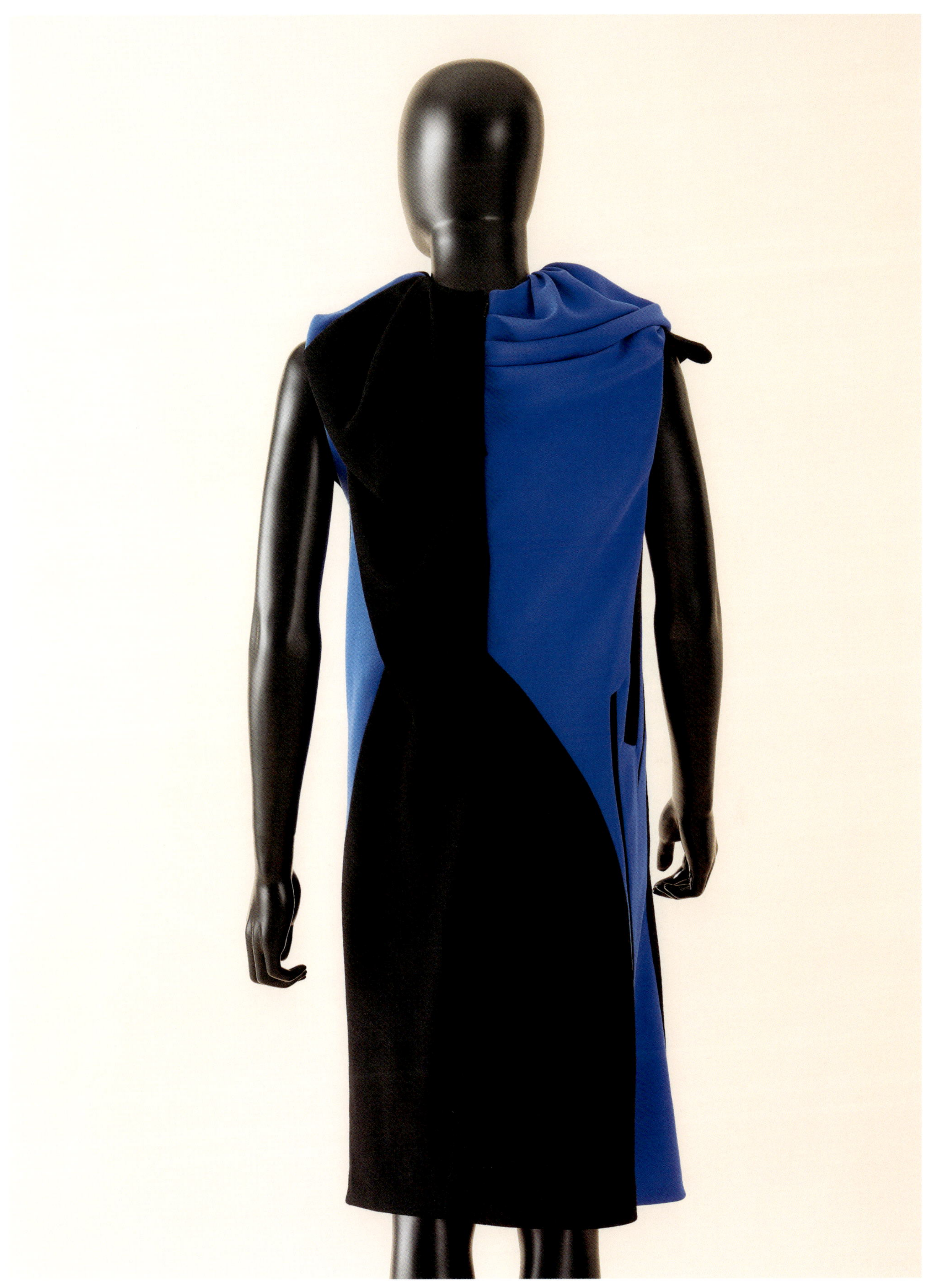

Untitled dress

CARMEN HERRERA

Carmen Herrera (b. 1915, Havana, Cuba; d. 2022) only sold her first painting in 2004, after many decades of working as an artist. By the time she found fame in her late eighties, she had amassed a vast body of work, both paintings and sculptures. She was influenced by early Russian Suprematists Kazimir Malevich, Olga Rozanova and Lyubov Popova, whom she discovered at the Salon des Réalités Nouvelles in Paris, where she spent her formative years. In the 1950s, her work became more minimalist as she simplified her style, likening the process to purification.

Opposite:
Equation, 1958, acrylic on canvas, 61 × 106.7cm (24 × 42in)

Blanco y Verde, 1956, acrylic on canvas, 124.5 × 124.5cm (49 × 49in)

Yesterday, 1987, acrylic on canvas, 121.9 × 152.4cm (48 × 60in)

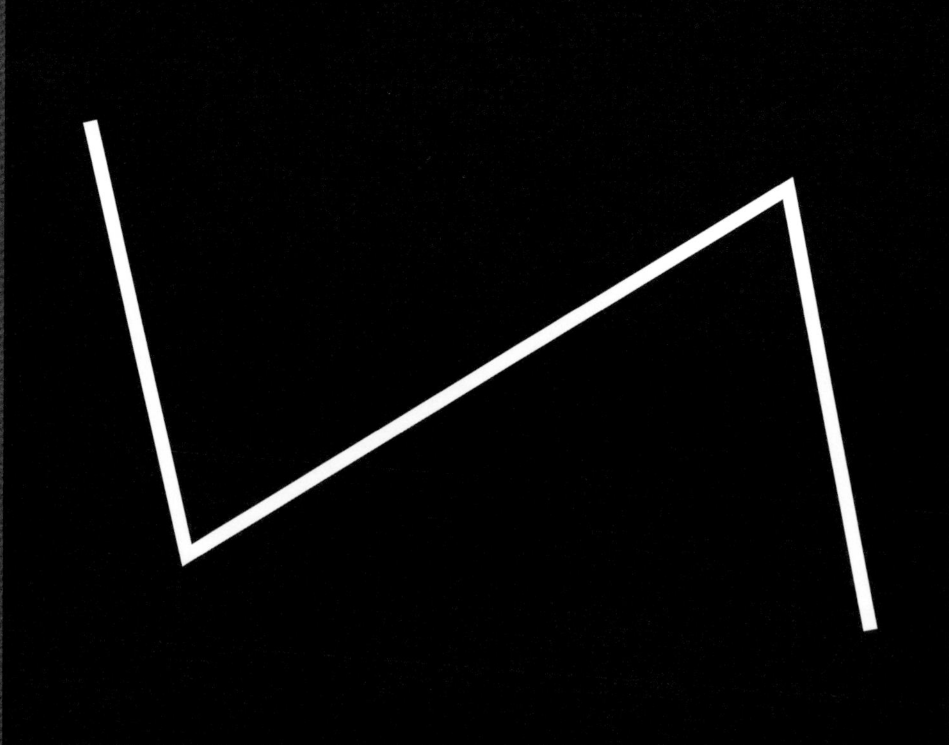

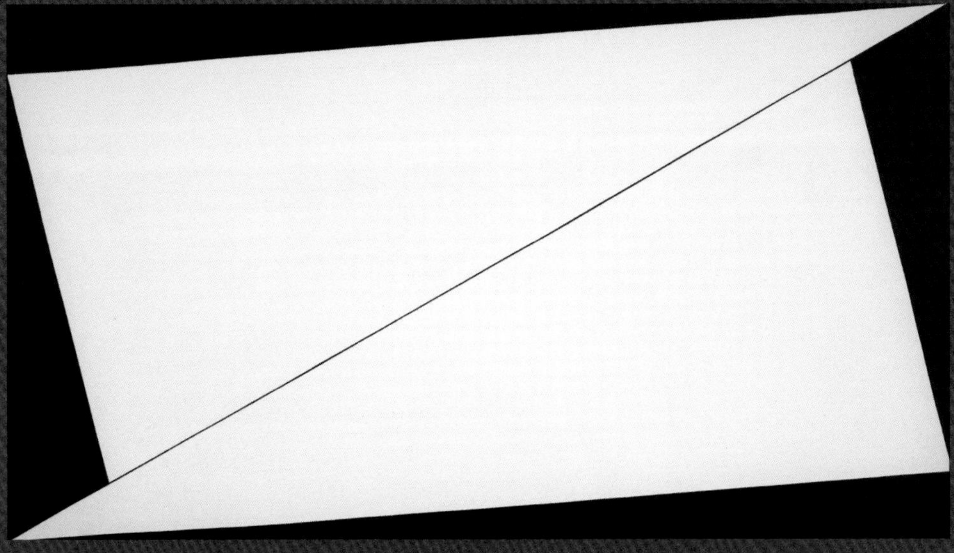

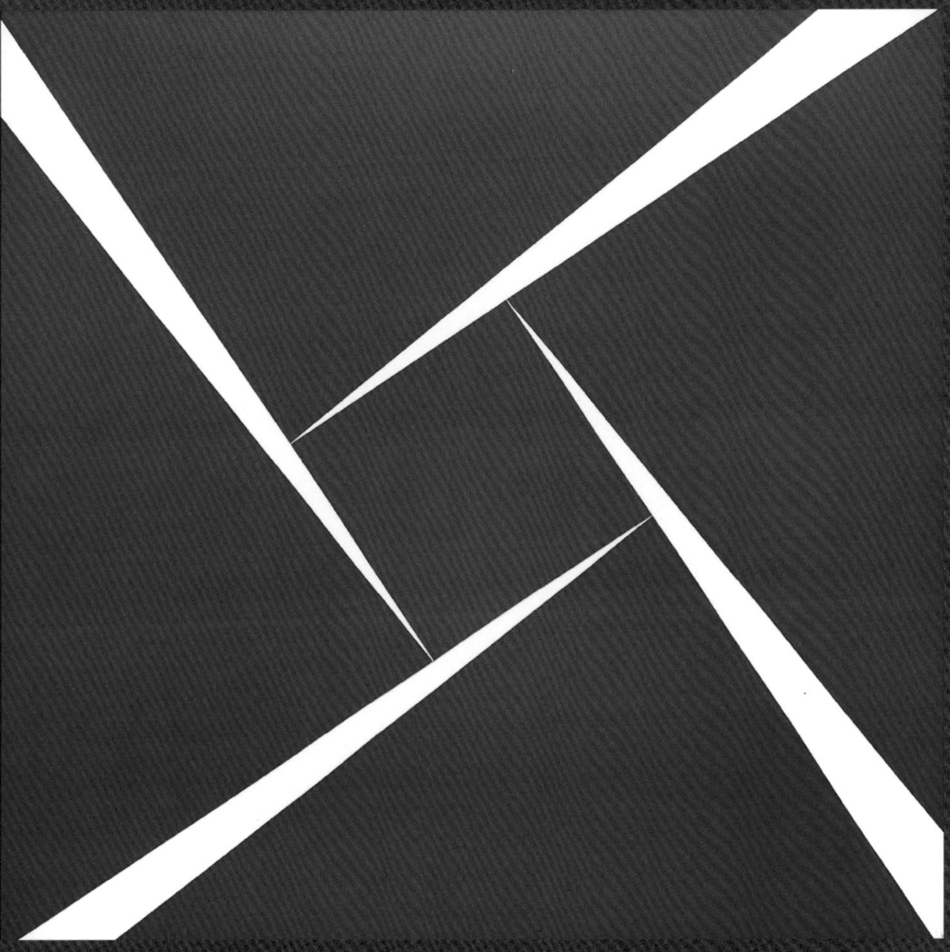

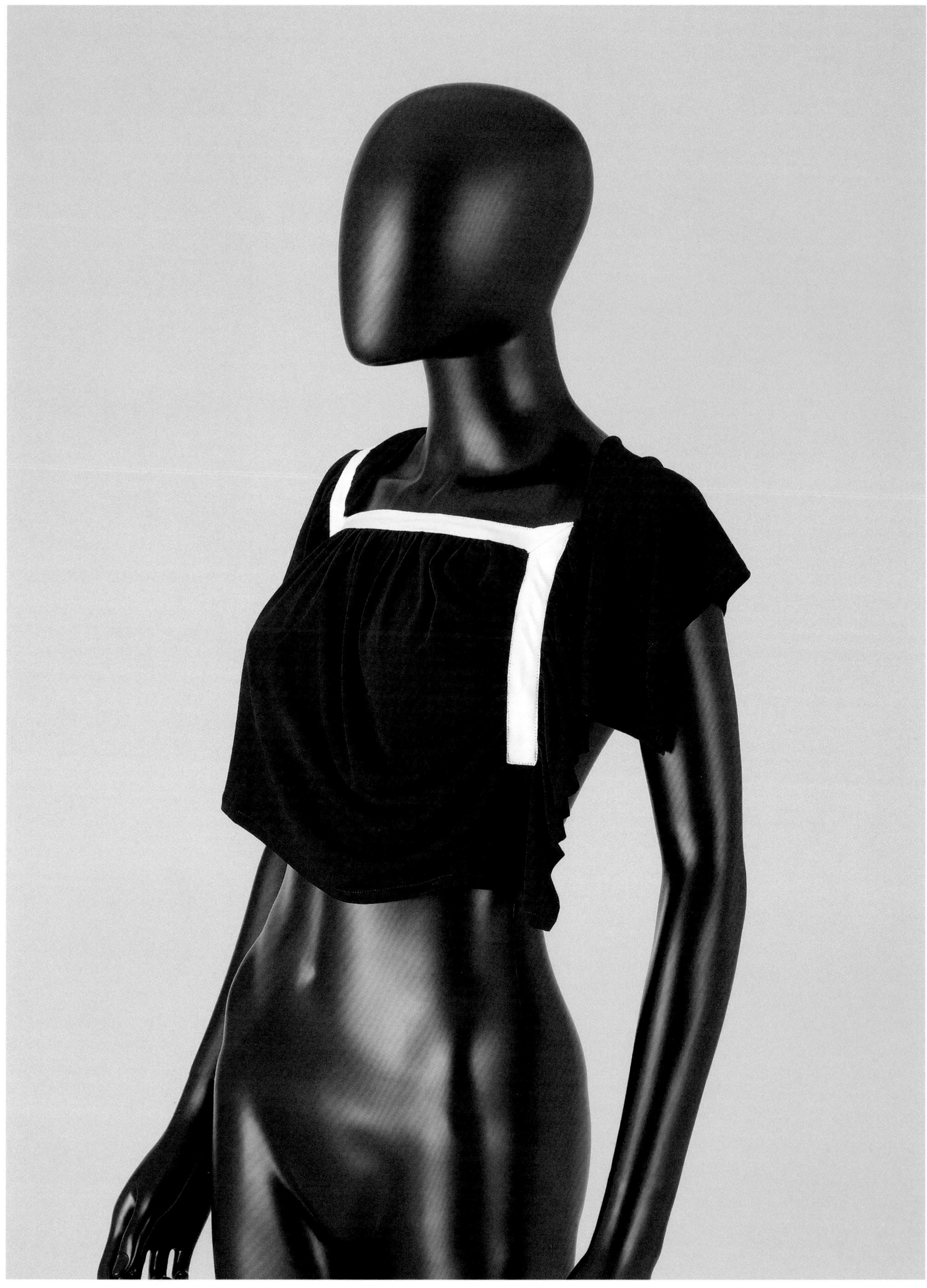

Yesterday top

For more designs based on this artwork, scan the QR code

Carmen Herrera's *Yesterday* is a flexible artwork that can be draped in a number of different ways for a variety of looks. Here I have created a top that uses the black rectangular shape as a shoulder drape with a cowl at the back. I scaled down the white zigzag in a nonlinear fashion and used it as a frame to hold gathers on the black section. The design can be turned around so that the cowl is worn at the front, or it can be worn vertically with the cowl over one shoulder (see p. 50).

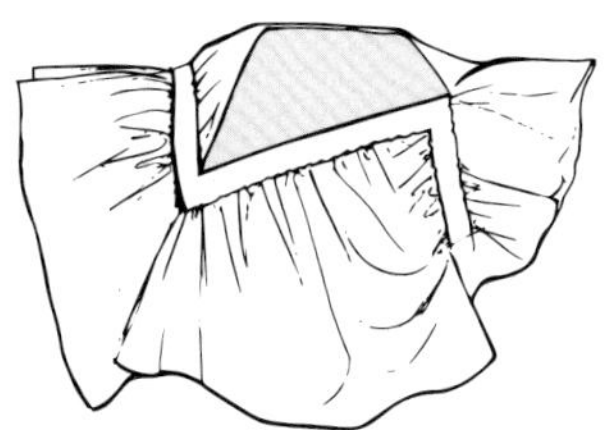

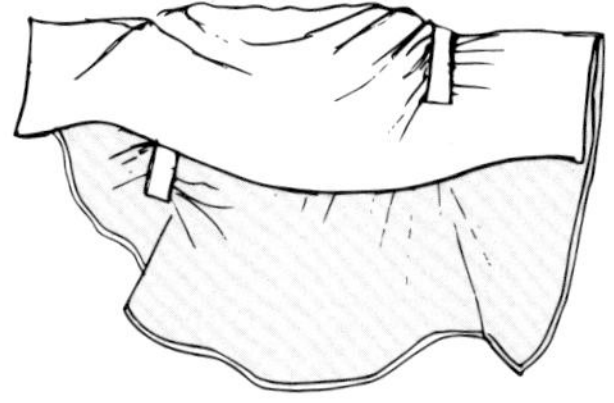

SIZING

The example here is a size B (12–16; US 8–12).

Measurements:

Finished length from front shoulder: 37cm (14⅝in)

Finished length from back shoulder: 27cm (10⅝in)

To create additional sizes, grade the pattern (see p. 10).

FABRIC SUGGESTIONS

Black: Drape jersey, viscose, cotton jersey with minimal stretch.

White: Crisp linen, cotton, silk.

For the sample I used deadstock drape jersey in black and white.

COLOUR REFERENCES

Black #000000

White #FFFFFF

1

Examine the artwork shapes.

Black = **A**

White = **B**

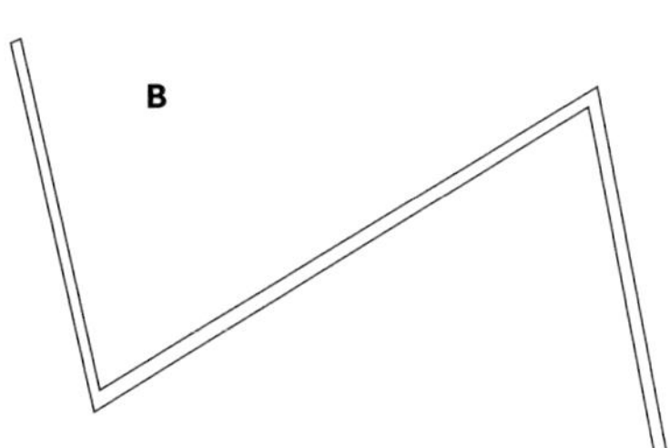

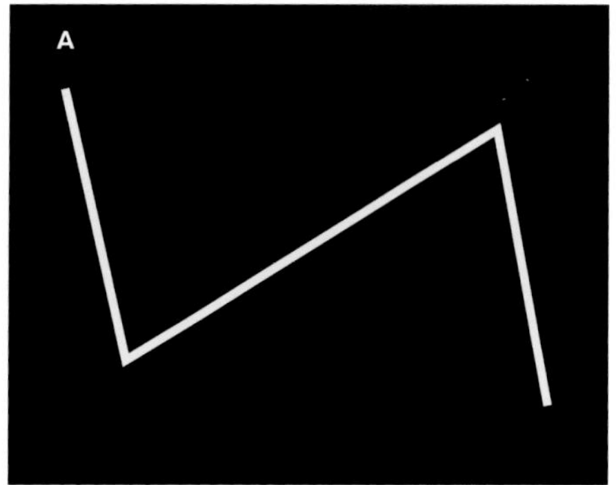

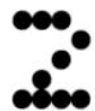

Plot the outlines of the shapes onto plain pattern paper. Place 5cm (2in) squared paper underneath the pattern paper as a guide.

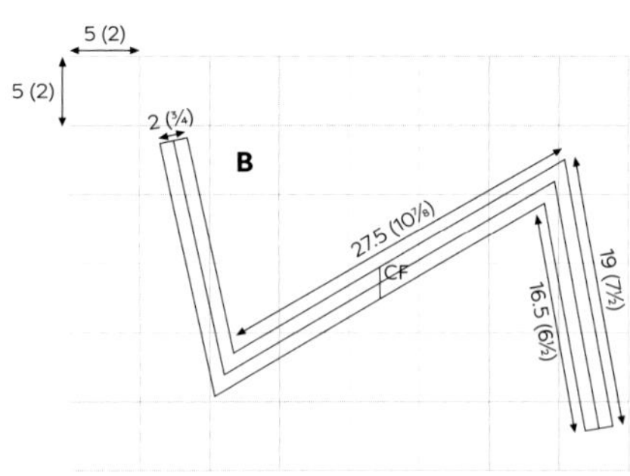

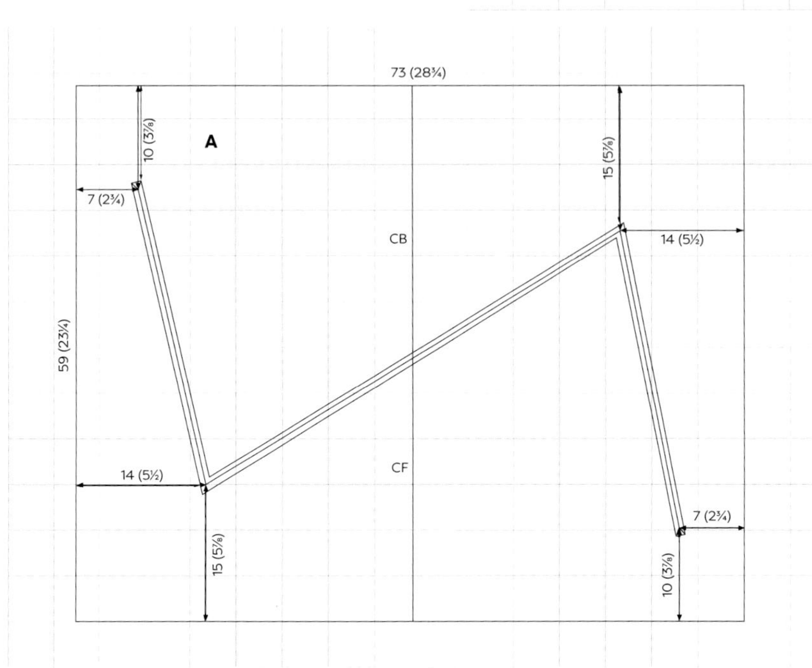

Mark grainlines, CF and CB on each pattern piece.

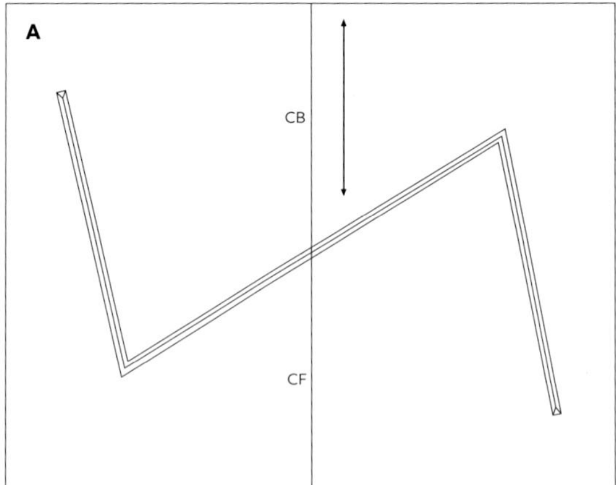

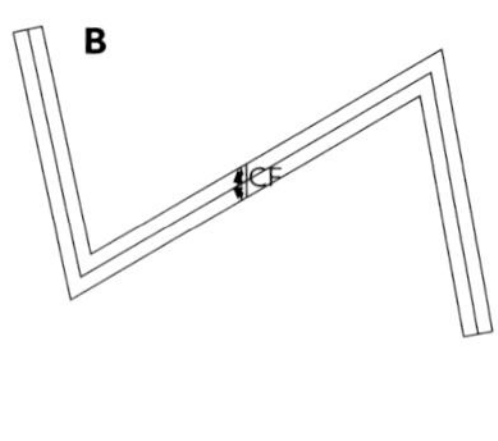

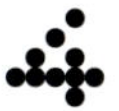

Mark notches and gather references. Add a 1cm (⅜in) seam allowance around each pattern piece. Cut out the pieces in jersey or lightweight calico (muslin).

A (Front and back) x 1 RSU
B x (Facing) x 1 RSU

Using a tracing wheel and carbon paper, transfer grainlines, CF and CB, notches and gather references onto BOTH sides of the fabric.

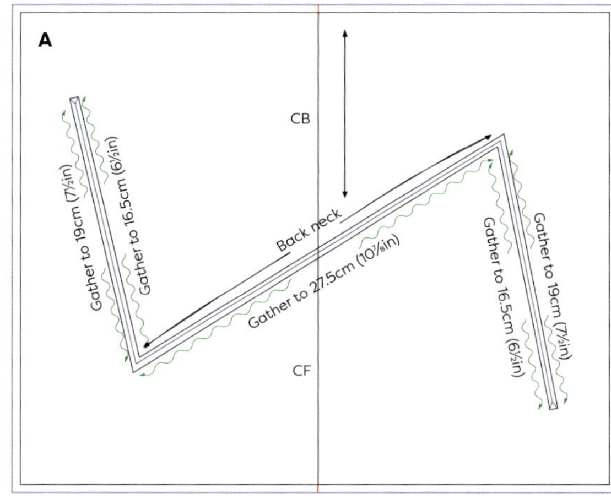

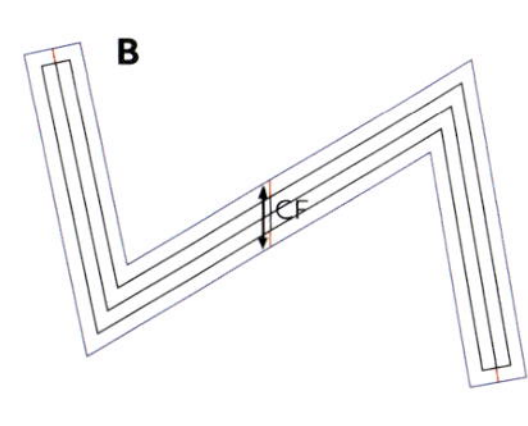

DRAPING THE SHAPES

Prepare the shapes following steps 2–4 of the pattern-cutting instructions (pp. 48–49).

Here calico (muslin) is used to drape the top, with the final fabrication in jersey. Either type of fabric can be used: jersey will give softer gathers, while calico creates a crisper, more structured silhouette.

(i) Create the neck by folding over 1cm (⅜in) along the top edge of the horizontal section of B. Pin B to the dress form.

(ii) Make two rows of running stitches along all the areas on A that are marked for gathers. Attach the left side of A to B and gather to fit the marked sections on A.

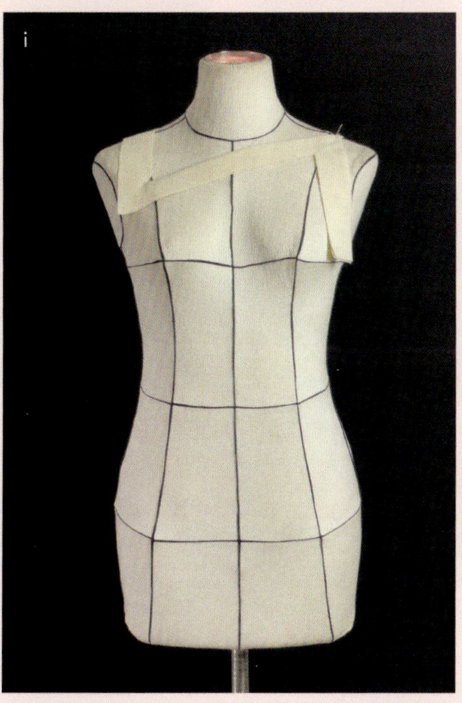

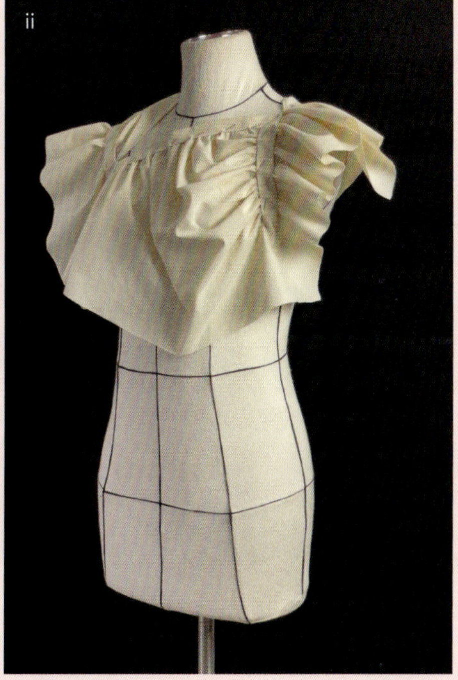

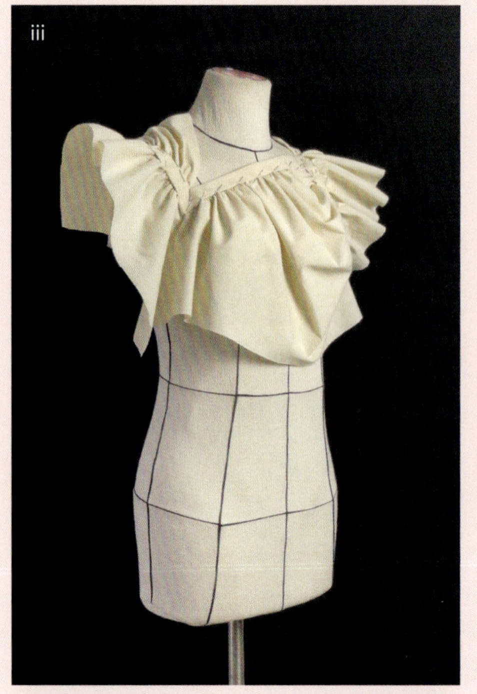

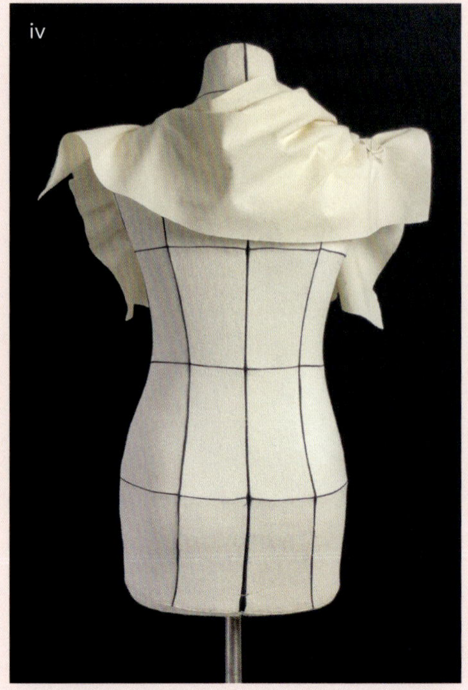

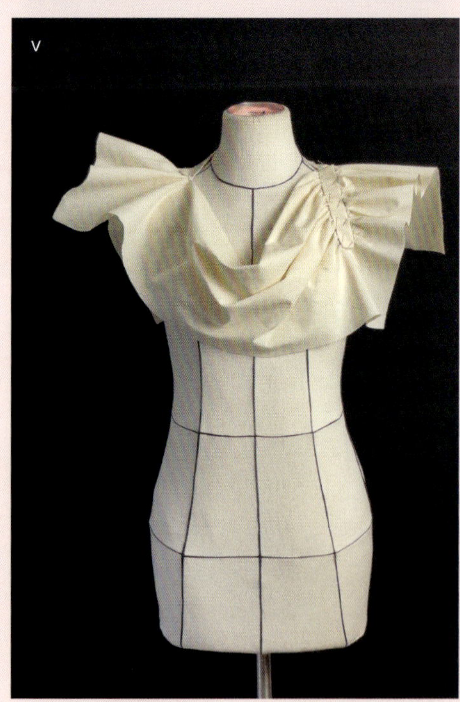

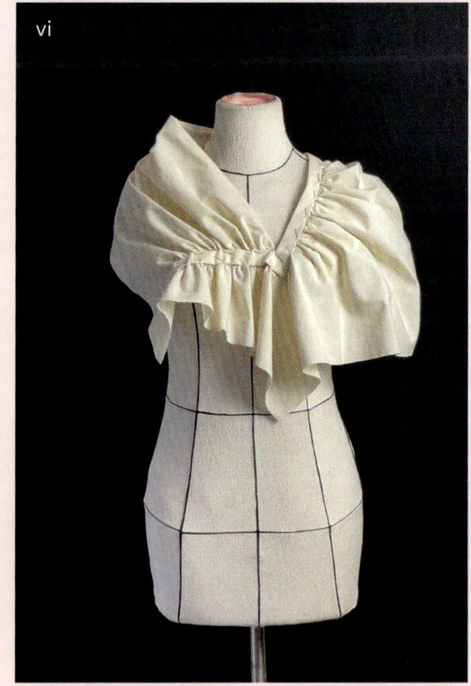

(iii) Attach the right side of A to B and gather to fit the marked sections on A.

(iv) Form a cowl from the back neck area.

(v) The top can be turned around, so that the cowl is worn at the front.

(vi) The top can also be worn with the cowl over one shoulder and the zigzag sitting vertically.

Equation top

I selected Herrera's painting *Equation* for its form and monochrome palette. I developed a top that is fastened at either side with large snap fasteners (press studs). I used the black background to make a rectangular front and back, and draped the triangles to create sleeves, using tucks to add volume in a form that is reminiscent of an articulated harp shell. The triangles are symmetrical in the artwork, so I needed to rotate one of them 180º to form the opposite sleeve.

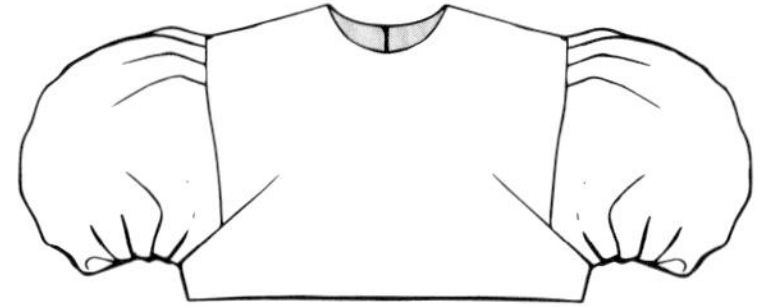

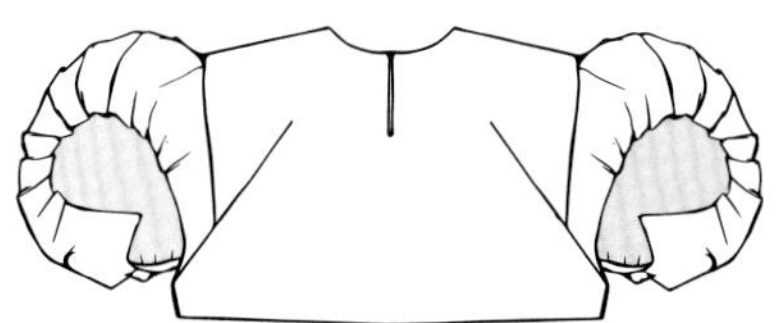

SIZING
The example here is a size B (12–16; US 8–12).
Measurements:
Length from shoulder:
42.5cm (16¾in)

To create additional sizes, grade the pattern (see p. 10).

FABRIC SUGGESTIONS
Black and white: Medium-weight woven fabrics, such as wool crepe, viscose, viscose or silk duchesse satin, organdie, heavy satin-backed crepe, linen, cotton shirting.

For the sample I used deadstock silk duchesse satin. Both sections were backed with tarlatan.

COLOUR REFERENCES
Black #000000
White #FFFFFF

1 Examine the artwork shapes.

Black = **A**
White = **B**

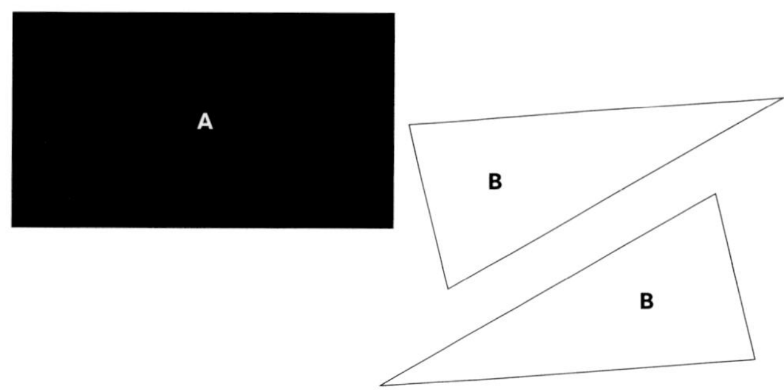

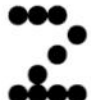

Plot the outlines of the shapes onto plain pattern paper. Place 5cm (2in) squared paper underneath the pattern paper as a guide.

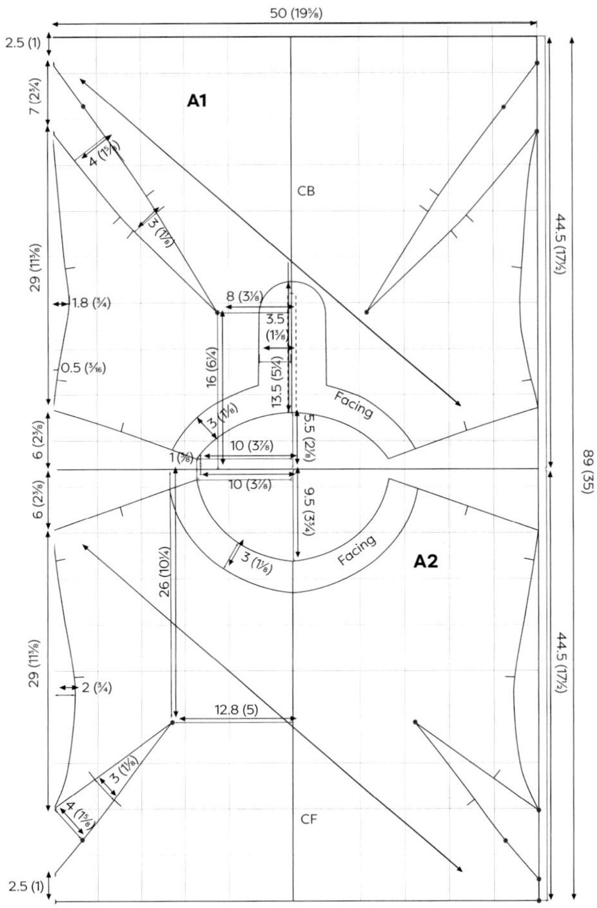

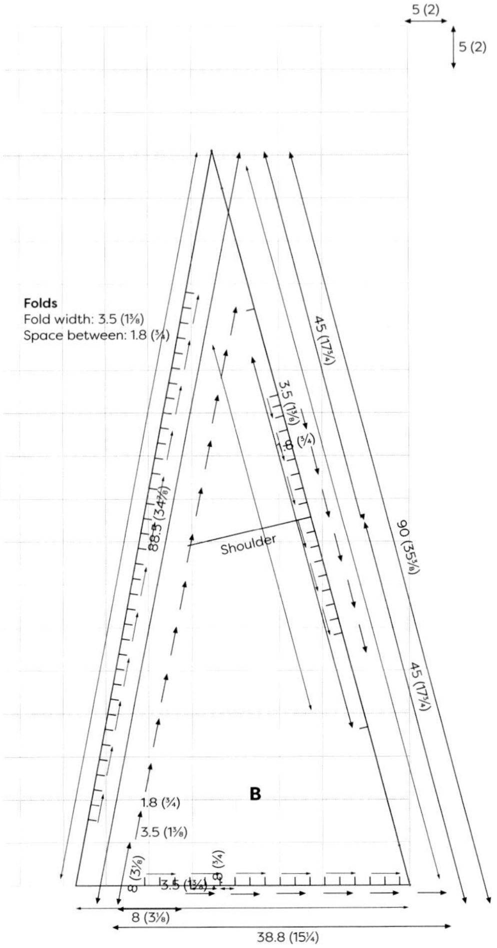

50 (19⅝)
2.5 (1)
7 (2¾)
A1
4 (1⅝)
CB
3 (1⅛)
29 (11⅜)
44.5 (17½)
1.8 (¾)
8 (3⅛)
3.5 (1⅜)
0.5 (³⁄₁₆)
16 (6¼)
13.5 (5¼)
Facing
3 (1⅛)
5.5 (2⅛)
6 (2⅜)
1 (⅜)
10 (3⅞)
89 (35)
10 (3⅞)
6 (2⅜)
9.5 (3¾)
Facing
3 (1⅛)
A2
26 (10¼)
29 (11⅜)
44.5 (17½)
2 (¾)
12.8 (5)
3 (1⅛)
4 (1⅝)
CF
2.5 (1)

5 (2)
5 (2)
Folds
Fold width: 3.5 (1⅜)
Space between: 1.8 (¾)
45 (17¾)
3.5 (1⅜)
1.8 (¾)
88.5 (34⅞)
Shoulder
90 (35⅝)
45 (17¾)
1.8 (¾)
3.5 (1⅜)
B
8 (3⅛)
3.5 (1⅜)
1.8 (¾)
8 (3⅛)
38.8 (15¼)

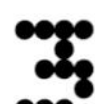

Mark bias grainlines, CF and CB, darts, tucks, drill holes and notches on the pattern pieces.

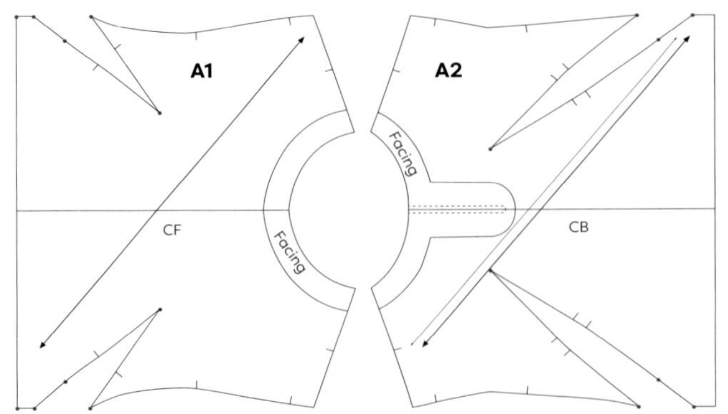

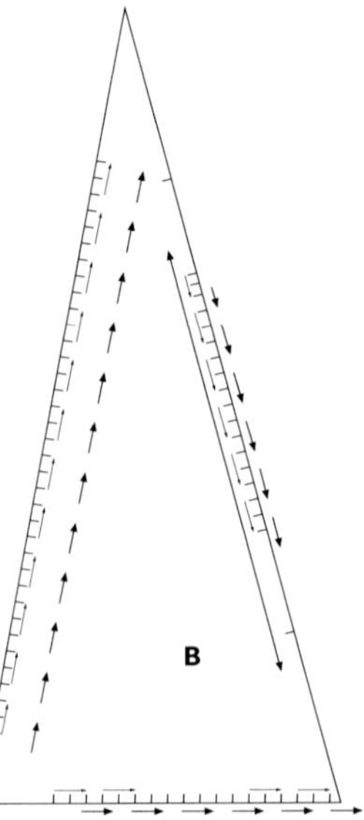

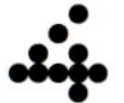

Trace the front and back neck facings (C and D) separately.

Add a 1cm (⅜in) seam allowance around each pattern piece. Cut out the pieces in calico (muslin).

A1 (Front) x 1 RSU
A2 (Back) x 1 RSU
B (Sleeve) x 2 RSU
C (Front facing) x 1
D (Back facing) x 1

Using a tracing wheel and carbon paper, transfer CF and CB, darts, tucks, drill holes and notches onto BOTH sides of the fabric.

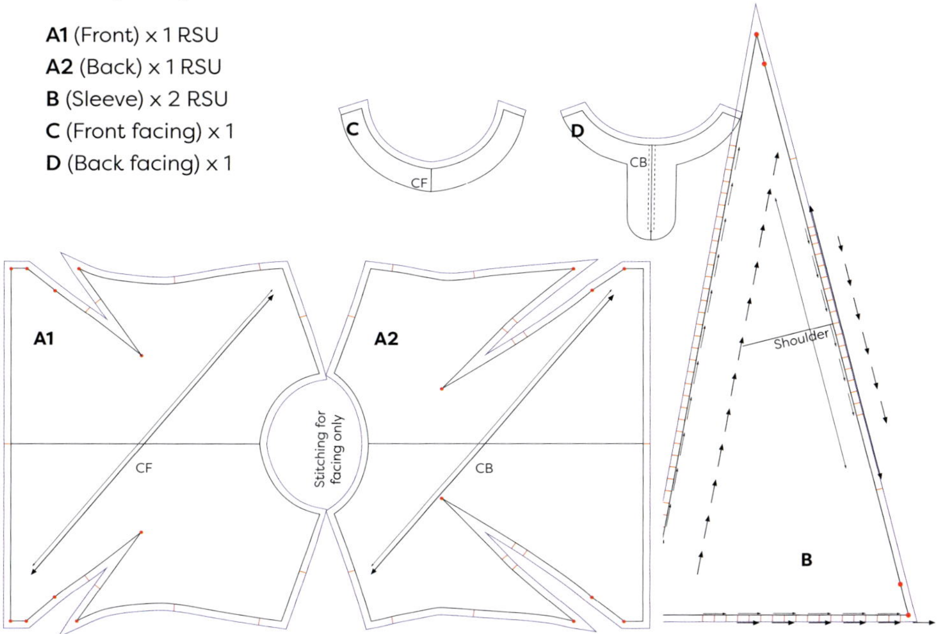

DRAPING THE SHAPES

To follow this draping process, cut out section A as a rectangle and mark the neckline, shoulder line, darts and armholes, as shown in step 2 of the pattern-cutting instructions on the opposite page.

(i) Fold section A in half horizontally and make a slash large enough to fit over the neck of the dress form. Make vertical slashes to open the neck area and make a neck hole.

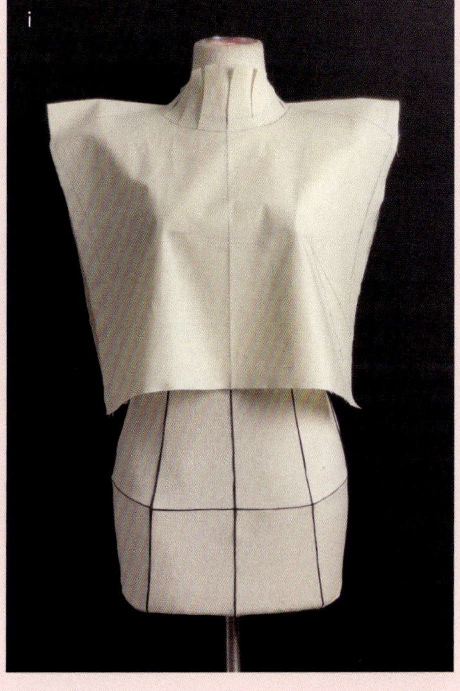

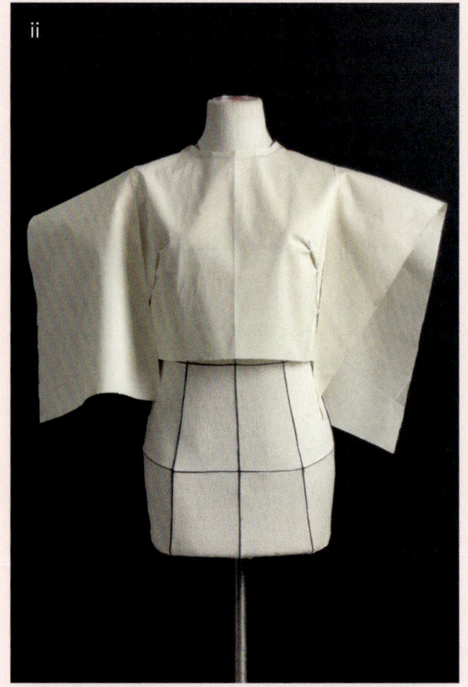

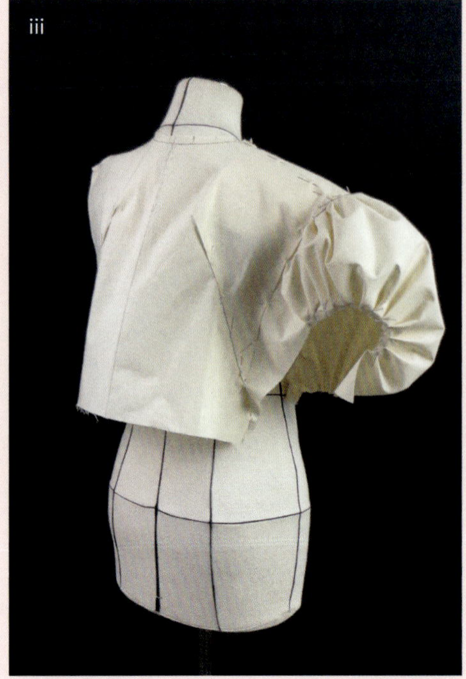

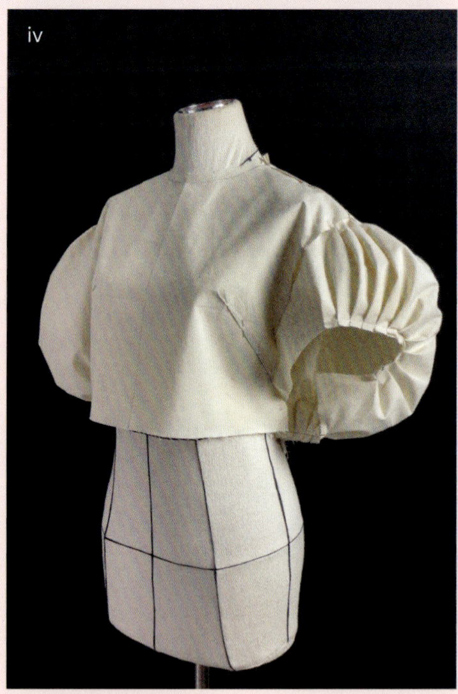

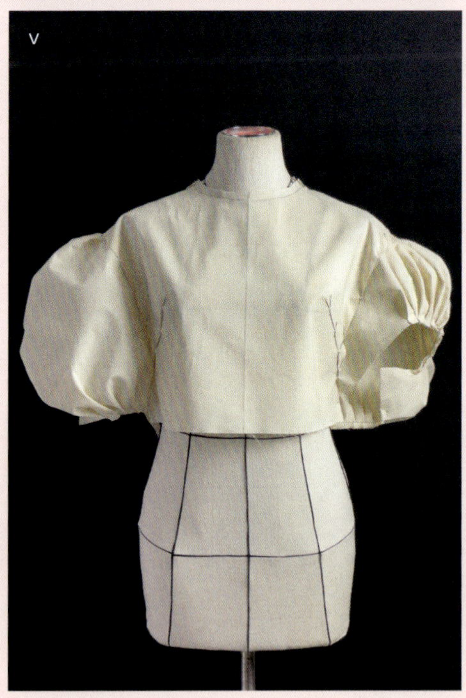

(ii) Pin the shoulders and cut away the excess fabric, leaving a 1cm seam allowance. Make the darts on the front and the back. Pin the sleeves to the middle of both shoulders.

(iii) Make the tucks on the right sleeve head, and on the lower sections.

(iv) Make the tucks on the left sleeve head, and on the lower sections.

(v) The finished drape.

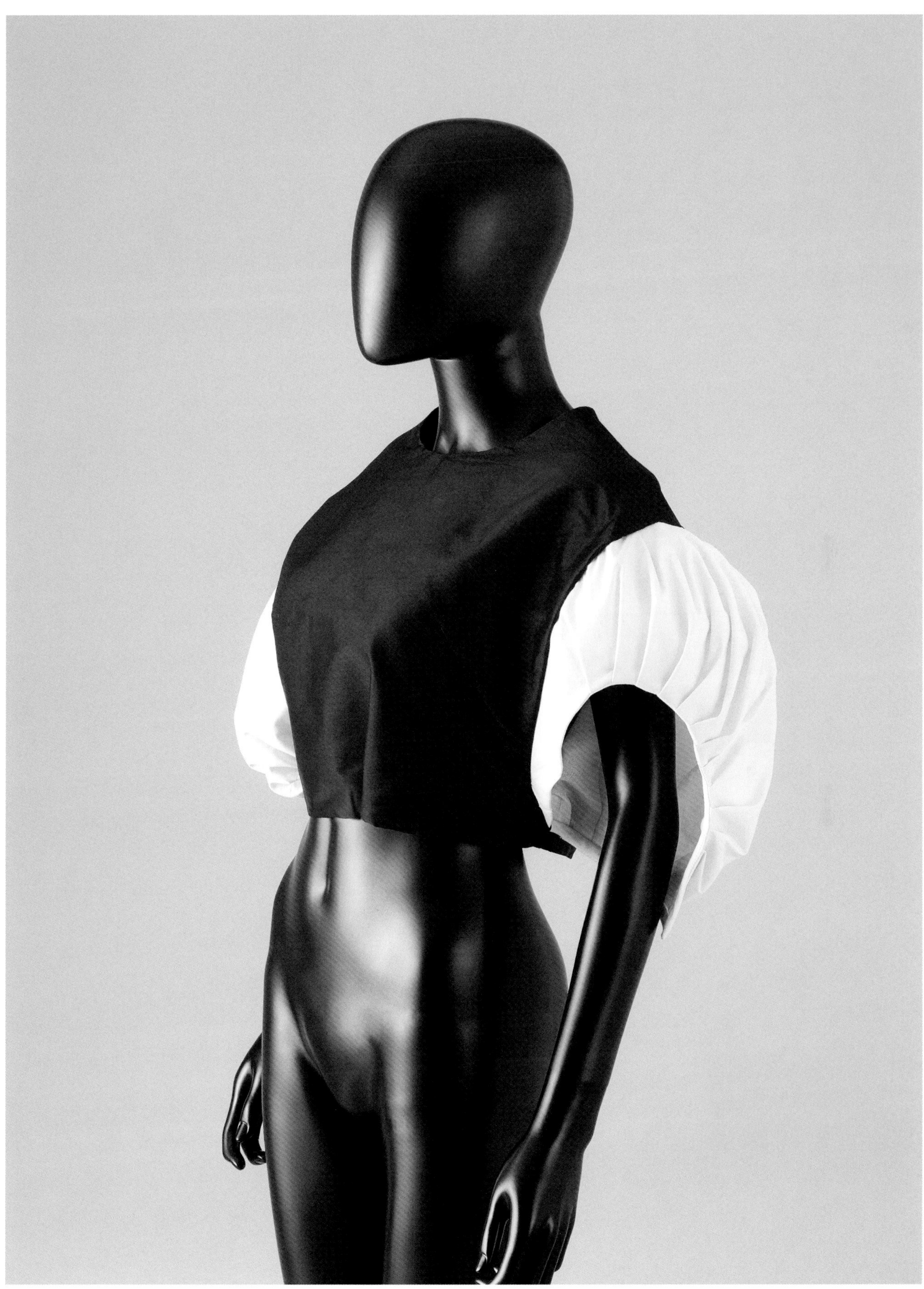

Equation top

Blanco y Verde dress

I turned the geometric shapes of Herrera's *Blanco y Verde* into a draped dress with a spiral skirt. The square in the centre of the painting becomes the front bodice of the dress and features an asymmetric cowl neck, held in place by an asymmetric facing. One of the triangles forms the skirt of the dress, and two are gathered at the neckline in a billowing cape that adds voluminous, structural interest. The fourth triangle can be fashioned into a head scarf or wrap. The finished design surprised me, as my initial sketches were taking me in a slightly different direction. The beauty of freestyle draping is that it allows you to see what the cloth wants to do.

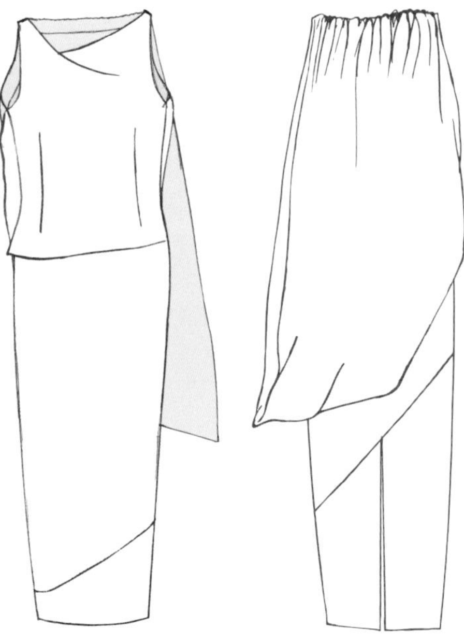

SIZING

The example here is a size 10 (US 6).

Measurements:

Bust: 94cm (37in)

Waist: 78cm (30¾in)

Hips: 96cm (37¾in)

Length: 120cm (47¼in)

To create additional sizes, grade the pattern (see p. 10).

FABRIC SUGGESTIONS

Wool or viscose crepe, silk satin, double wool crepe, satin-backed crepe.

COLOUR REFERENCES

Green #004EC7

Examine the artwork shapes.

Square = **A** and **B**
Triangles = **C**, **D**, **E** and **F**

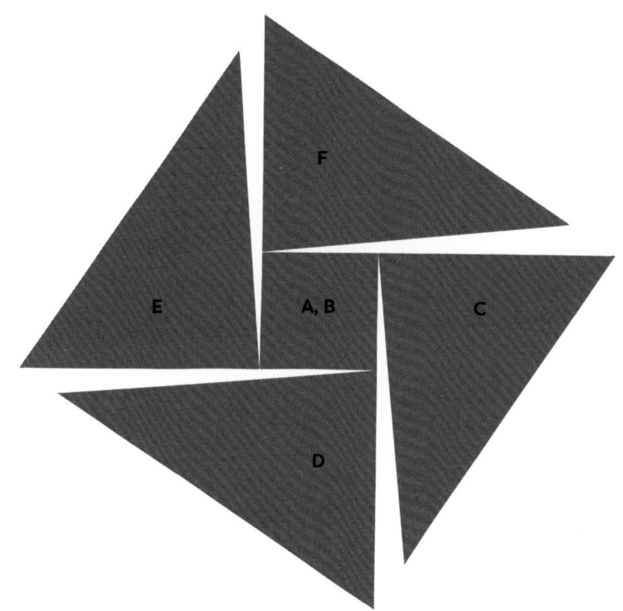

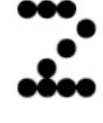

Plot the outlines of the shapes onto plain pattern paper. Place 5cm (2in) squared paper underneath the pattern paper as a guide.

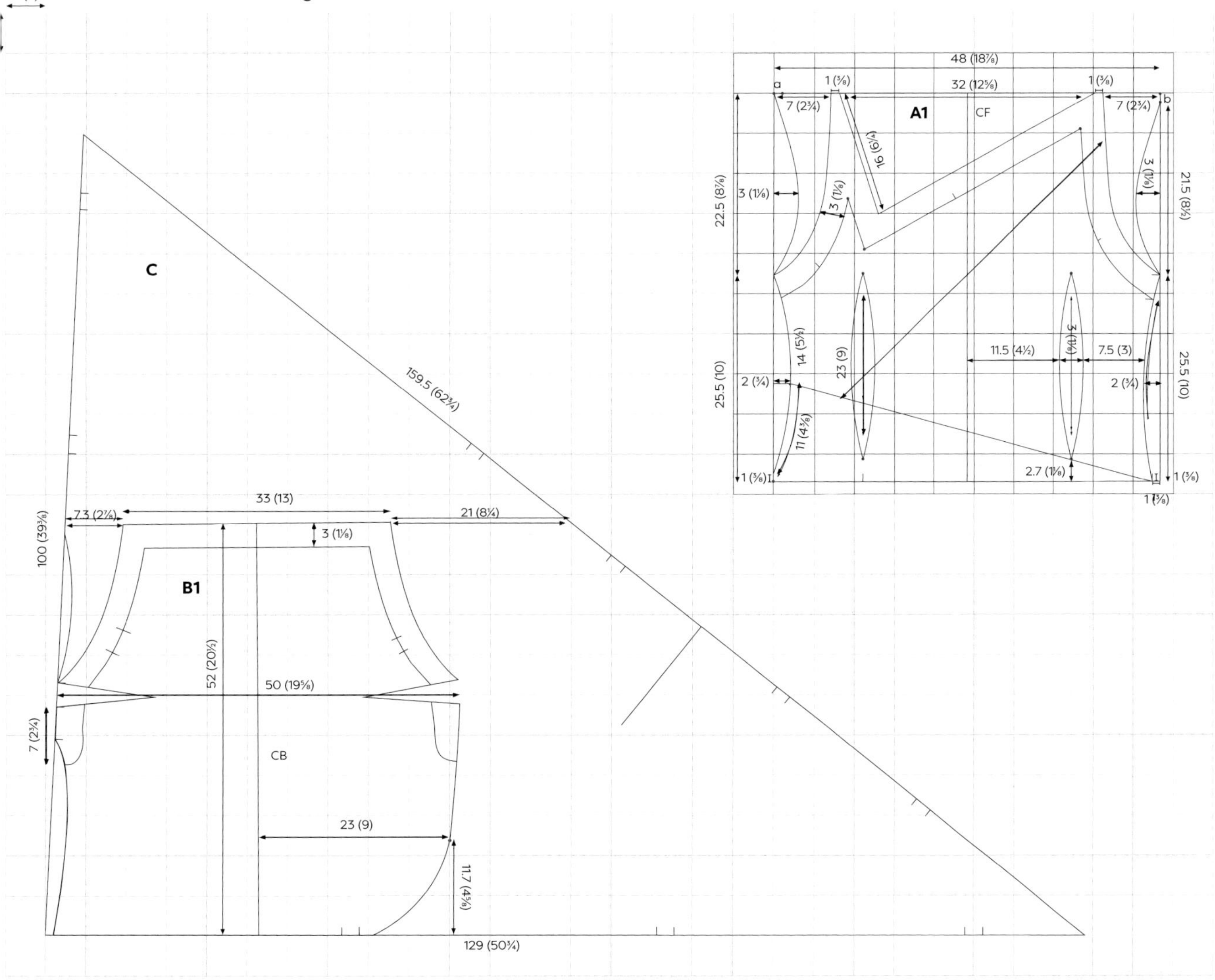

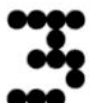

Trace section A1, the front bodice. Trace the bodice lining (A2) and the front facing (A3) and flip them horizontally.

Trace the back bodice lining section (B1) and the back facing (B2) and flip them horizontally.

Use the outline of triangle C to create two additional triangles – D1 and E.

Plot the darts and curves as shown in the diagrams below. Extract the facings (D2 and D3) from triangle D1.

Mark grainlines, CF and CB, darts, drill holes and notches on all pattern pieces.

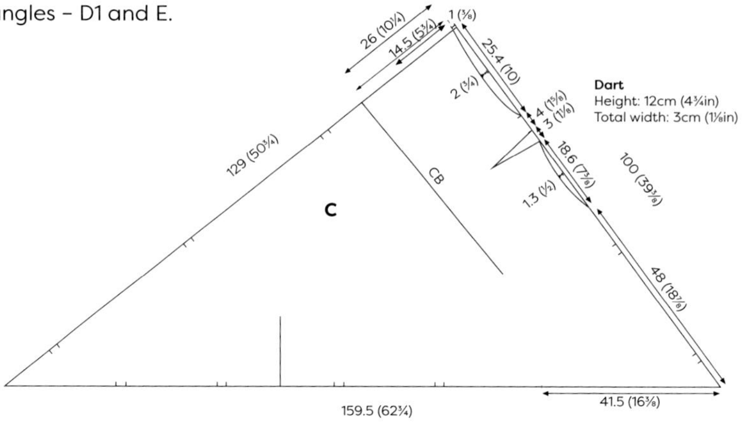

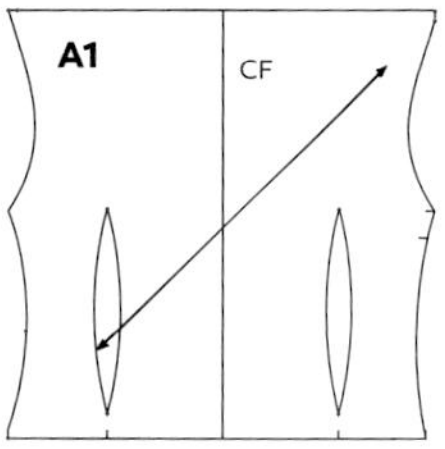

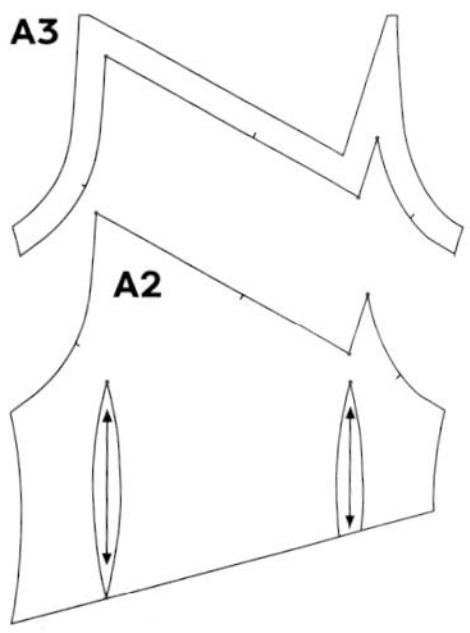

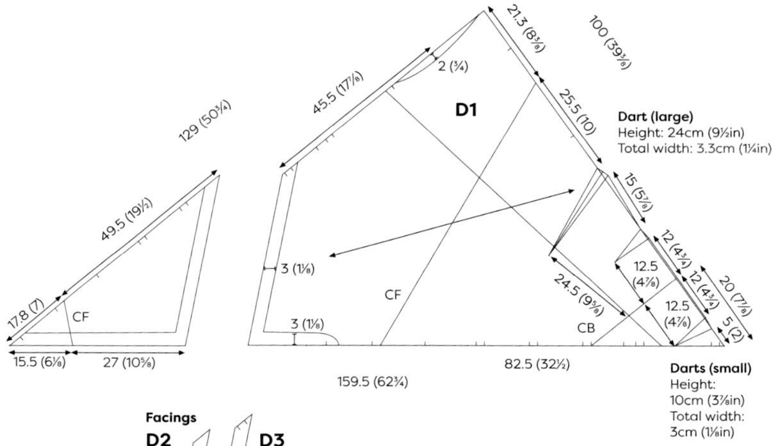

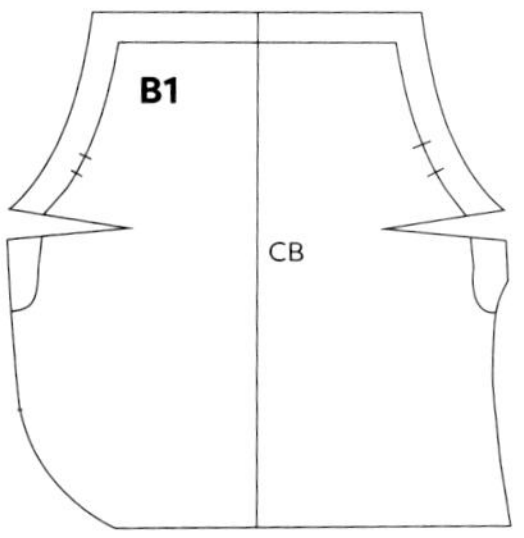

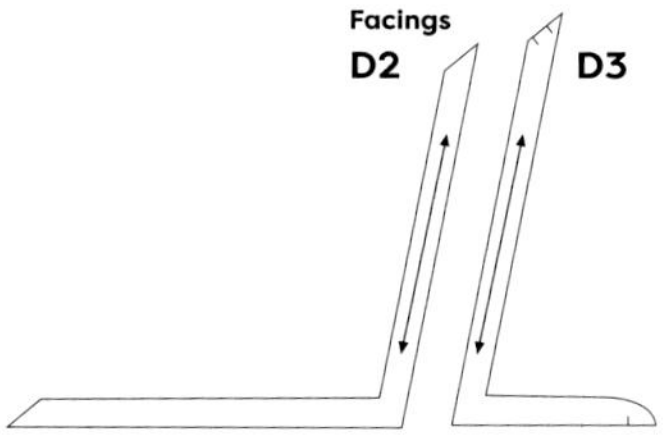

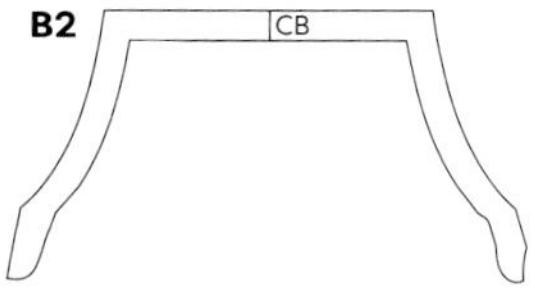

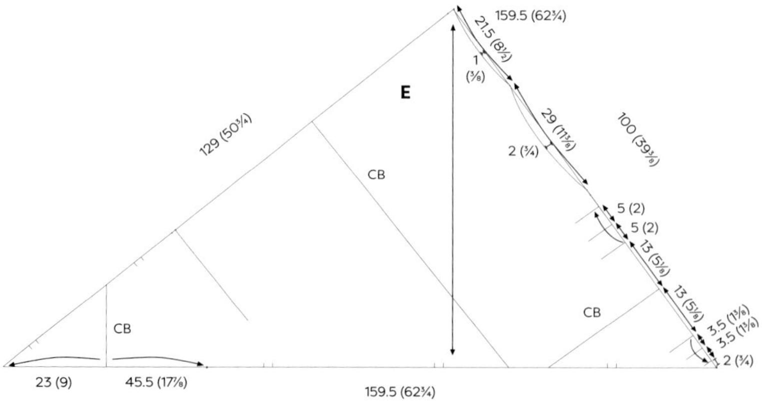

A1
CF

A3

A2

B1
CB

B2
CB

26 (10¼)
14.5 (5¾)
1 (⅜)
25.4 (10)
2 (¾)
4 (1⅝)
3 (1⅛)
18.6 (7⅜)
1.3 (½)
100 (39⅜)
48 (18⅞)
129 (50¾)
C
CB
159.5 (62¾)
41.5 (16⅜)

Dart
Height: 12cm (4¾in)
Total width: 3cm (1⅛in)

129 (50¾)
49.5 (19½)
17.8 (7)
CF
15.5 (6⅛)
27 (10⅝)

45.5 (17⅞)
21.3 (8⅜)
100 (39⅜)
2 (¾)
D1
25.5 (10)
15 (5⅞)
3 (1⅛)
CF
3 (1⅛)
24.5 (9⅝)
CB
12.5 (4⅞)
12.5 (4⅞)
12 (4¾)
12 (4¾)
20 (7⅞)
5 (2)
159.5 (62¾)
82.5 (32½)

Dart (large)
Height: 24cm (9½in)
Total width: 3.3cm (1¼in)

Darts (small)
Height:
10cm (3⅞in)
Total width:
3cm (1⅛in)

Facings
D2
D3

159.5 (62¾)
21.5 (8½)
1 (⅜)
E
29 (11⅜)
2 (¾)
100 (39⅜)
129 (50¾)
CB
5 (2)
5 (2)
13 (5⅛)
13 (5⅛)
3.5 (1⅜)
3.5 (1⅜)
2 (¾)
CB
CB
23 (9)
45.5 (17⅞)
159.5 (62¾)

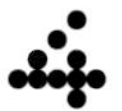

Add a 1cm (⅜in) seam allowance around each pattern piece.

Cut out the pattern pieces in calico (muslin). Using a tracing wheel and carbon paper, transfer grainlines, CF and CB, darts, drill holes and notches onto BOTH sides of the fabric.

A1 (Front) x 1 RSU
A2 (Front lining) x 1 RSU
A3 (Front facing) x 1 RSU
B1 (Back lining) x 1 RSU
B2 (Back facing) x 1 RSU
C (Cape) x 1 RSU
D1 (Skirt) x 1 RSU
D2 (Facing) x 1 RSU
D3 (Facing) x 1 RSU
E (Cape) x 1 RSU
F (Scarf) x 1 RSU

C
Zip
Drop waist
CF
Armhole
a
Gather to 33cm (13in)
CB
Fold
① ② ③

D2
D3
CF

D1
Bag out
Attach bodice lining here
Adjust length here
CF
CB

A1
CF
Zip
Bag out

A3
A2

E
b
Armhole
Side seam
CB
Join to front left shoulder
a
Gather to 33cm (13in)
Fold
Gather to 33cm (13in)
Ease to fit C
CB
Drop waist
③ ①

B2
CB

B1
CB

F
129 (50¾)
100 (39⅜)
Pin hem
Pin hem
Pin hem
159.5 (62¾)

DRAPING THE SHAPES

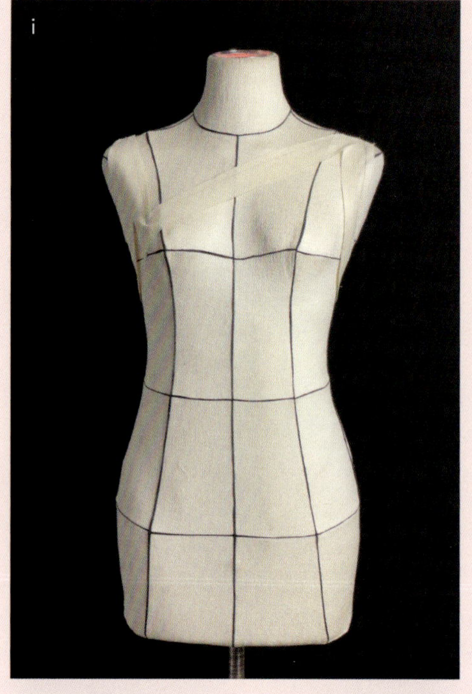
i

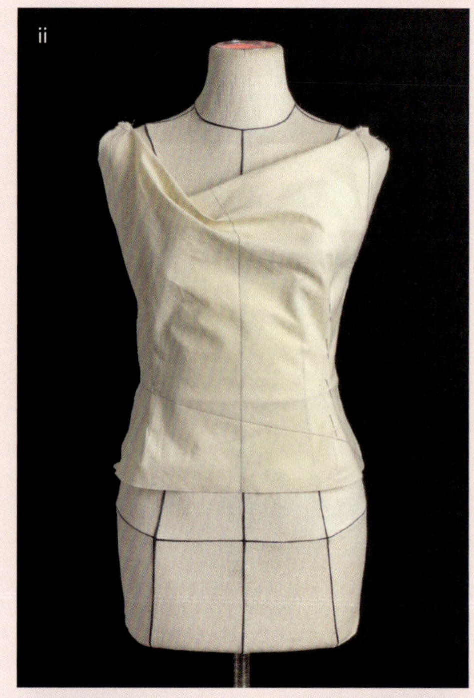
ii

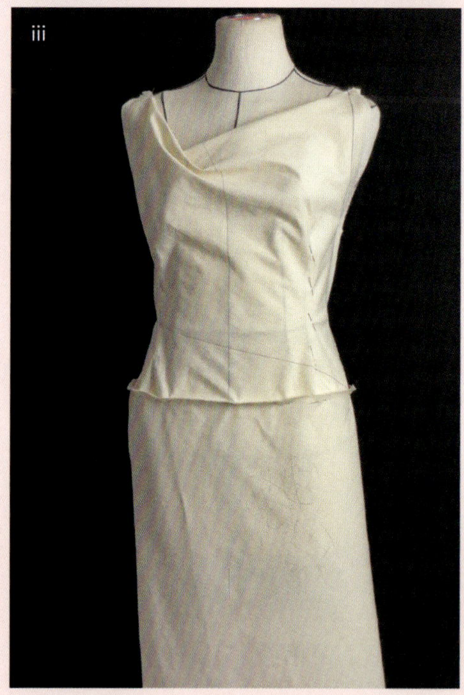
iii

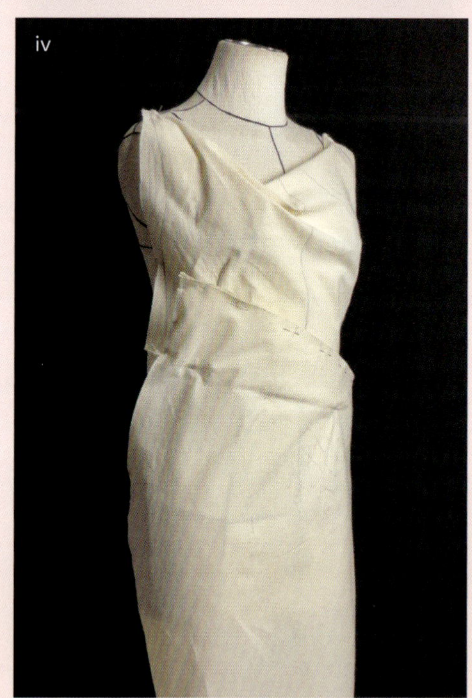
iv

Prepare the shapes following steps 2–4 of the pattern-cutting instructions (pp. 57–59).

(i) Pin the front facing (A3) to the dress form.

(ii) Make the fisheye darts on the bodice (A1) and attach to the facing.

(iii) Attach skirt D1 to the bottom of the bodice.

(iv) Attach the area labelled BAG OUT on the bodice to skirt D1.

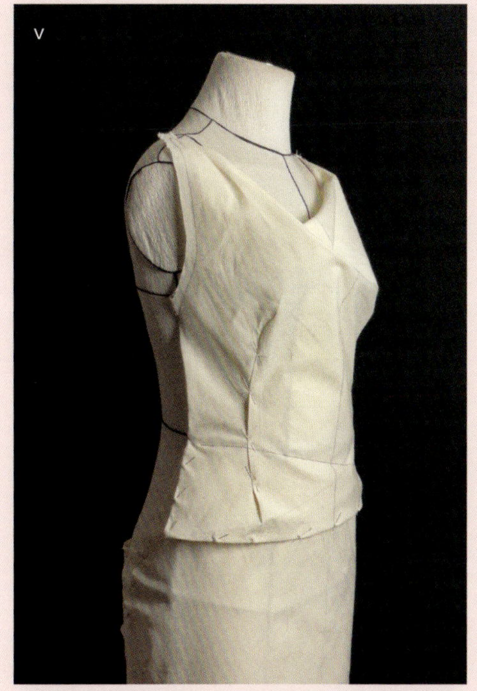

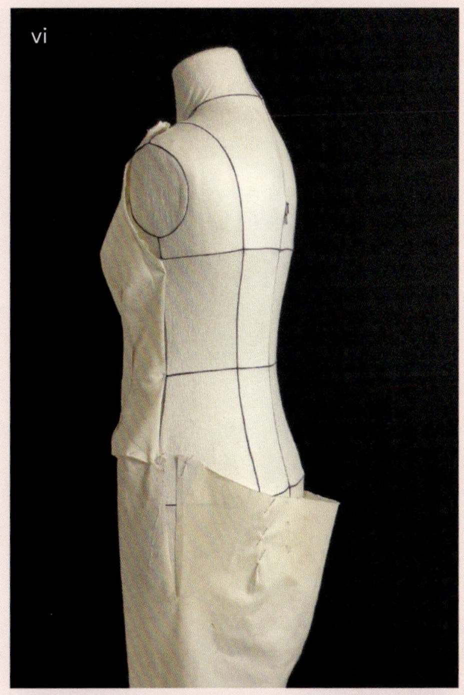

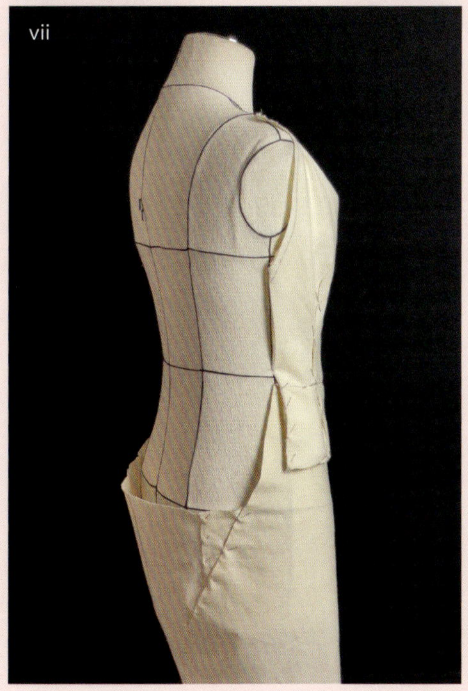

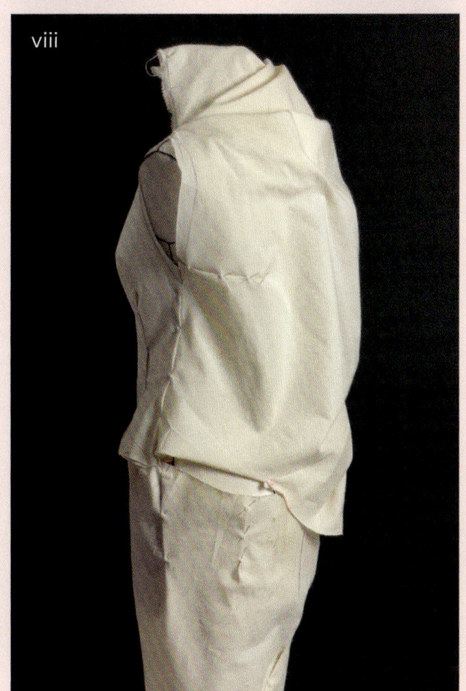

(v) View of the asymmetrical peplum.

(vi) Make the darts at the hip area of skirt D1.

(vii) Match the notches and close the back right.

(viii) Sew two rows of gathering stitches where marked on sections C and E. Make the armhole dart and attach to the bodice (A1) at the side seam. (Note: A zip should be inserted on the left bodice and skirt.) Attach the left shoulder. Join C and E together at area 1.

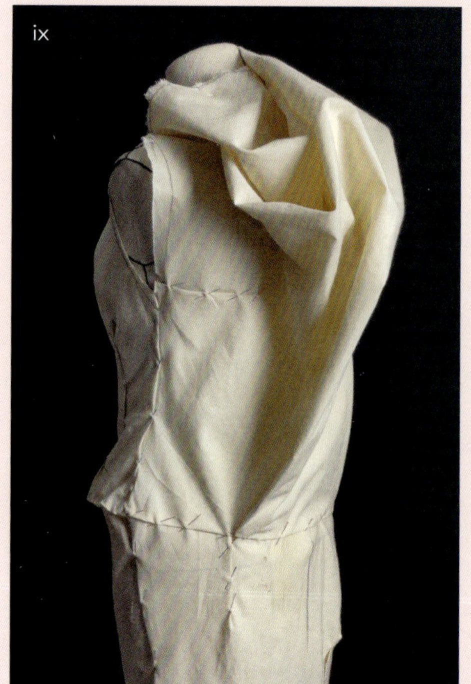

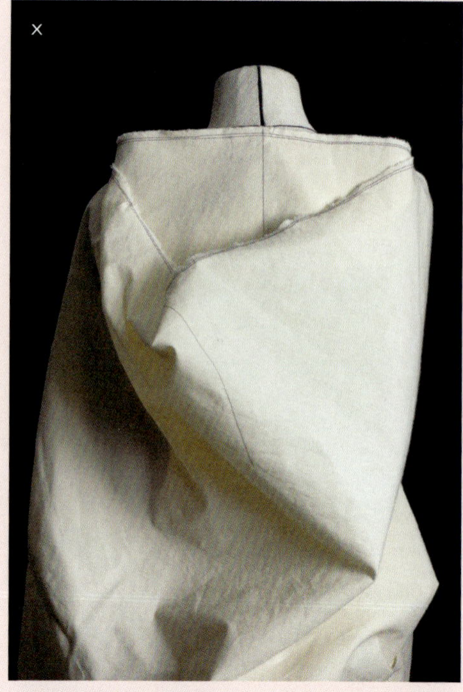

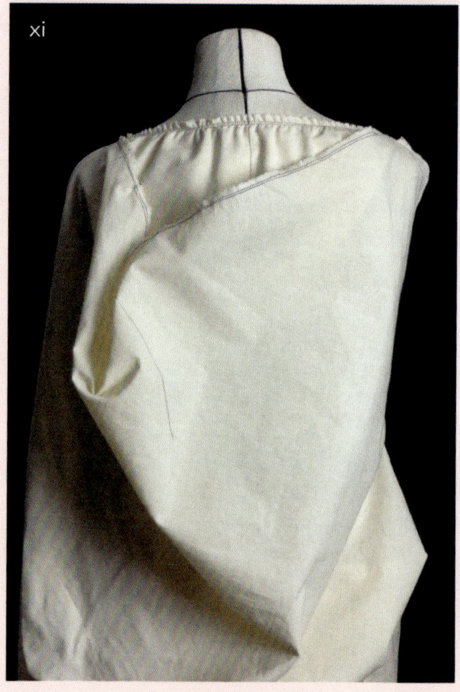

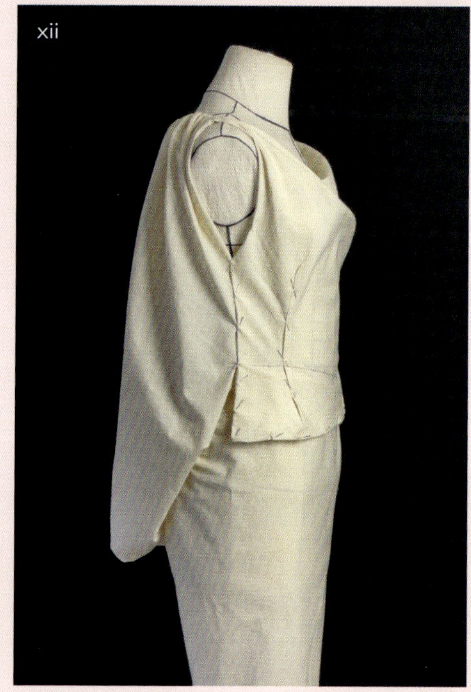

(ix) Attach the lower left back of section C to the skirt. Fold area 2 on section C. Ease area 3 on section E to fit area 3 on section C.

(x) Fold section E where marked and pin the back into place in preparation for completing the gathering.

(xi) Gather the lower back neck to fit. Gather the upper back to fit.

(xii) Attach the back sections to the front at the shoulders.

The fourth triangle, section F, can be used to make a scarf, finished with a pin hem, which can be attached to point *b* on section E (not shown).

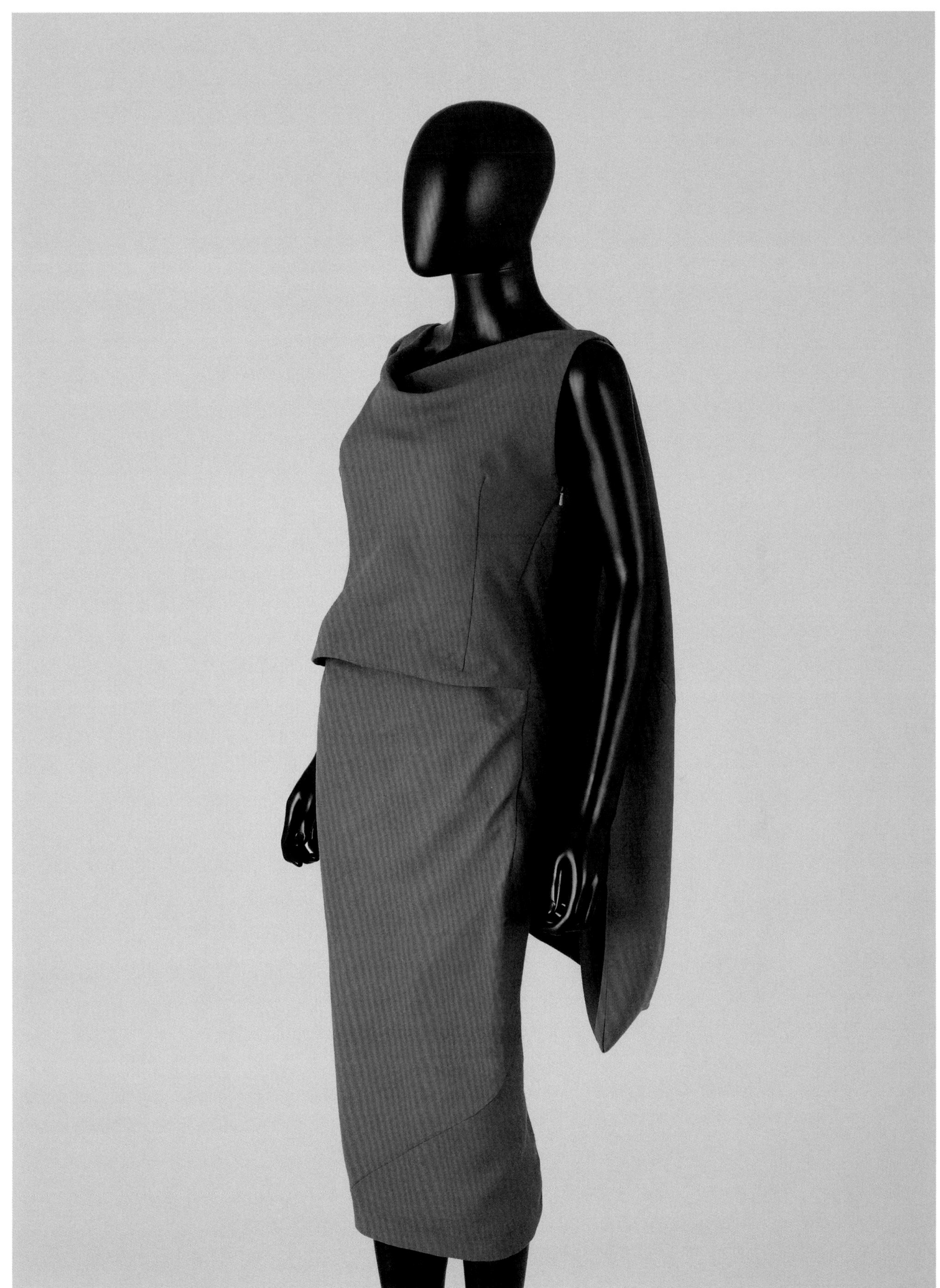

Blanco y Verde dress

LUBAINA HIMID

British artist and curator Lubaina Himid (b. 1954, Sultanate of Zanzibar) studied theatre design at the Wimbledon College of Art and cultural history at the Royal College of Art in London. She was an influential member of the Black arts movement in the UK in the 1980s and in 2018 was appointed a Commander of the Order of the British Empire (CBE) for her contributions to Black women's art. Himid uses everyday items such as old cardboard, boxes, pieces of wood and old chests of drawers to create paintings, drawings, prints and installations exploring Black heritage and uncovering the stories of marginalized figures. Her approach to colour and shape is influenced by her mother's work as a textile artist.

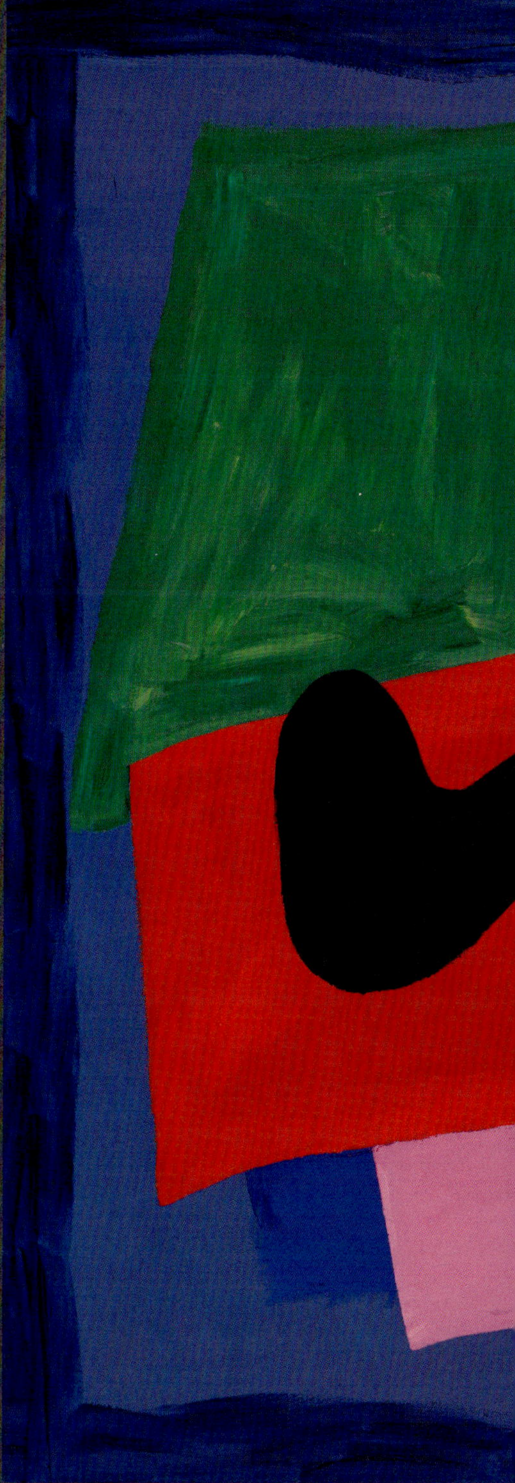

Carpet, 1992, acrylic paint on canvas, 121.9 × 152.4cm (48 × 60in), Tate

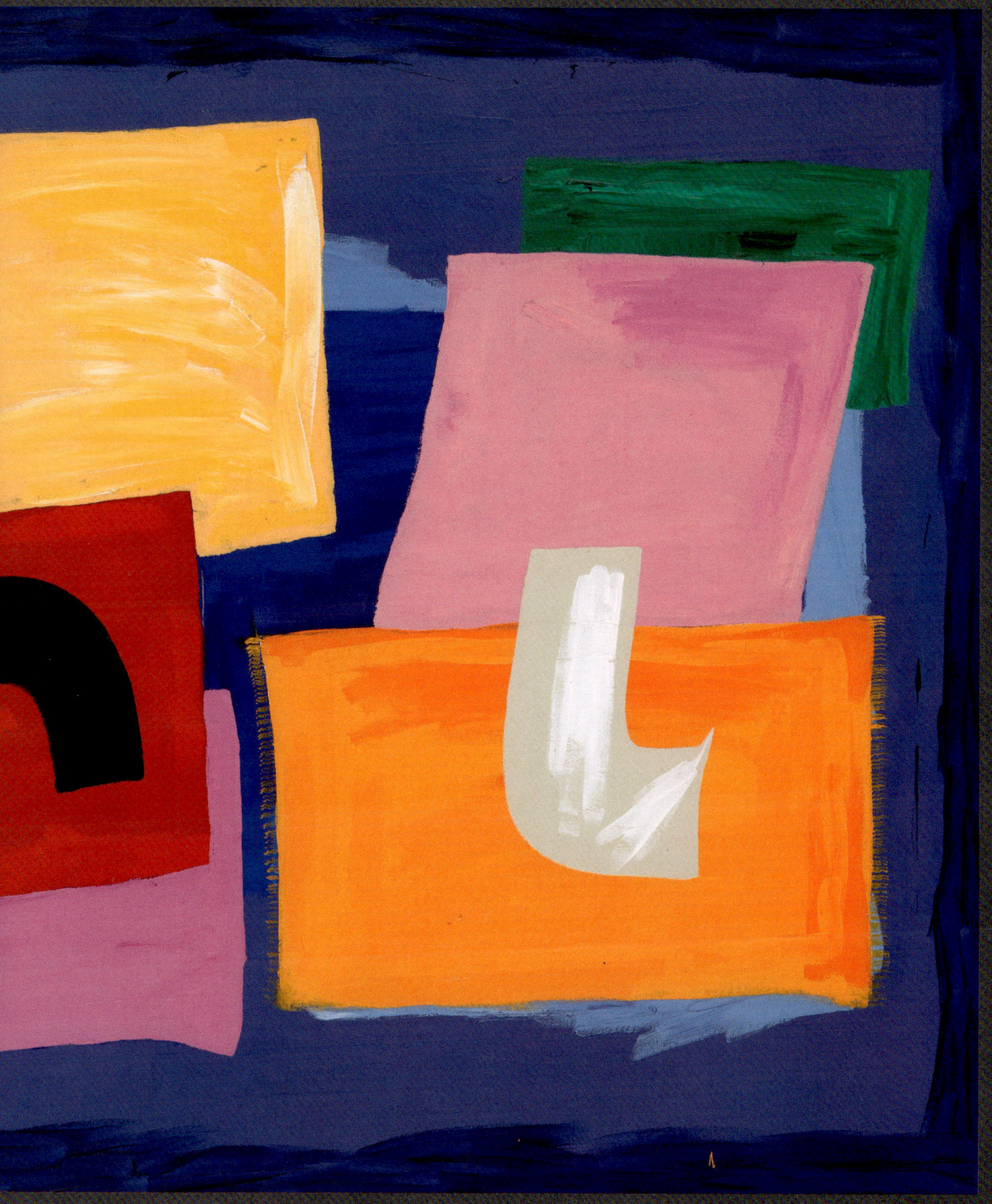

Carpet jacket

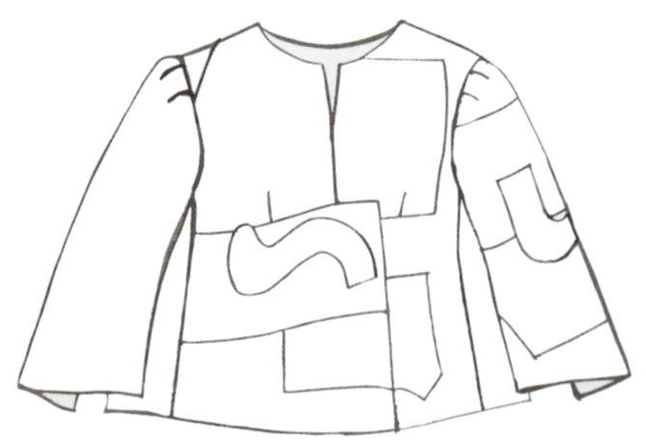

Himid describes her painting *Carpet* in terms of patchwork and cloth. With this in mind, I created a patchwork tweed jacket with cape-like sleeves. I shaped the multicoloured blocks to fit the body at the front and in one sleeve, and used the rectangular blue background for the back of the jacket. The gathered neck constricts the upper back, creating a sculptural silhouette.

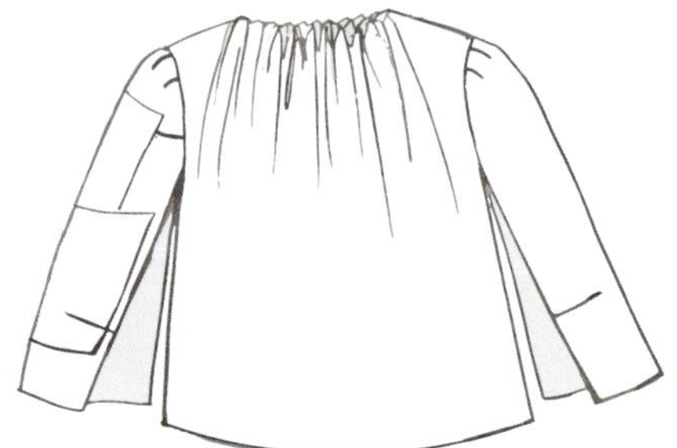

SIZING

The example here is a size 14 (US 10).

Measurements:

Bust: 106cm (41¾in)

Waist: 110cm (43¼in)

Hips: 122cm (48in)

Length: 60cm (23⅝in)

Sleeve length: 55cm (21⅝in)

To create additional sizes, grade the pattern (see p. 10).

FABRIC SUGGESTIONS

All colours: Tweed

COLOUR REFERENCES

Blue #1D2A7D

Green #317351

Yellow #F2B205

Pink #CF8AA6

Red #A00015

Black #000000

Beige #D3CBB7

Orange #E48902

1

Examine the artwork shapes.

Blue = **A**

Green = **B** and **E**

Yellow = **C**

Pink = **D** and **I**

Red = **F**

Black = **G**

Beige = **H**

Orange = **J**

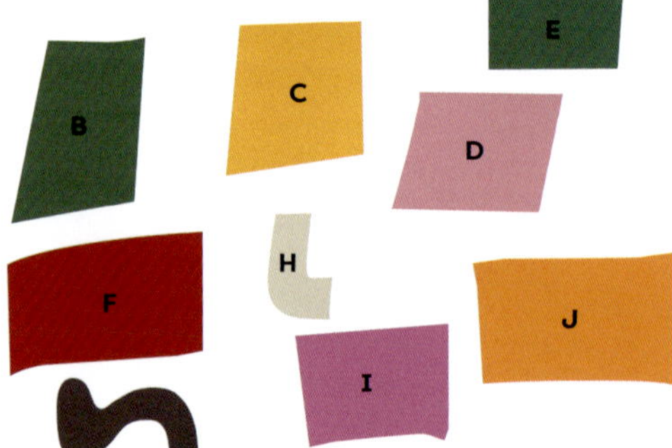

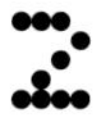

Plot the outlines of the shapes onto plain pattern paper. Place 5cm (2in) squared paper underneath the pattern paper as a guide.

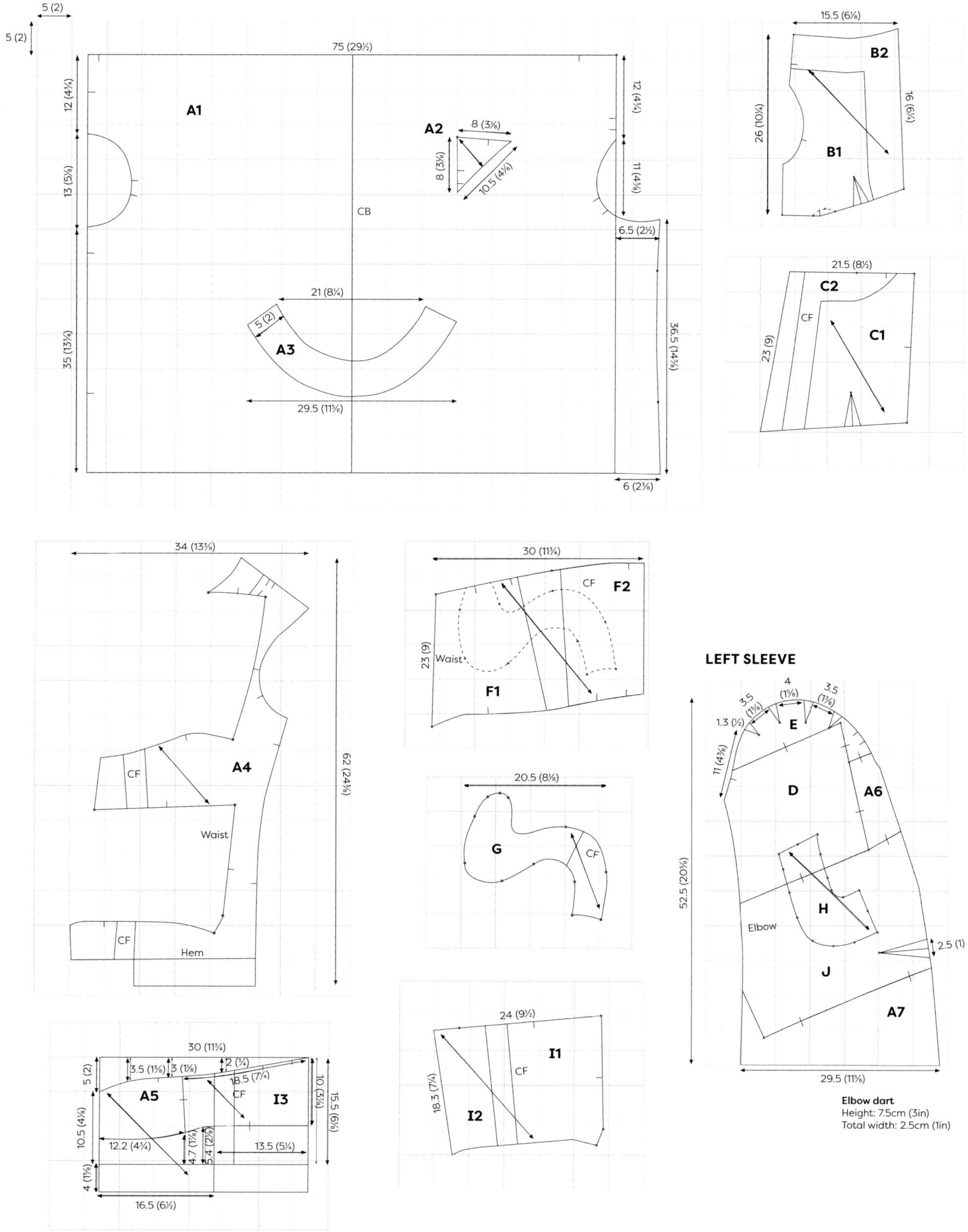

LEFT SLEEVE

Elbow dart
Height: 7.5cm (3in)
Total width: 2.5cm (1in)

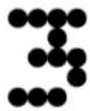

Trace the outline of the left sleeve and flip it horizontally to form the right sleeve. Trace the marked right facing sections (B2, F2 and I4) from pieces B1, F1 and I3, flip them horizontally, and join them together. Trace the marked left facing sections (A10, A11, A12, C2 and I2) from pieces A4, C1 and I1, flip them horizontally, and join them together. Mark grainlines, CF and CB, elbow and waist lines, darts, drill holes and notches on all pattern pieces.

RIGHT FRONT

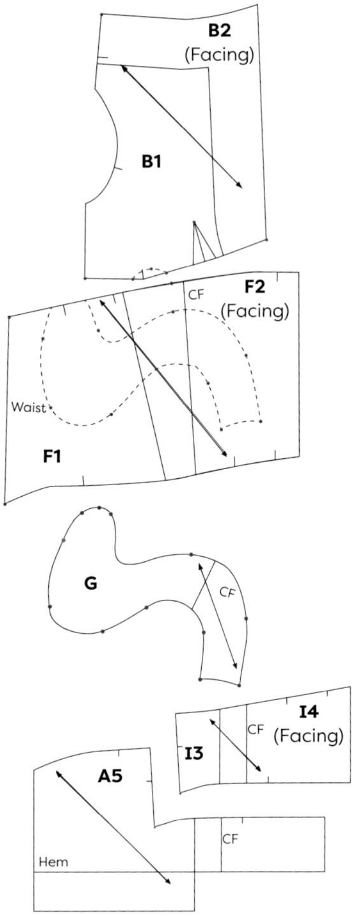

B2 (Facing) B1 CF F2 (Facing) Waist F1 G CF I4 CF (Facing) I3 A5 CF Hem

(Facing) A10 **LEFT FRONT** C2 (Facing) CF C1 CF A4 (Facing) A11 Waist I1 CF (Facing) A12 CF I2 (Facing)

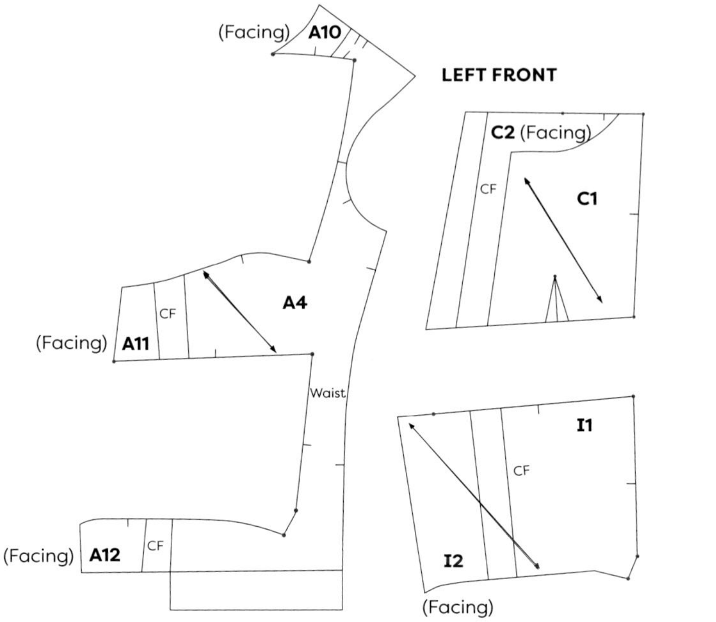

RIGHT FRONT FACING

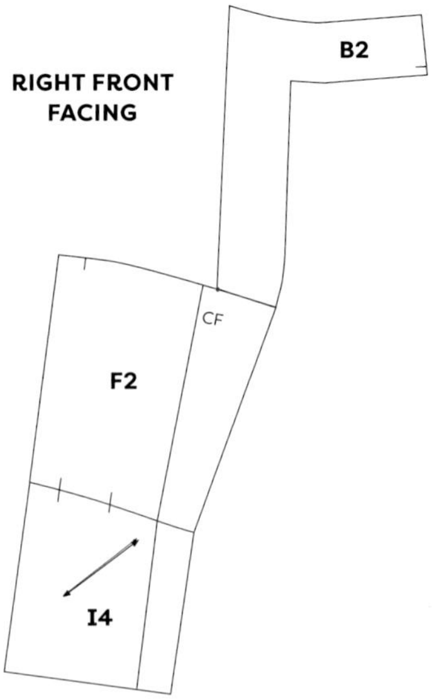

B2 CF F2 I4

LEFT FRONT FACING

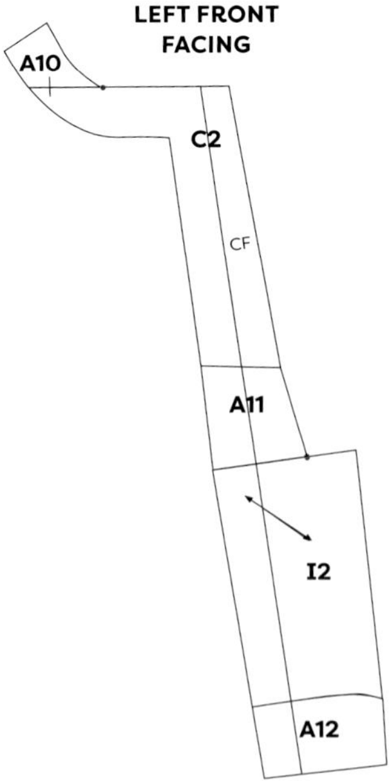

A10 C2 CF A11 I2 A12

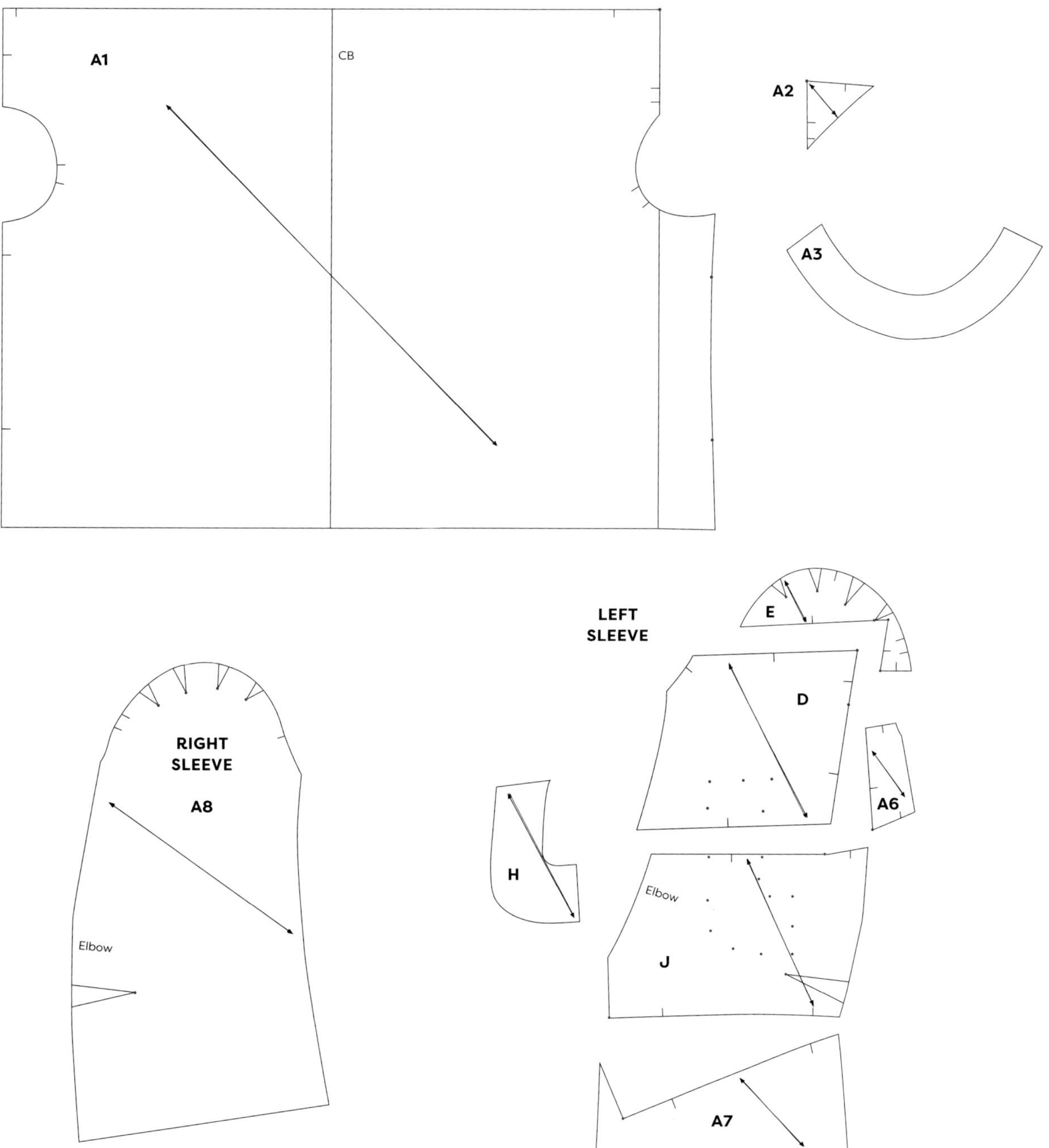
BACK
A1
CB
A2
A3
LEFT SLEEVE
E
D
A6
H
Elbow
J
A7
RIGHT SLEEVE
A8
Elbow

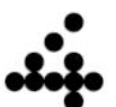

Mark gather references on A1. Add a 1cm (⅜in) seam allowance around each pattern piece. Add a 4cm (1⅝in) hem allowance to the back (A1), the left front section (A4), the right front section (A5) and the sleeves (A7, A8). Cut out the pattern pieces in calico (muslin).

A1 (Back) x 1 RSU
A2 (Right shoulder) x 1 RSU
A3 (Back neck lining) x 1 RSU

A4 (Left front) x 1 RSU
C1 (Left upper front) x 1 RSU
I1 (Left lower front) x 1 RSU

B1 (Right upper front) x 1 RSU
F1 (Right centre front) x 1 RSU
G (Right centre front) x 1 RSU + lining
I3 (Right lower front) x 1 RSU
A5 (Right lower front) x 1 RSU

E, **D**, **A6**, **J**, **A7** (Left sleeve) x 1 RSU
H (Left sleeve) x 1 RSU + lining
A8 (Right sleeve) x 1 RSU
A9 (Sleeve lining) x 1 pair

A10, **C2**, **A11**, **I2**, **A12** (Left front facing) x 1 RSU
B2, **F2**, **I4** (Right front facing) x 1 RSU

Using a tracing wheel and carbon paper, transfer grainlines, CF and CB, elbow and waist lines, darts, drill holes, notches, and gather and ease references onto BOTH sides of the fabric.

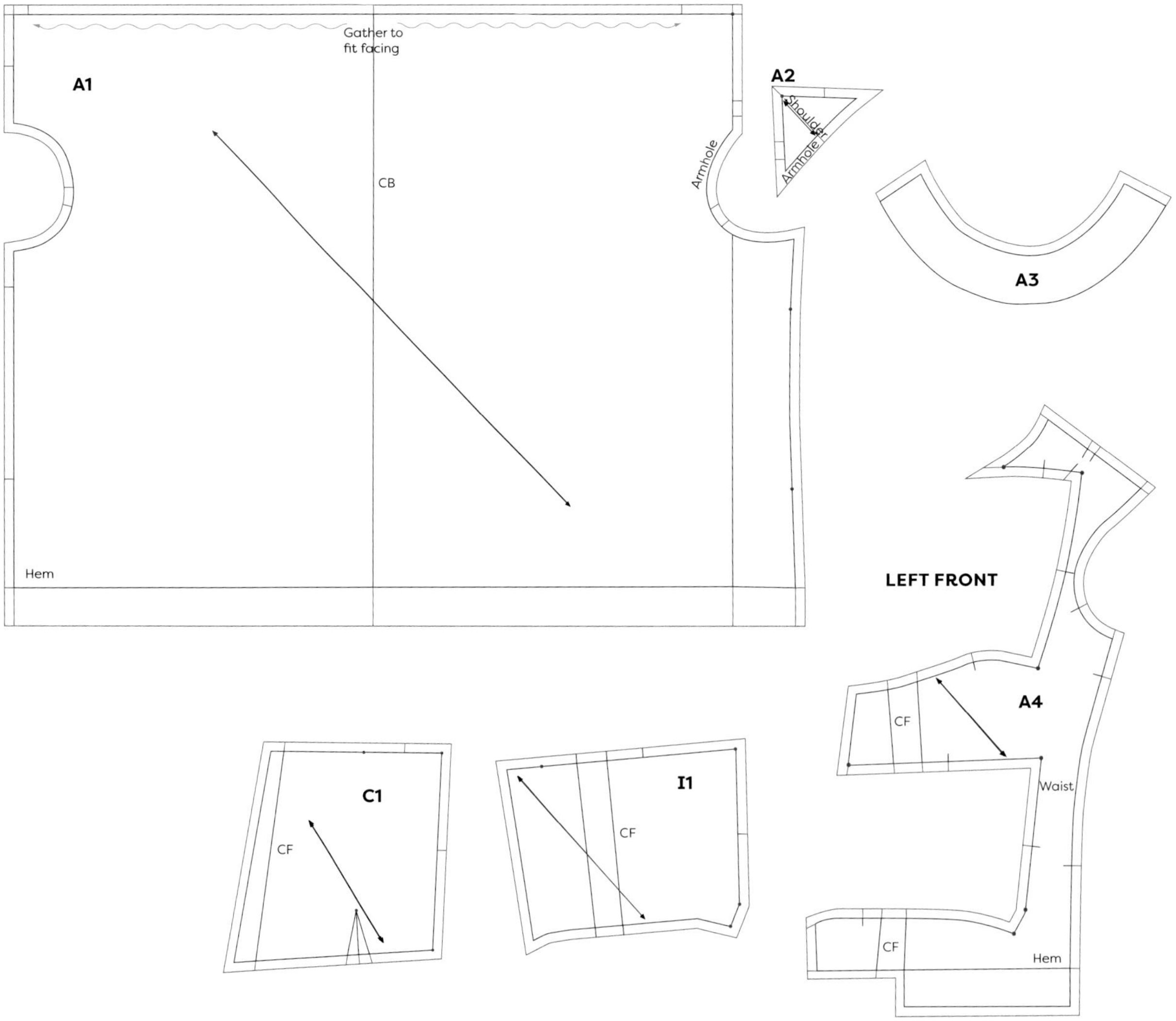

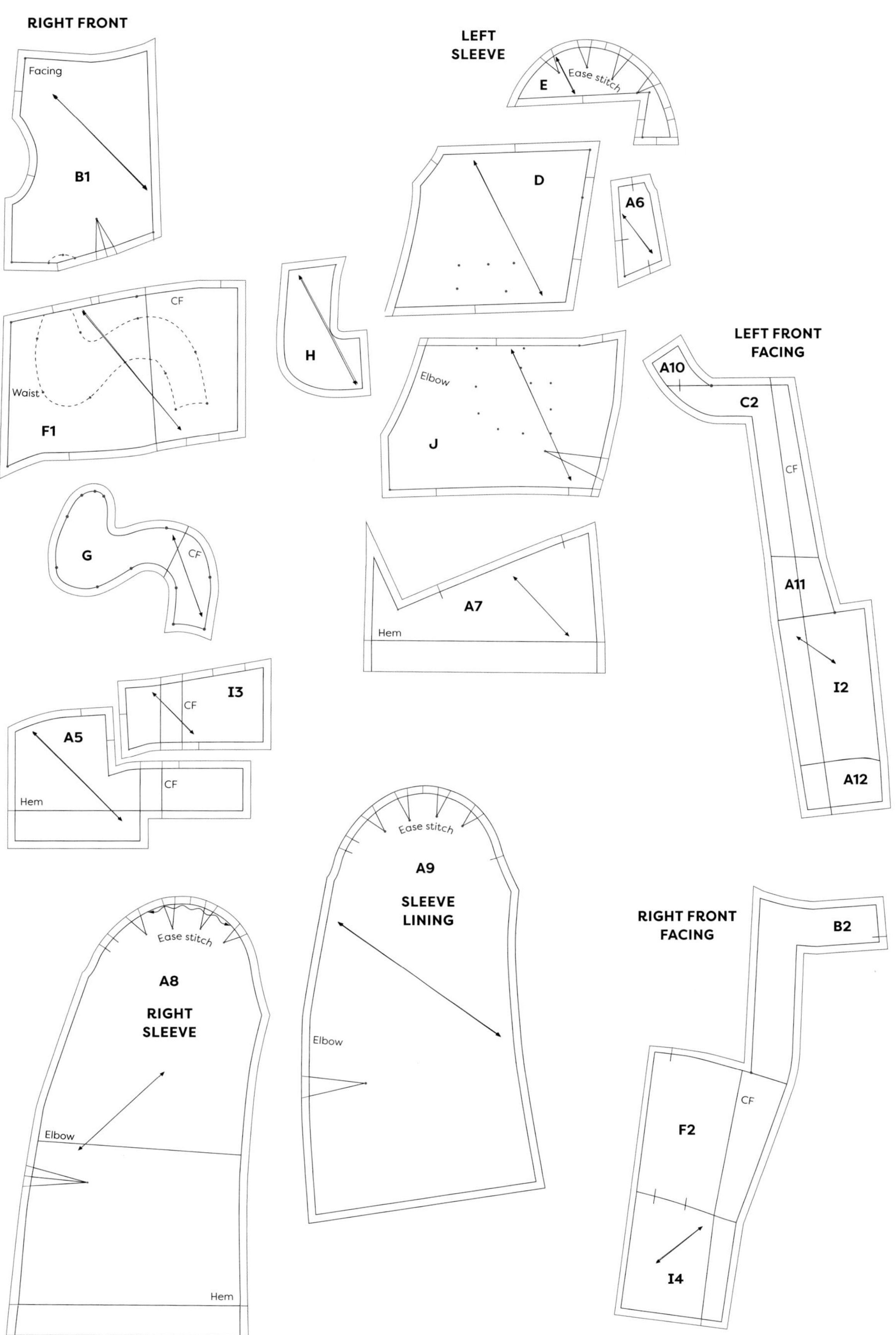
RIGHT FRONT
Facing
B1
LEFT SLEEVE
E
Ease stitch
D
A6
F1
CF
Waist
H
J
Elbow
LEFT FRONT FACING
A10
C2
CF
G
CF
A7
Hem
A11
I2
I3
CF
A5
CF
Hem
A12
Ease stitch
A9
SLEEVE LINING
RIGHT FRONT FACING
B2
Ease stitch
A8
RIGHT SLEEVE
Elbow
Elbow
CF
F2
I4
Hem

DRAPING THE SHAPES

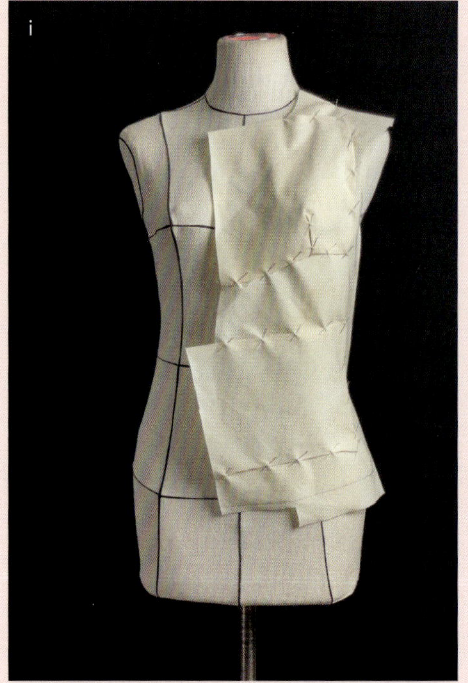
i

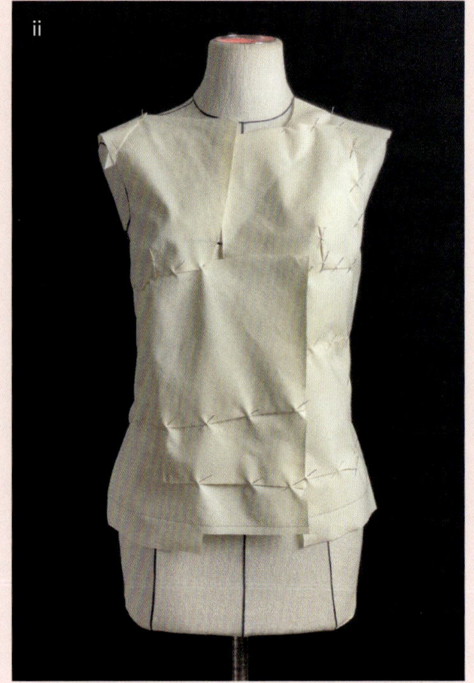
ii

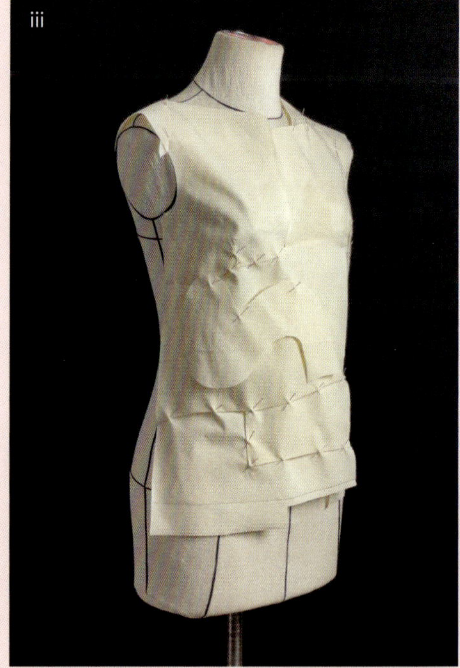
iii

Prepare the shapes following the pattern-cutting instructions in steps 2–4 (pp. 67–71).

(i) Pin the left front of the jacket (A4) onto the dress form. Make the bust dart on C1 and pin into position on A4. Place I1 onto A4 and pin into place.

(ii) Join A1, A2, A5, B1, F1 and I2 together to form the right front. Pin to the dress form.

(iii) Attach G to the front, aligning the drill hole markings.

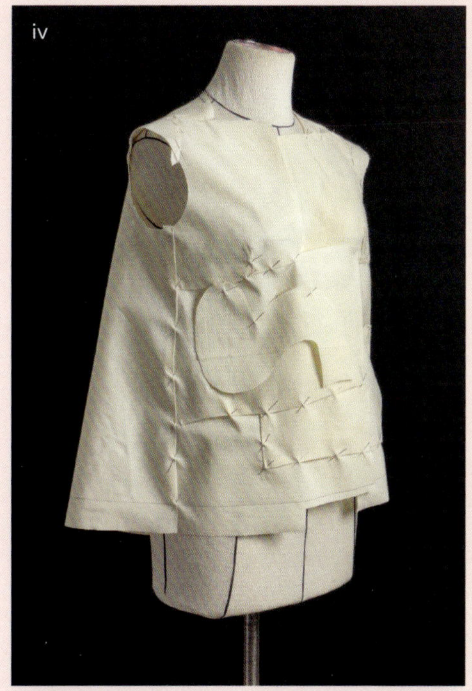

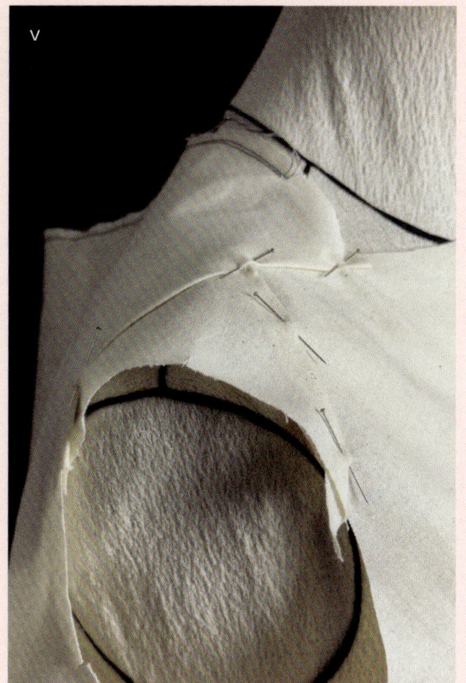

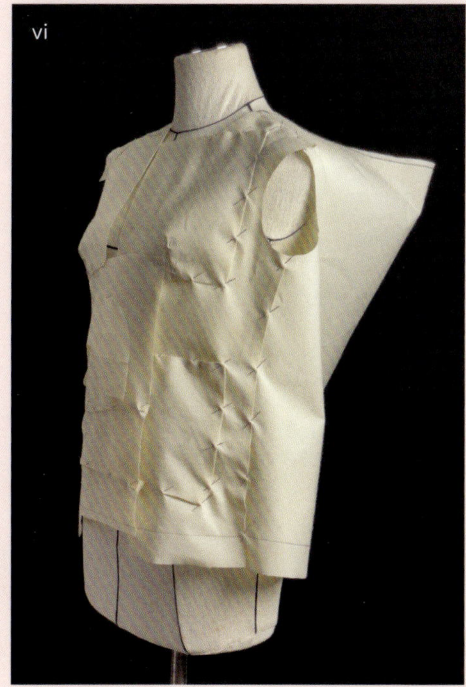

(iv) Sew two rows of gathering stitches between the notches on the back (A1). Attach A1 to the right side of the front.

(v) Pin the back shoulder to the triangle (A2).

(vi) Attach the back (A1) to the left front (A4) along the side seam and the shoulder.

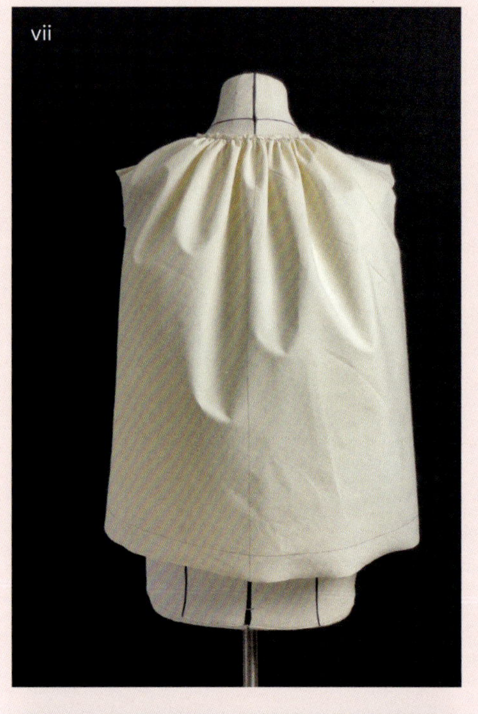

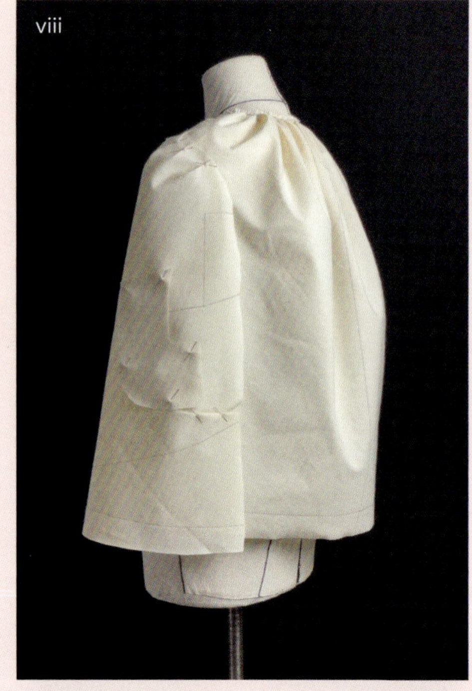

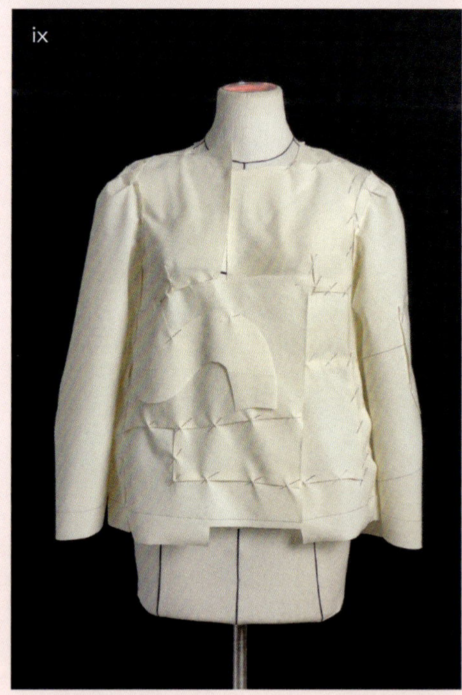

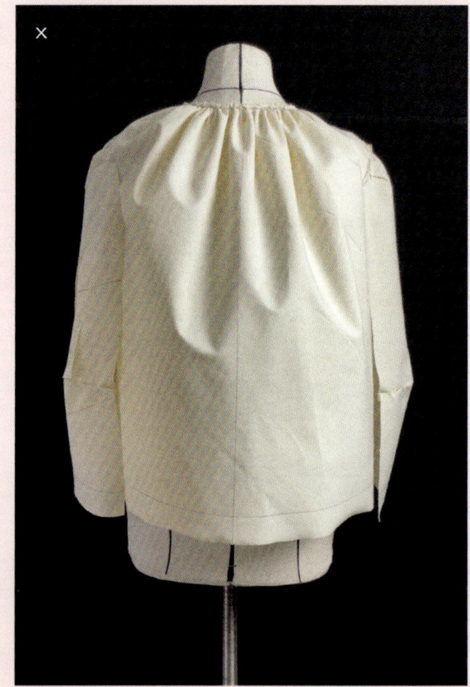

(vii) Gather the back neck to fit the dress form.

(viii) Patch together the left sleeve pieces (E, D, A6, J, A7 and H). Make the darts on the sleeve head (E) and add a row of ease stitching. Make the dart at the elbow (J). Attach the sleeve to the jacket.

(ix) Make the darts on the right sleeve head (A8) and add a row of ease stitching. Make the dart at the elbow. Attach the sleeve to the jacket.

(x) Back view of the finished drape.

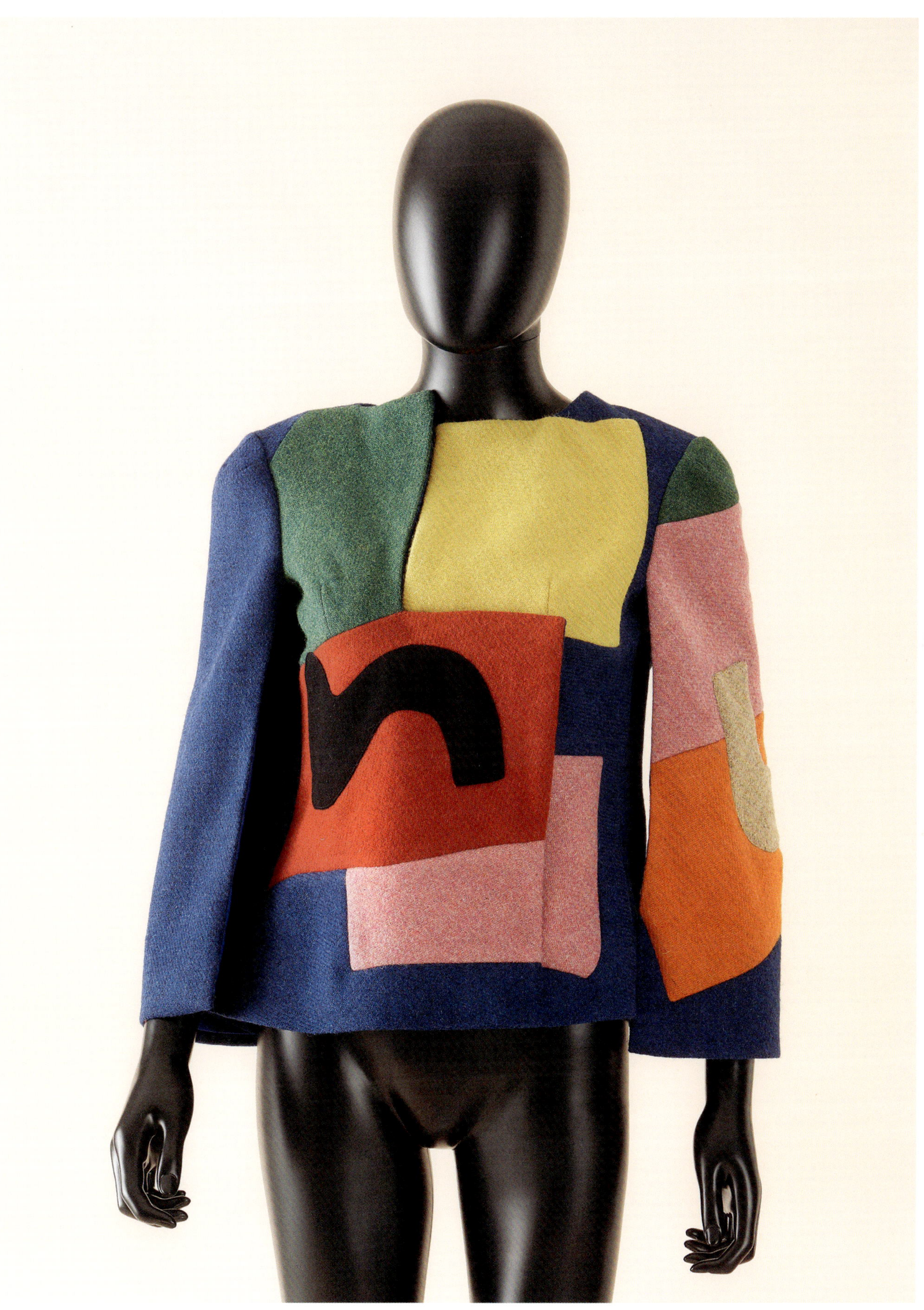

Carpet jacket

HENRI MATISSE

Henri Matisse (b. 1869, Le Cateau-Cambrésis, France; d. 1954) was one of the leading figures of modern art. Though most famous for his paintings, he was also a draughtsman, printmaker, and sculptor. In the early 1930s he began to simplify his forms. In 1941, surgery for abdominal cancer left him with restricted mobility. Painting and sculpture became difficult and Matisse turned to collage, which he created with the help of assistants, who would paint sheets of paper with gouache for him to cut and arrange into compositions. During the last fourteen years of his life, he created a significant body of cut-outs.

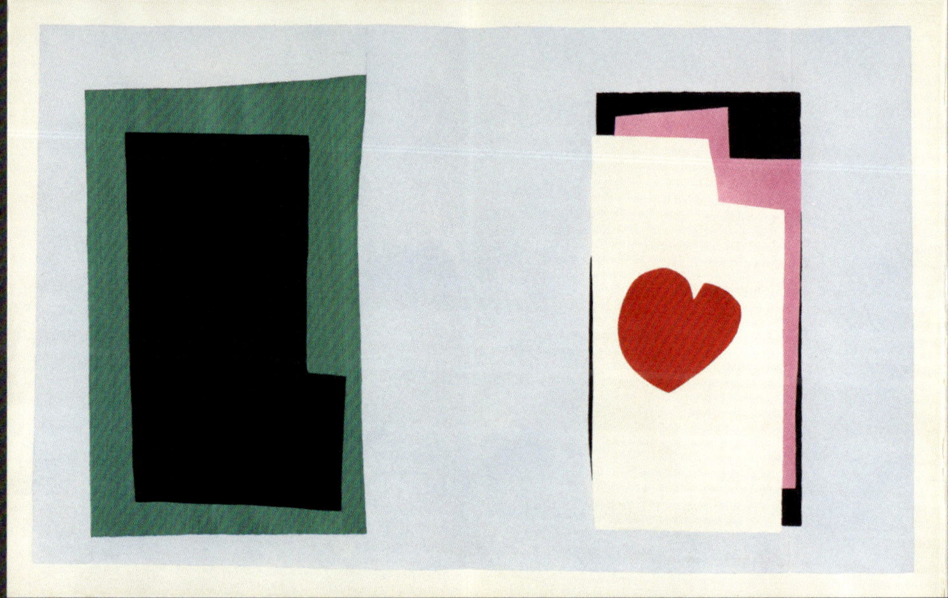

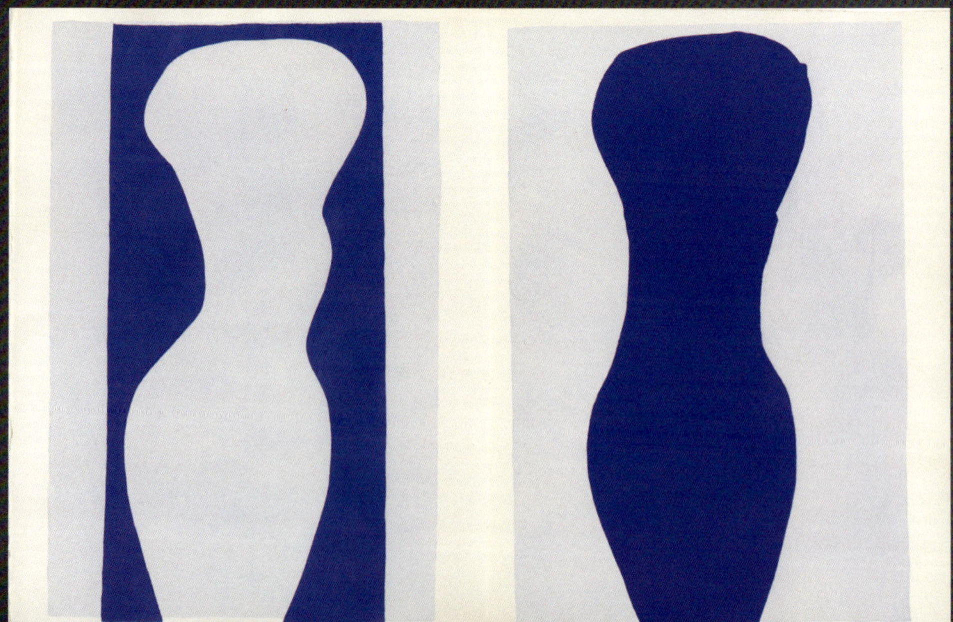

Top: *Le Coeur (The Heart)*, 1947, plate 7 from the portfolio *Jazz*, color pochoir with gouache on ivory wove paper, sheet 42.2 × 65.1cm (16⅝ × 25⅝in)

Bottom: *Formes (Forms)*, 1947, plate 9 from the portfolio *Jazz*, color pochoir with gouache on ivory wove paper, sheet 42.2 × 65.1cm (16⅝ × 25⅝in)

Berggruen et Cie poster featuring one of Matisse's *Papiers Découpés*, 1953, 61 × 40cm (24 × 15¾in)

MATISSE

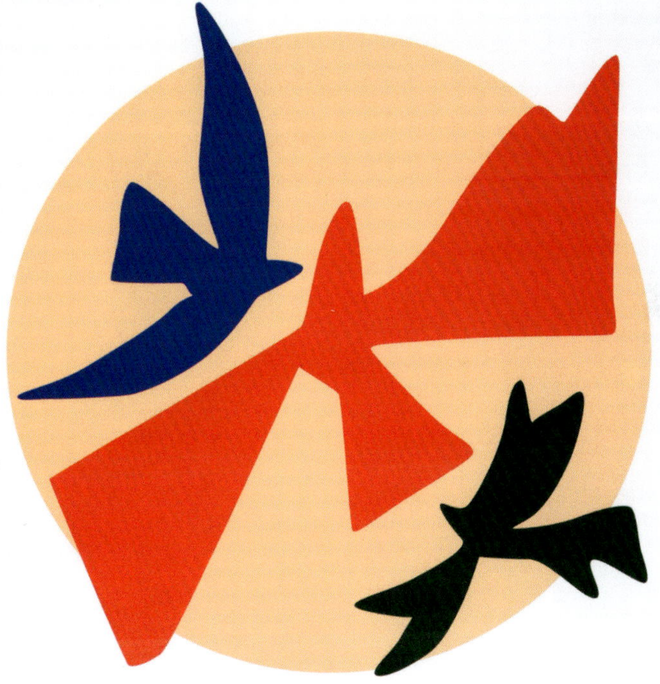

BERGGRUEN & CIE

70, RUE DE L'UNIVERSITE, PARIS - VII

Du Vendredi 27 Fevrier au Samedi 28 Mars 1953

Le Coeur dress

I find Matisse's cut-paper collages evocative of the Hard-Edge painting style. *Le Coeur (The Heart)* features a sharp block of black juxtaposed with striking emerald green. I slashed and spread the pattern for the black section and added small tucks vertically on each side and along the neck to create a seductive draped column in jersey. The green background was transformed into a rectangular support for the jersey section and stands rigid, maintaining its original shape.

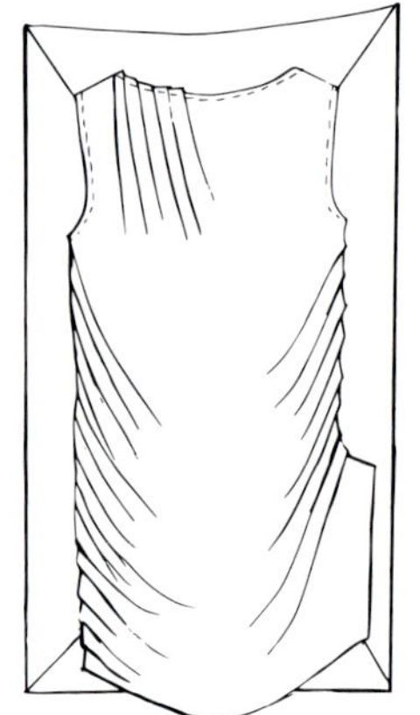

SIZING

The example here is a size 12 (US 8).
Measurements:
Bust: 91cm (35⅞in)
Waist: 91cm (35⅞in)
Hips: 101cm (39¾in)
Length: 72cm (28⅜in)

To create additional sizes, grade the pattern (see p. 10).

FABRIC SUGGESTIONS

Green: Medium-weight woven fabrics, such as wool crepe, drill, cotton.
Black: Drape jersey, viscose, cotton jersey with minimal stretch.

COLOUR REFERENCES

Green #0B9372
Black #000000

1 Examine the artwork shapes.

Green = **A**
Black = **B**

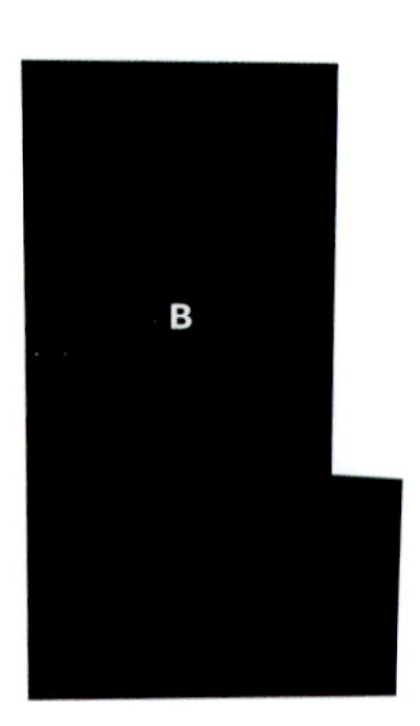

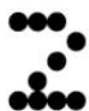

Plot the outlines of the shapes onto plain pattern paper. Place 5cm (2in) squared paper underneath the pattern paper as a guide.

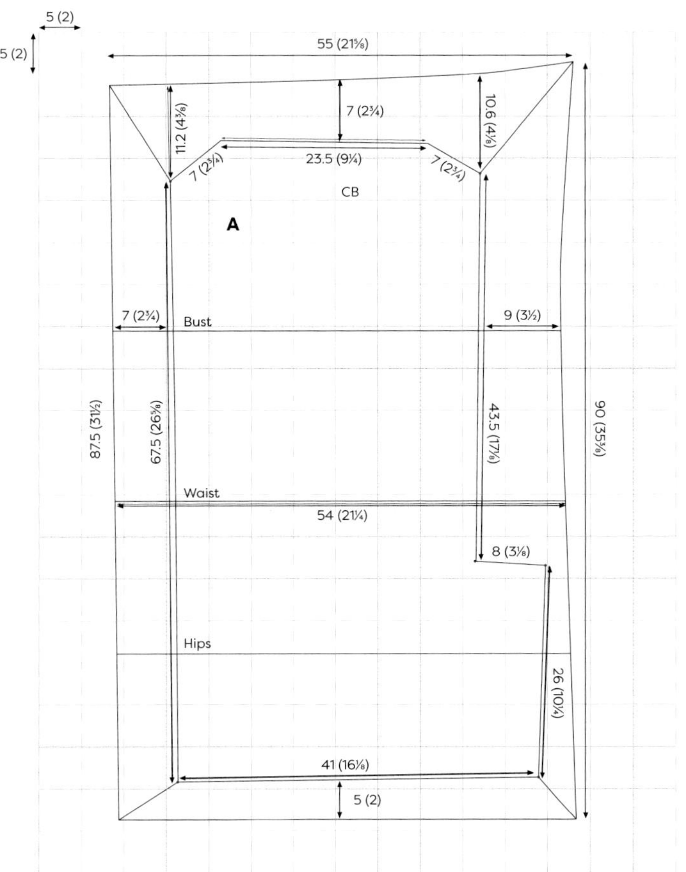

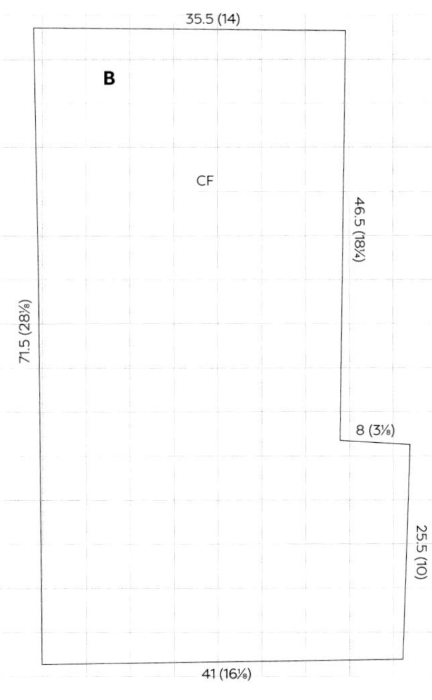

Trace the outline of the back section (A) and flip it horizontally. Divide it into sections as illustrated. Slash and spread the sections.

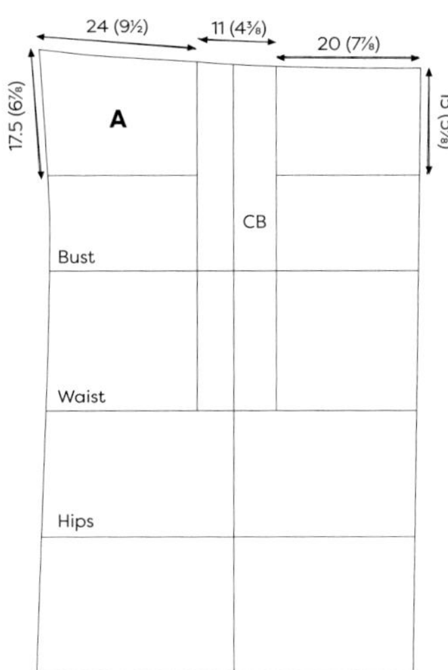

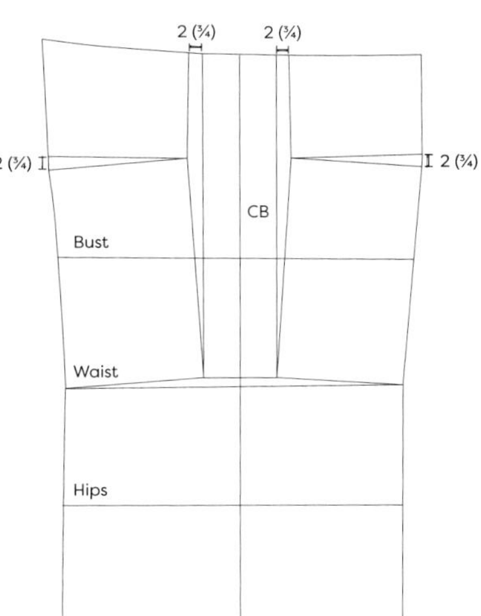

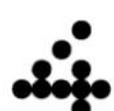

Trace the outline of the front section (B) and divide the shape vertically into three sections: a, b and c. Then divide the shape horizontally into seven sections and label them 1 to 7.

The next step is to slash and spread. Cut through the two vertical lines to separate sections a, b and c, then lay them out on pattern paper. Add 11.5cm (4½in) to the top between sections a and b, and between sections b and c.

Add 6cm (2⅜in) to the bottom between sections a and b, and between sections b and c.

Glue the sections onto the paper.

Cut sections 1 and 2 from right to left – do not separate.

Cut section 3 away from section 2.

Cut sections 4 to 7 from left to right – do not separate.

Fan out the pattern onto paper and add the required measurements.

Glue into place.

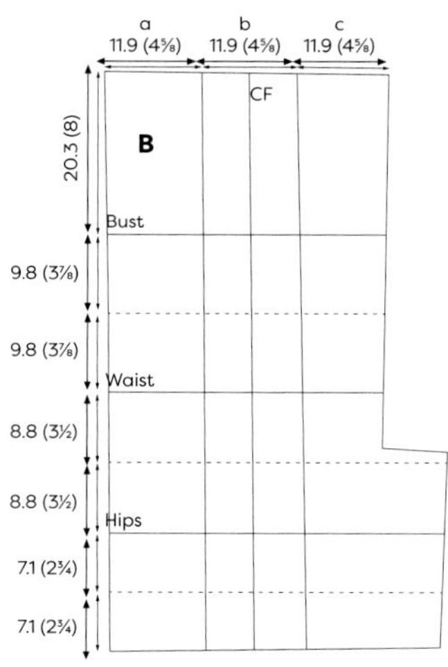

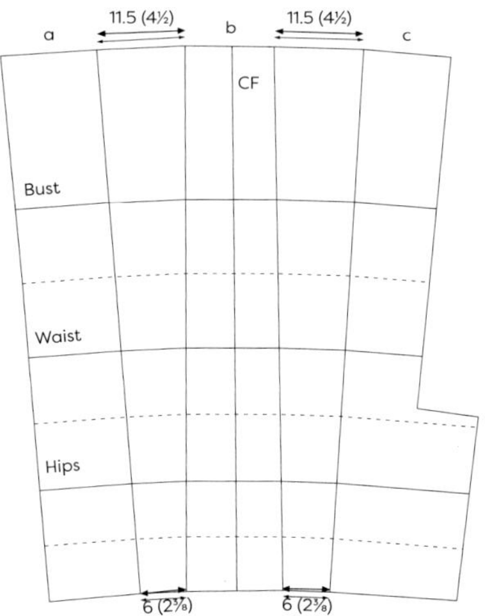

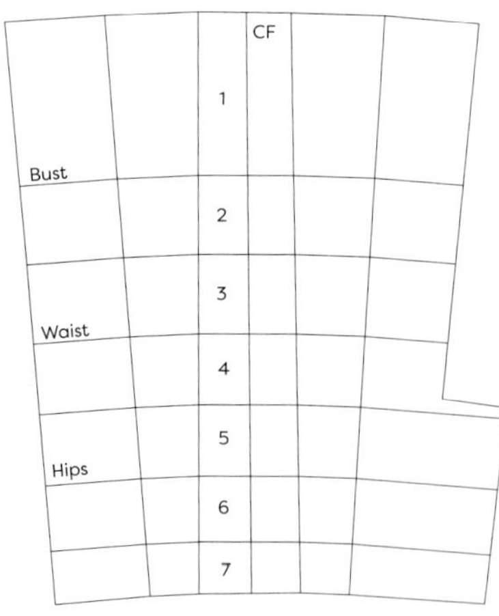

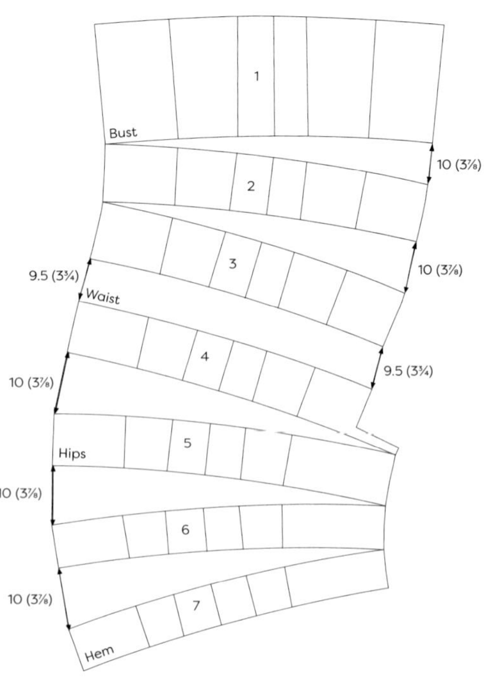

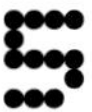

Trace and extract the facing sections from the back section (A) and number them A1 to A5. Mark the notches.

On A, mark the darts.

On the front section (B), mark the tucks.

Mark grainlines; CF and CB; bust, waist and hip lines; drill holes and notches.

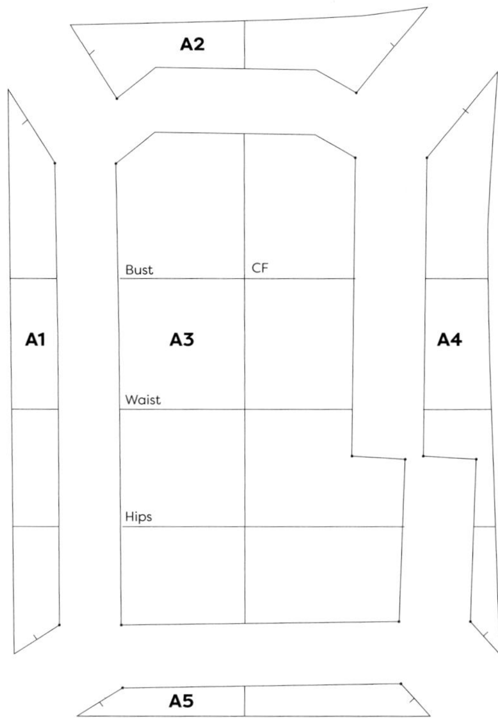

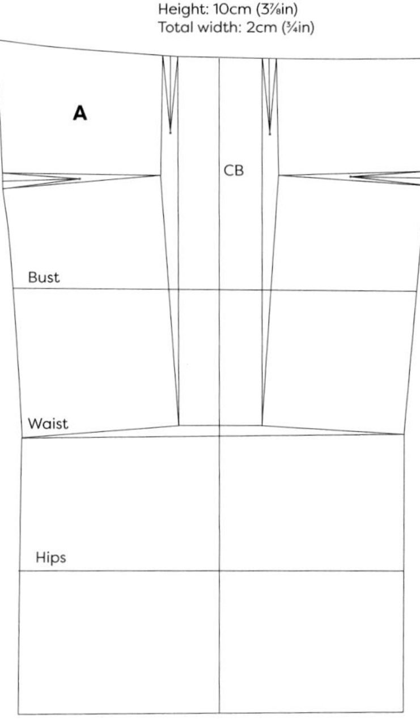

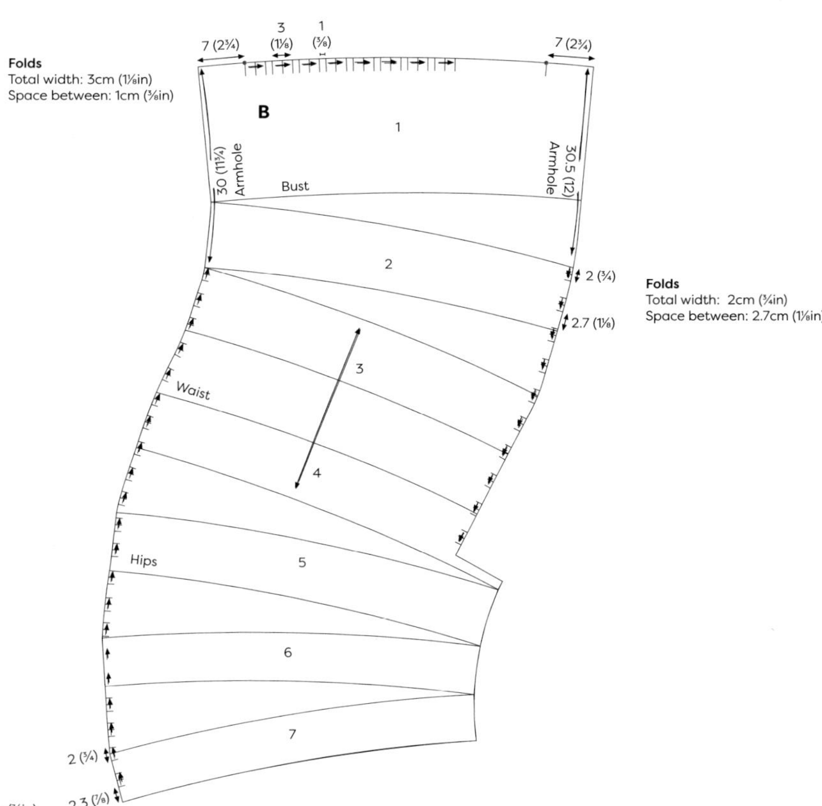

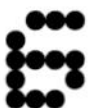

Add a 1cm (⅜in) seam allowance to each pattern piece. Add a 4cm (1⅝in) hem allowance to B.

Cut out the back section (A) and facings (A1–A5) in calico (muslin) and the front section (B) in drape jersey.

A (Back) x 1 RSU
A1 (Right side facing) x 1 RSU + fusing
A2 (Top facing) x 1 RSU + fusing
A3 (Back facing) x 1 RSU
A4 (Left side facing) x 1 RSU + fusing
A5 (Bottom facing) x 1 RSU + fusing
B (Front) x 1 RSU

Using a tracing wheel and carbon paper, transfer grainlines; CF and CB; bust, waist and hip lines; dart; tucks; drill holes and notches onto BOTH sides of the fabric.

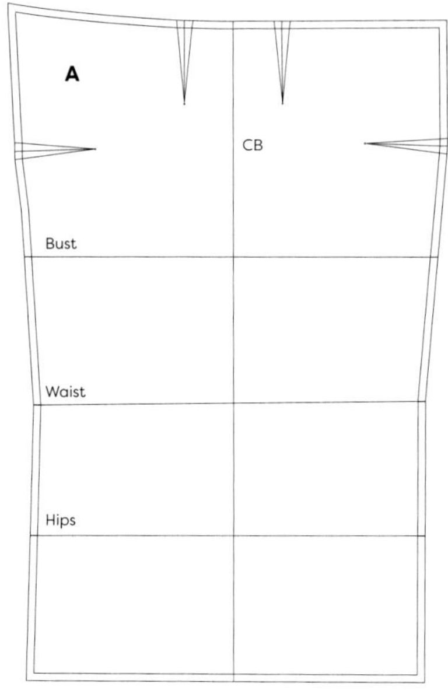

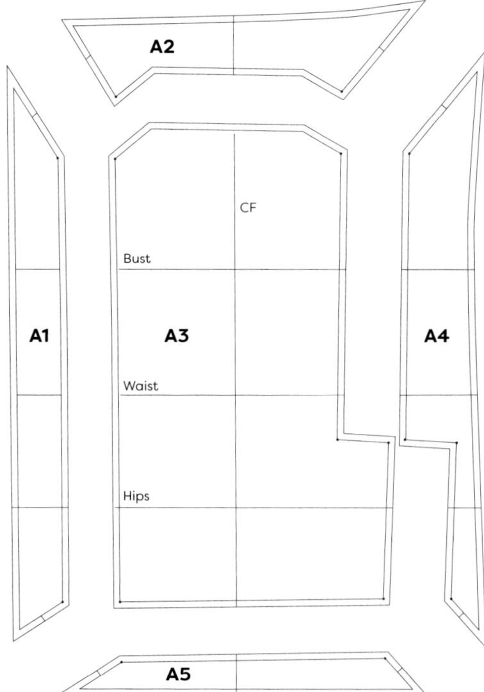

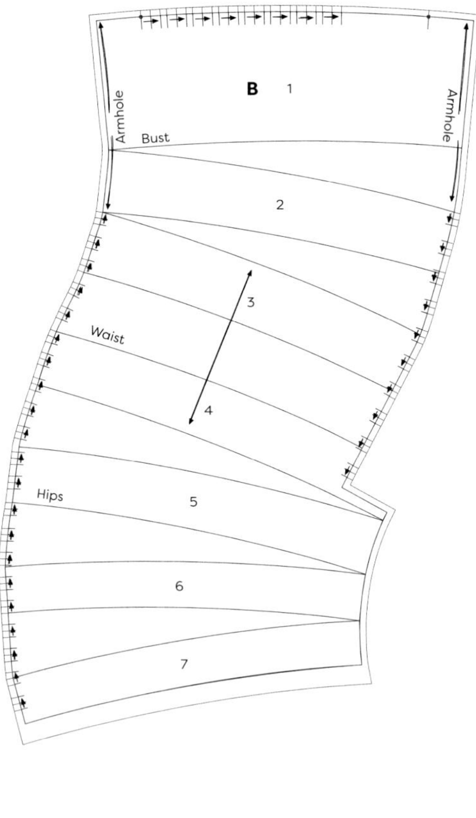

DRAPING THE SHAPES

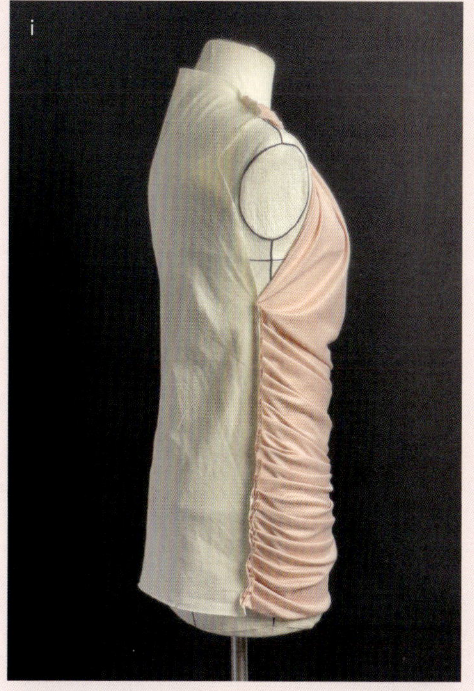

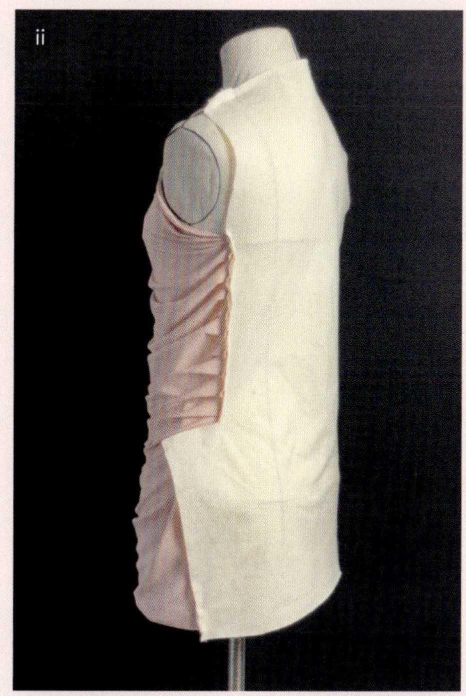

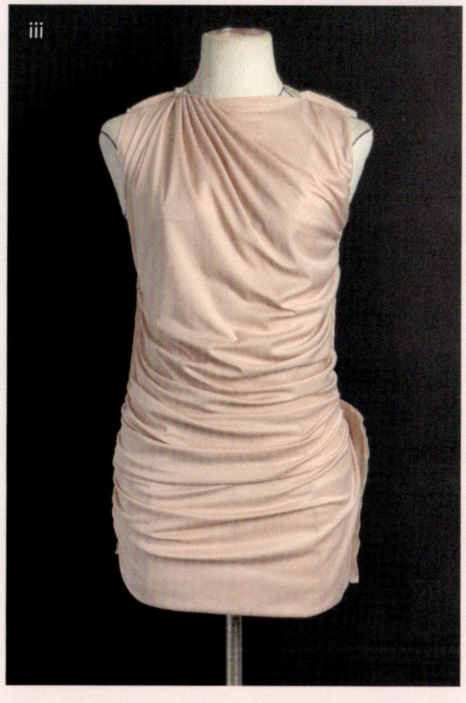

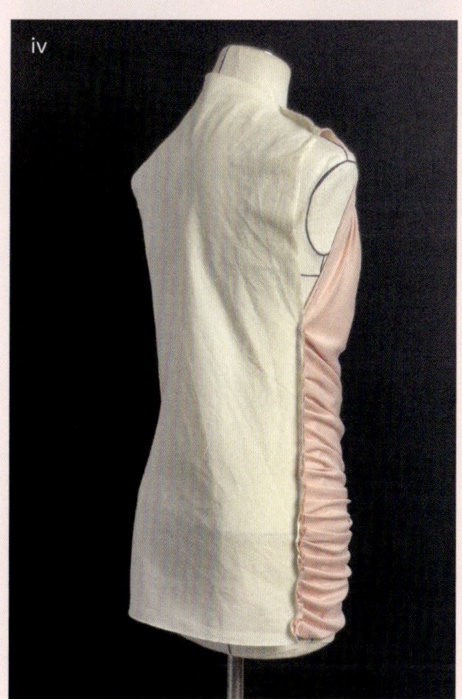

Prepare the shapes following steps 2–6 of the pattern-cutting instructions (pp. 79–82).

(i) Attach the calico (muslin) back facing A3 to the dress form. Make the tucks on the right side of the jersey front section (B). Attach B to A3. Join the shoulders.

(ii) Make the tucks on the left side of B and attach to A3. Join the shoulders.

(iii) Make the neck tucks on B.

(iv) Back view.

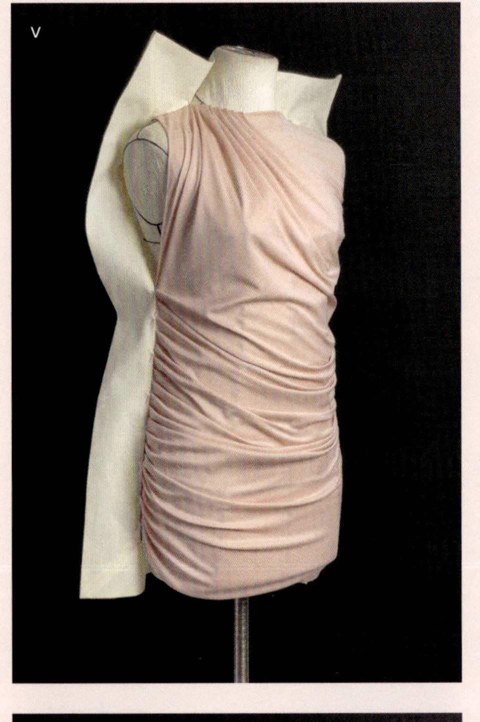

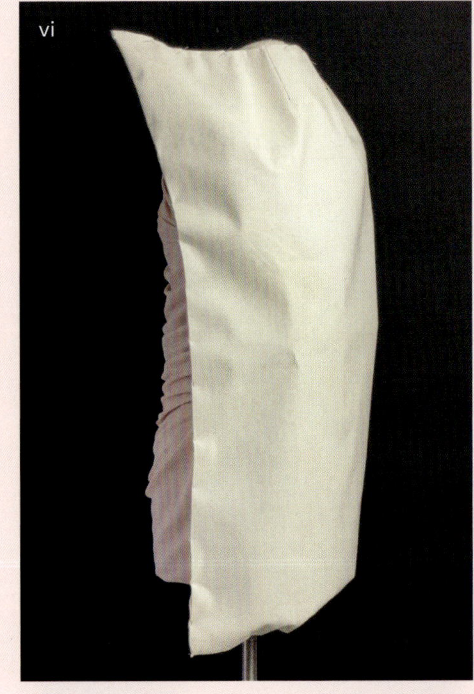

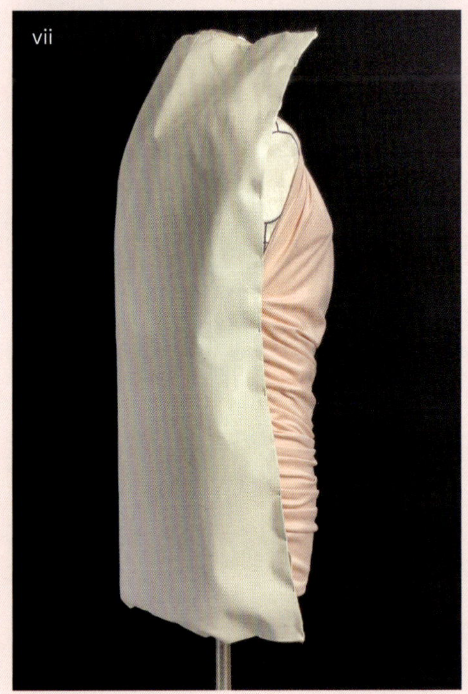

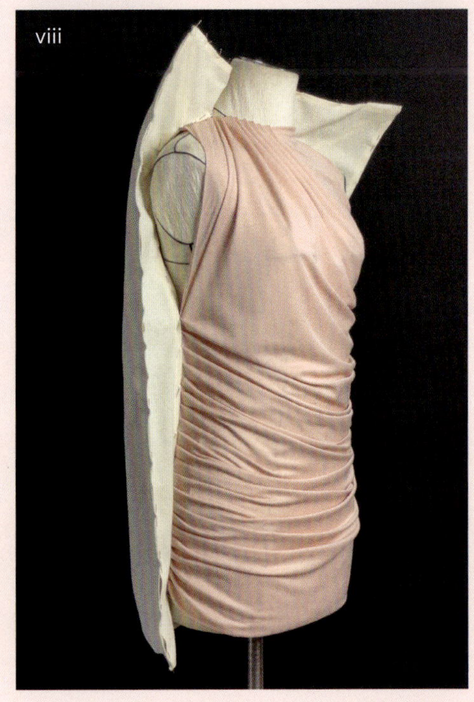

(v) Sew the facing sections A1, A2, A4 and A5 together to form a frame and attach it to A3 and B.

(vi) Make the four darts on back section A.

(vii) Attach A to the facing frame.

(viii) The finished drape from the side front.

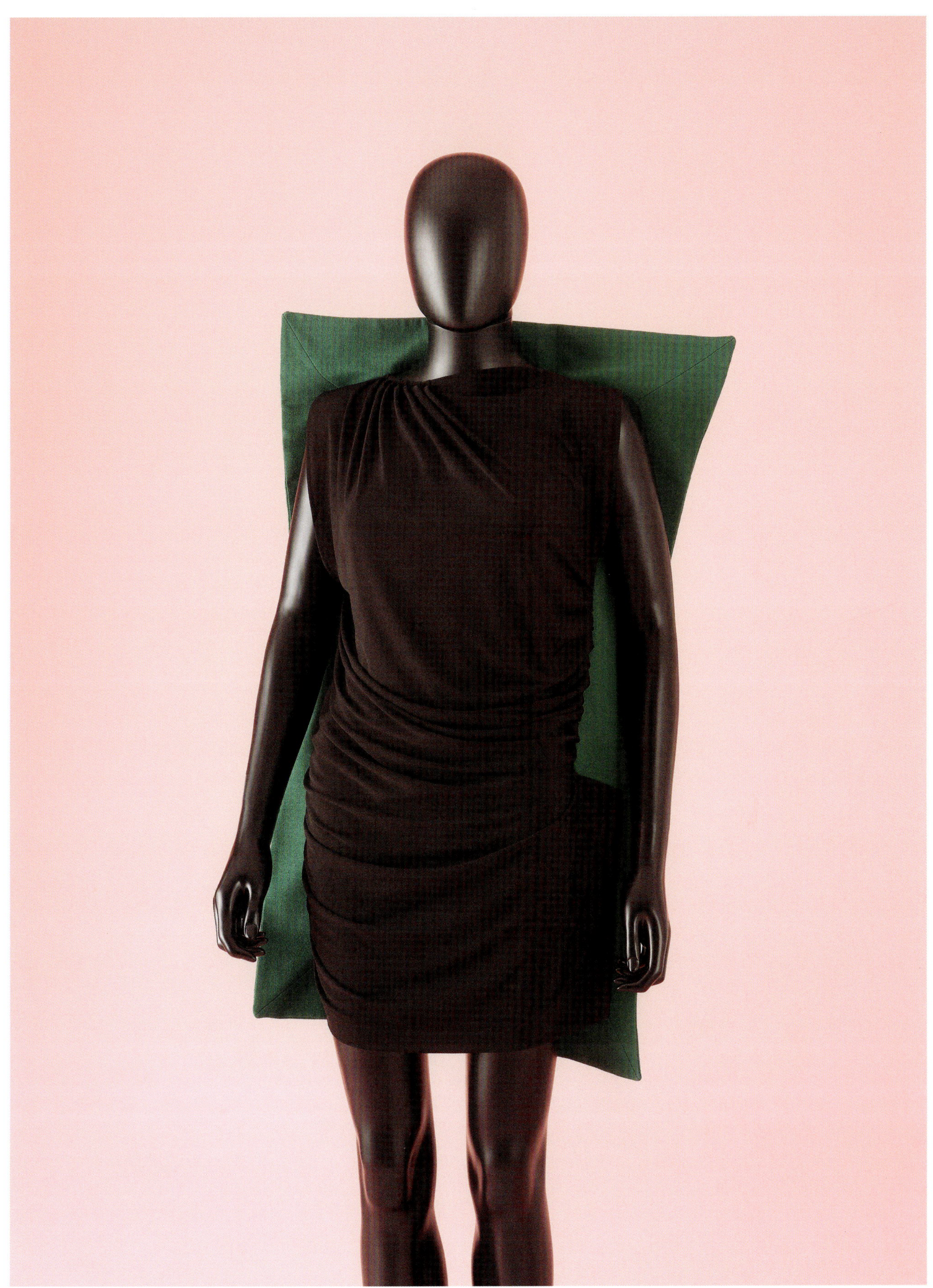

Le Coeur dress

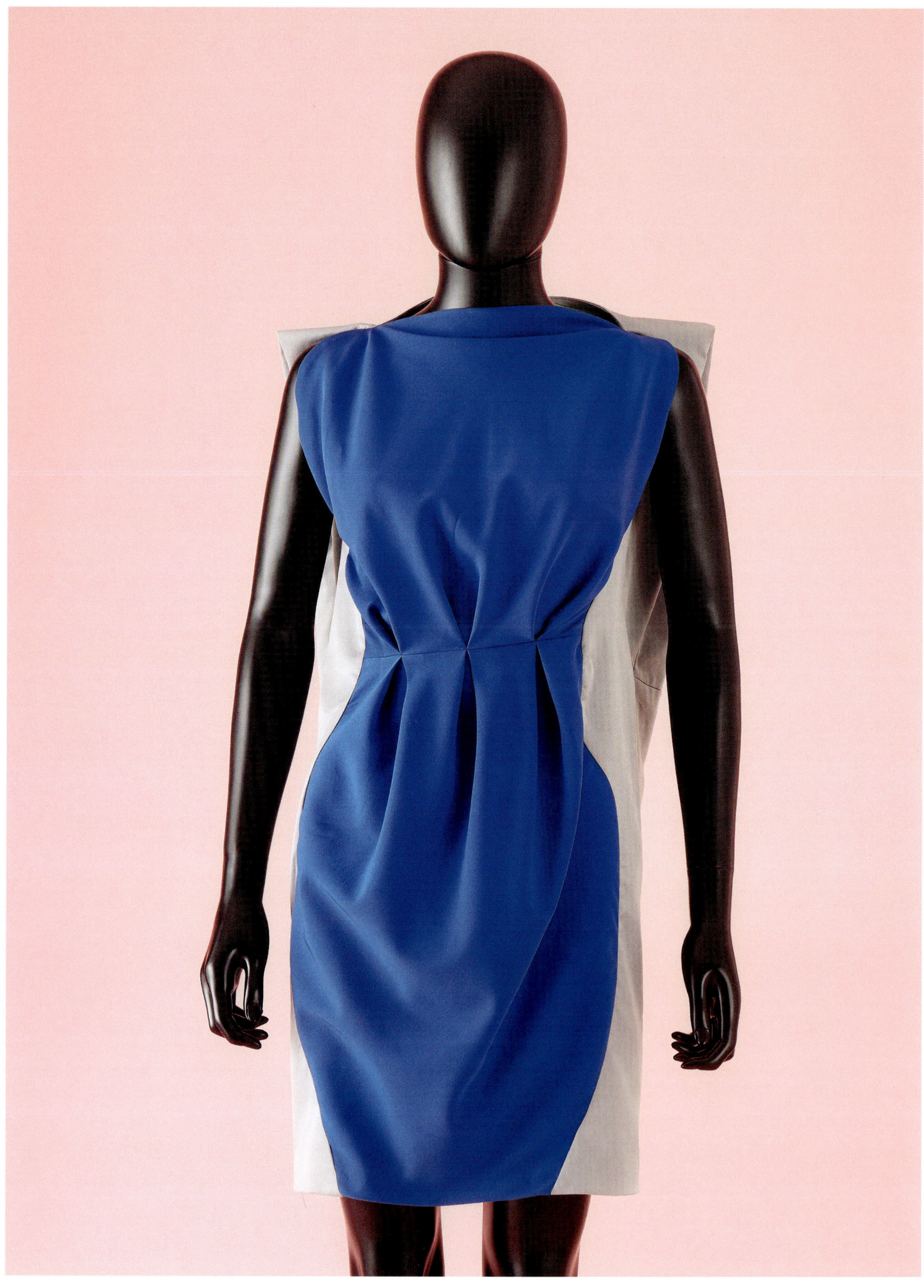

Formes dress

I fashioned Matisse's *Formes* into a sack-back dress. I added volume to the grey rectangle – used for the back of the dress – at the neckline and shoulder blades, which made it stand proud from the body. I cut the electric-blue block in half horizontally – above the waistline – and added tucks to the upper and lower sections. Openings were made for the head, arms and legs, and the blue block was inserted into the grey section.

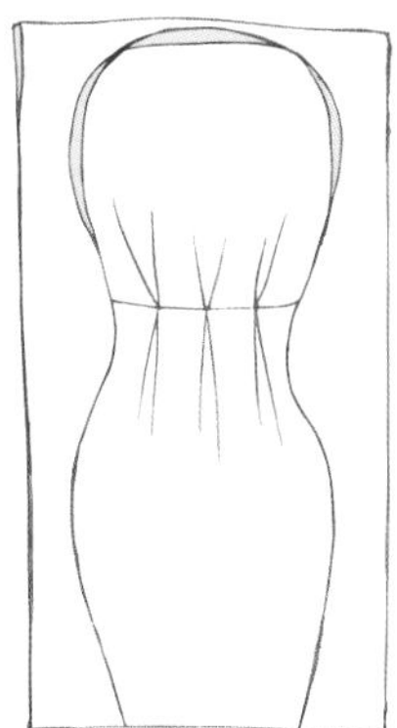

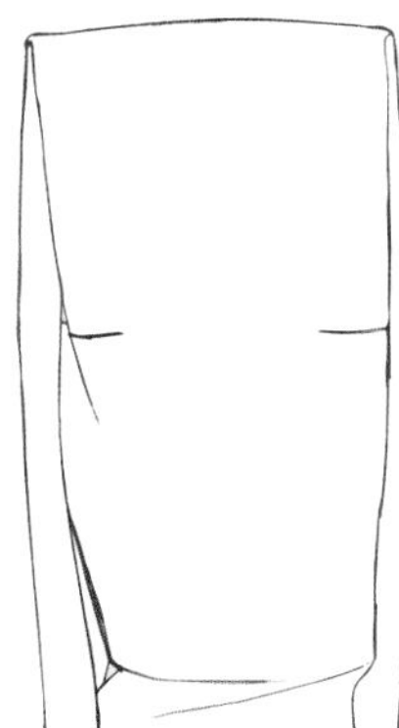

SIZING

The example here is a size 12 (US 8).
Measurements:
Bust: 64cm (25¼in)
Waist: 64cm (25¼in)
Hips: 64cm (25¼in)
Length: 88.5cm (34⅞in)

To create additional sizes, grade the pattern (see p. 10).

FABRIC SUGGESTIONS

Blue: Drape jersey, viscose, cotton jersey with minimal stretch.
Grey: Scuba (Neoprene).

For the sample I used deadstock jersey in blue and scuba (Neoprene) in grey.

COLOUR REFERENCES

Blue #004EC7
Grey #DCD8D0

1

Examine the artwork shapes.

Blue = **A**
Grey = **B**

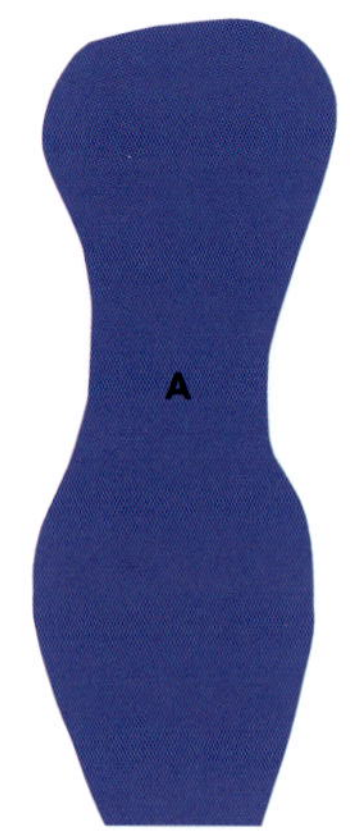

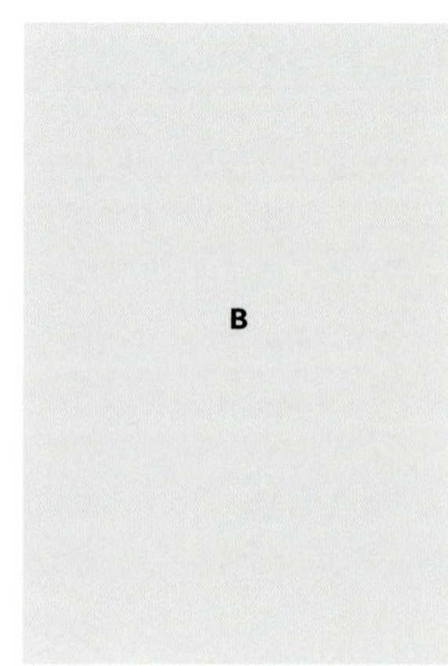

Plot the outlines of the shapes onto plain pattern paper. Place 5cm (2in) squared paper underneath the pattern paper as a guide.

Mark CF and darts. Divide the blue section at the waist darts to create two sections (A1 and A2), as shown.

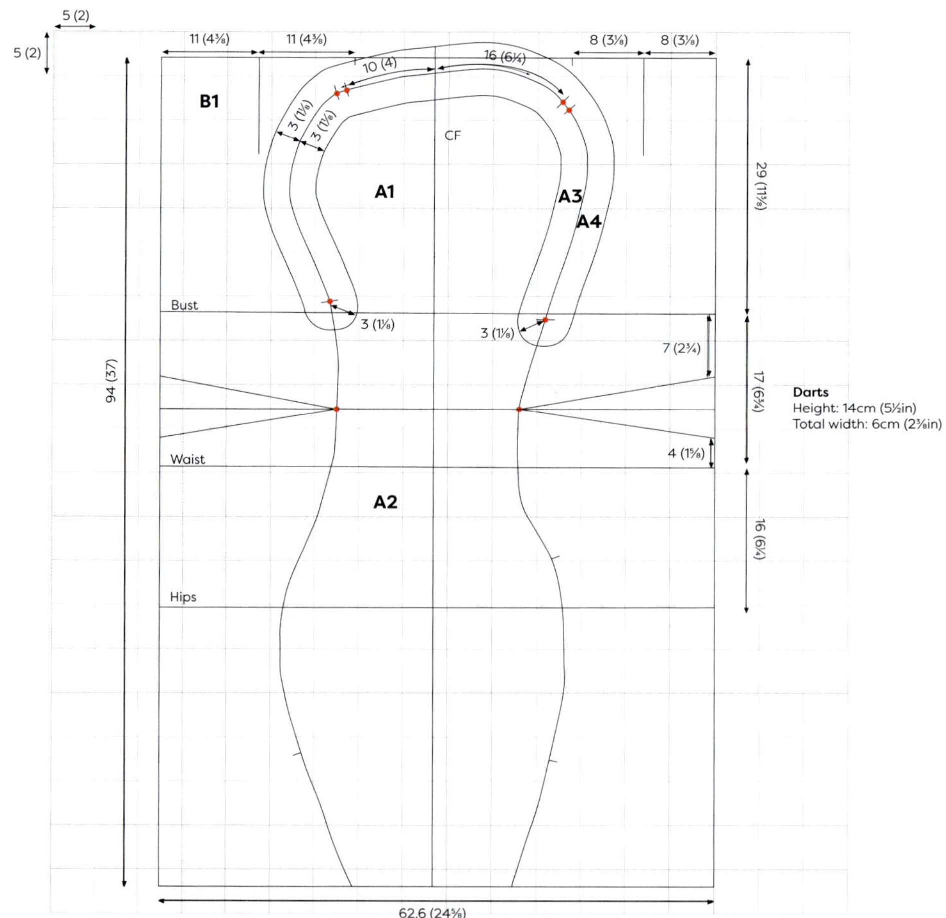

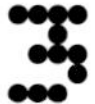

Trace section B1.

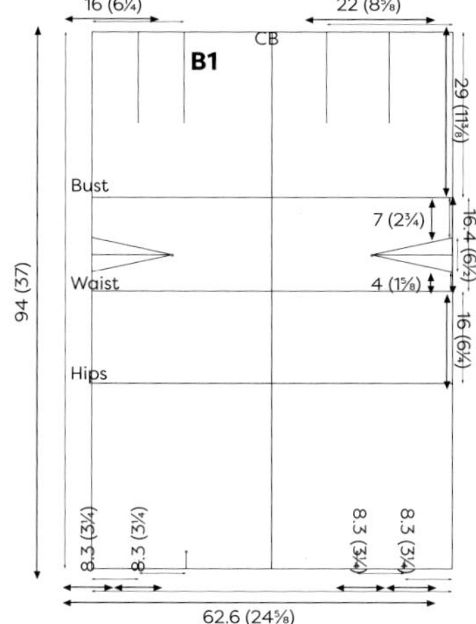

Darts
Height: 14cm (5½in)
Total width: 6cm (2⅜in)

Trace B1 again, this time cutting out the central shape formed by A1 and A2, to make section B2. Close the darts.

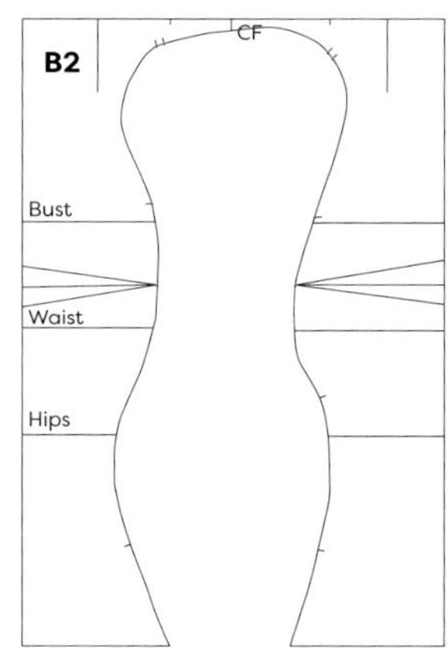

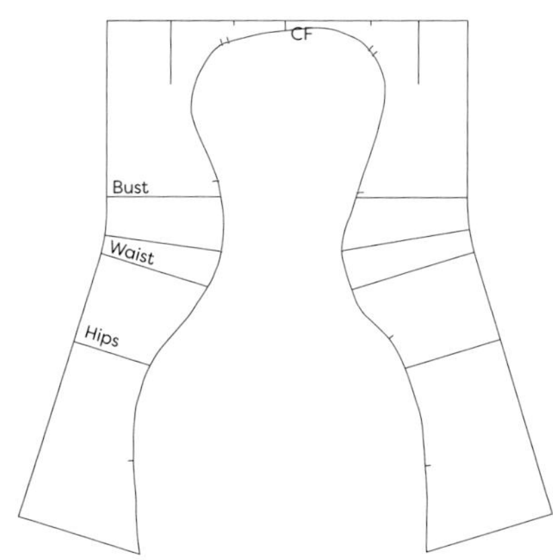

Trace sections A1 and A2. Divide both sections vertically, then slash and spread them as shown.

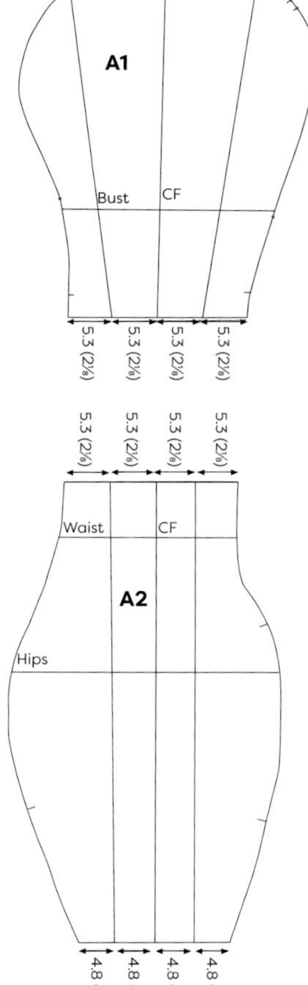

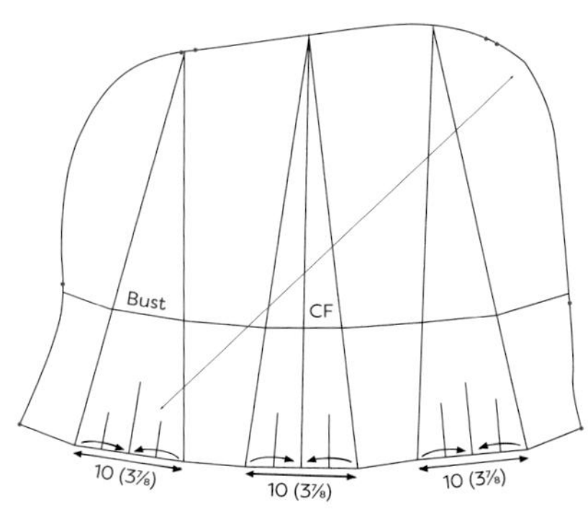

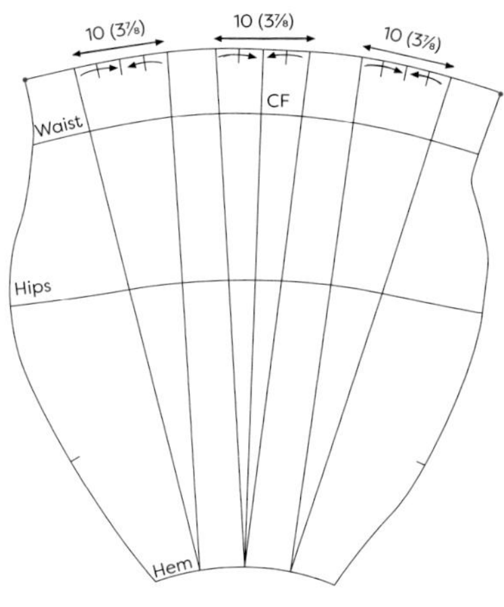

Trace the facings (A3 and A4) from the grid illustration and flip them horizontally.

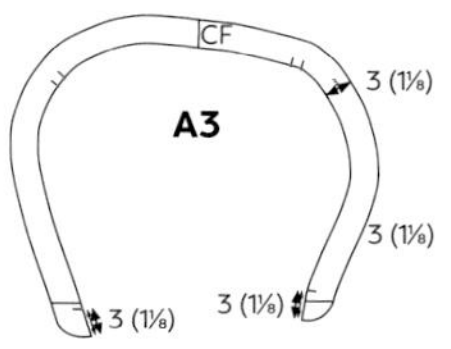

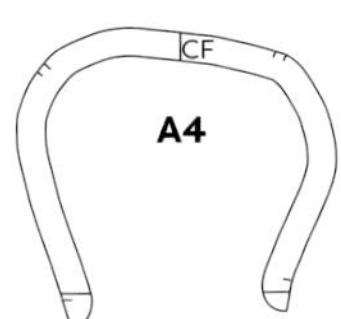

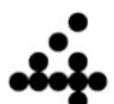

Mark the grainline on A1. Mark drill holes and notches on all pattern pieces. Add a 1cm (⅜in) seam allowance to each piece.

Cut out the pieces: grey pieces B1 and B2 in calico (muslin); blue pieces A1, A2, A3 and A4 in drape jersey.

A1 (Front upper) x 1 RSU
A2 (Front lower) x 1 RSU
A3 (Facing) x 1 RSU
A4 (Mid facing) x 1 RSU
B1 (Back) x 1 RSU
B2 (Front) x 1 RSU

Using a tracing wheel and carbon paper, transfer the grainline; CF and CB; tucks; darts; folds; bust, waist and hip lines; drill holes and notches onto BOTH sides of the fabric.

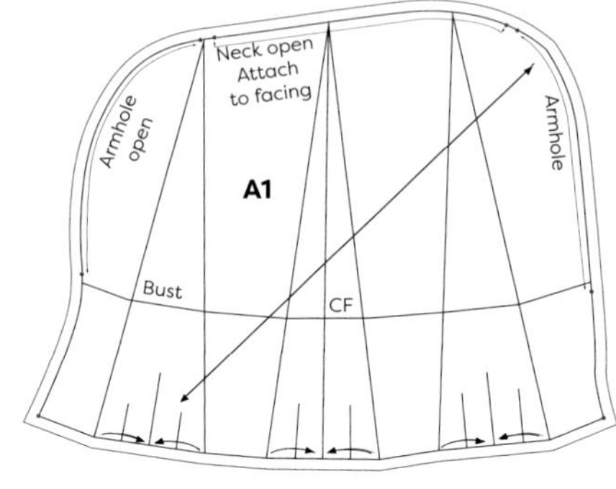

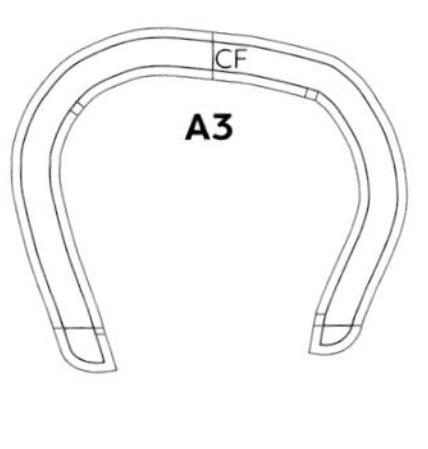

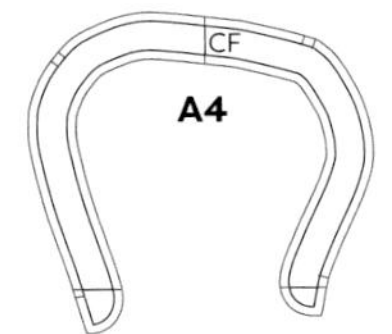

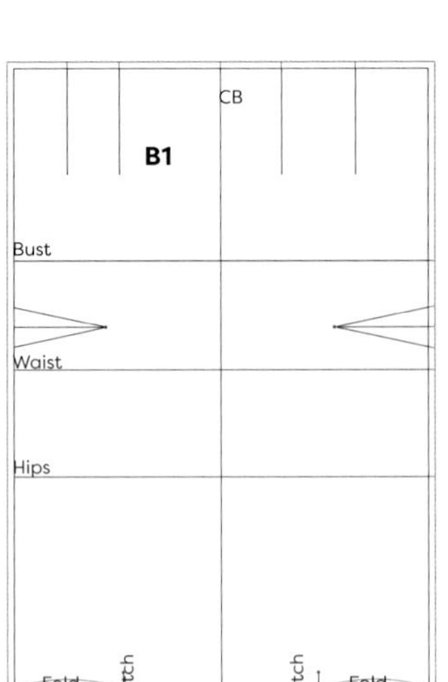

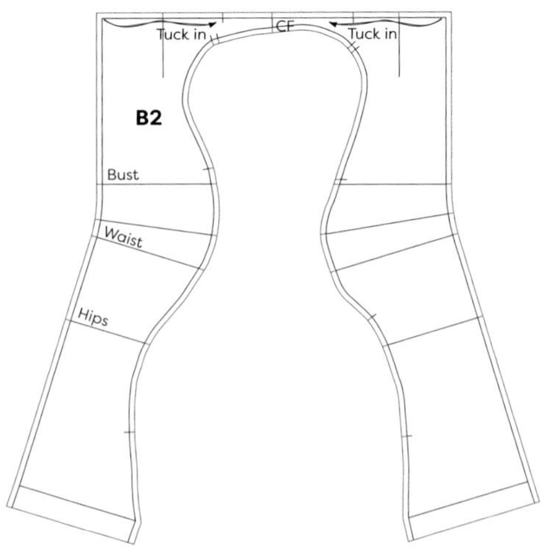

DRAPING THE SHAPES

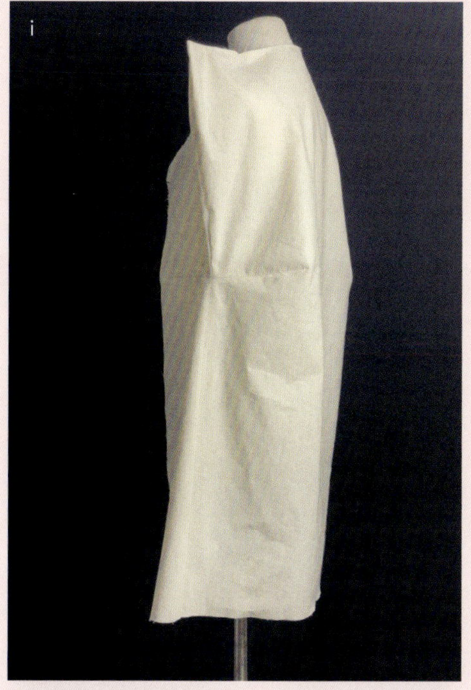
i

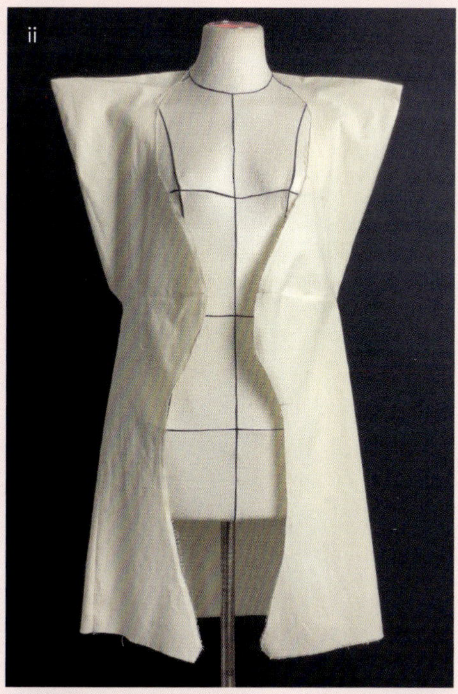
ii

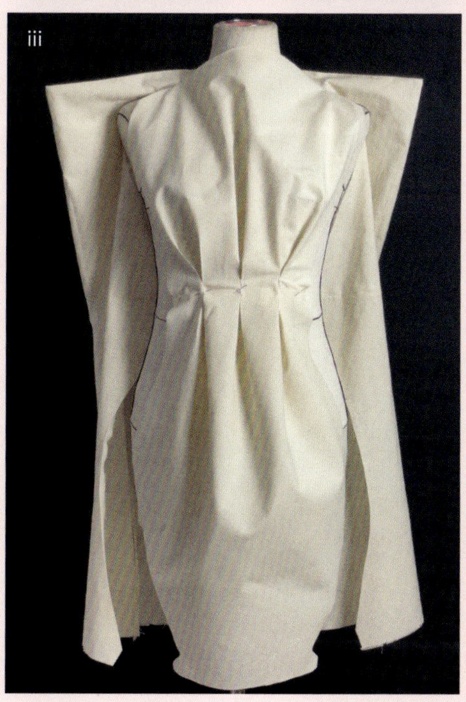
iii

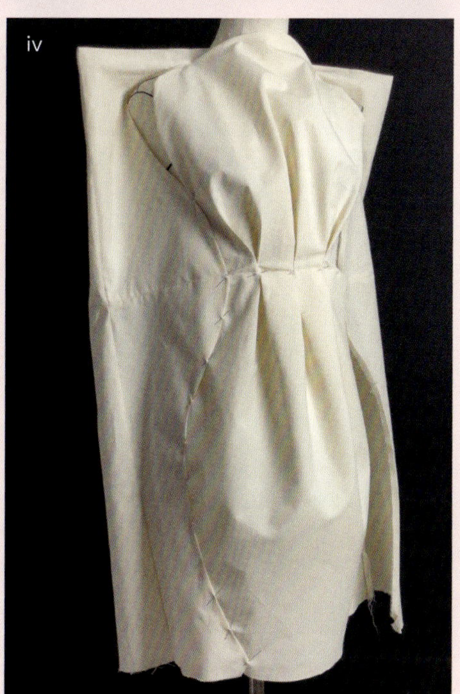
iv

Prepare the shapes following steps 2–4 of the pattern-cutting instructions (pp. 88–90).

(i) Make the darts on section B1. Attach B1 to B2 to make a new single section B.

(ii) Section B seen from the front.

(iii) Make the waist tucks on sections A1 and A2. Join A1 and A2 together to make a new single section A. Attach section A to section B at the shoulder points.

(iv) Join the right side of section B to the right side of section A at the front.

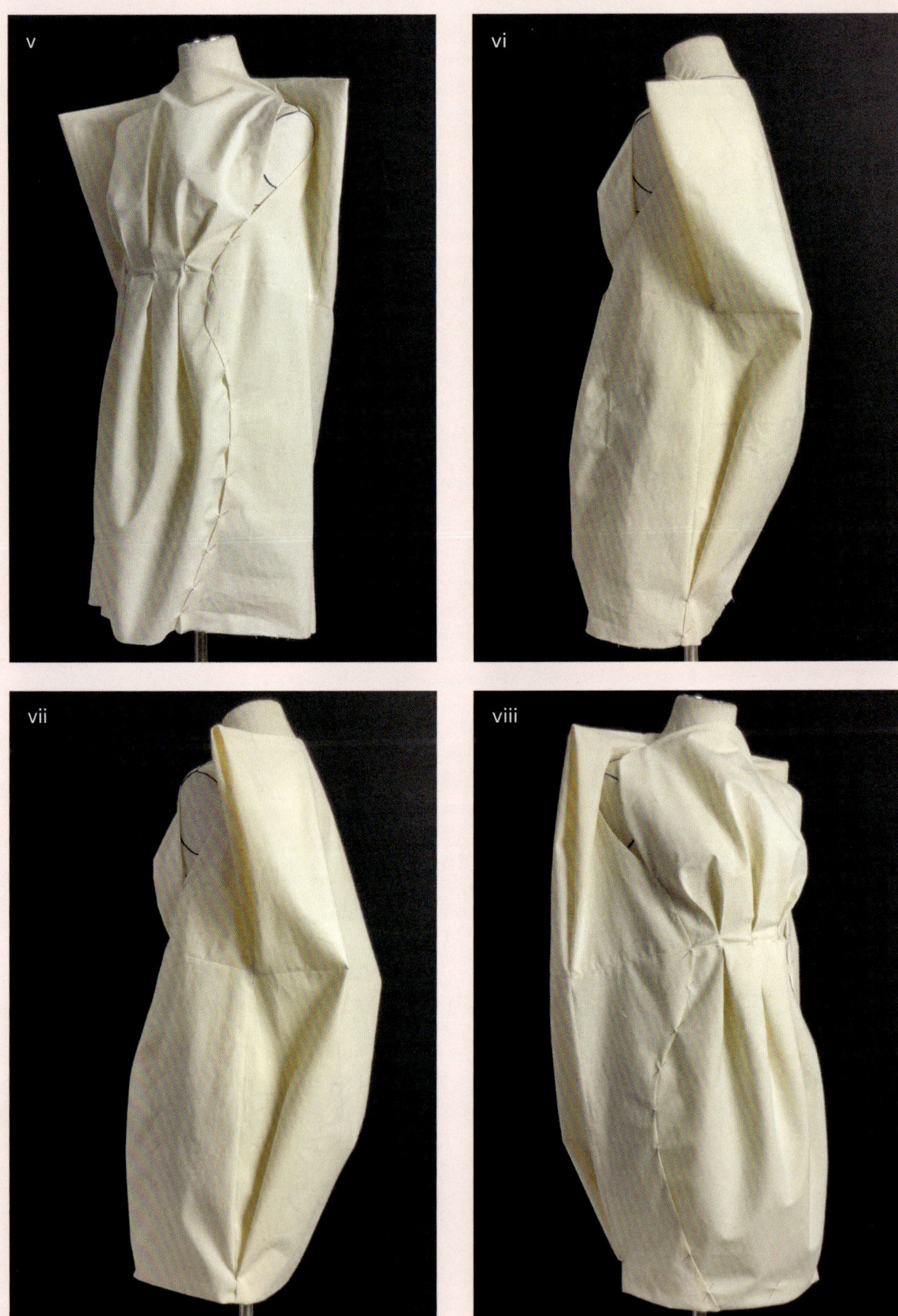

(v) Join the left side of section B to the left side of section A.

(vi) Make the tucks at the hem of section B.

(vii) Push in the folds at the shoulder of section B. Turn up the hem.

(viii) The finished drape.

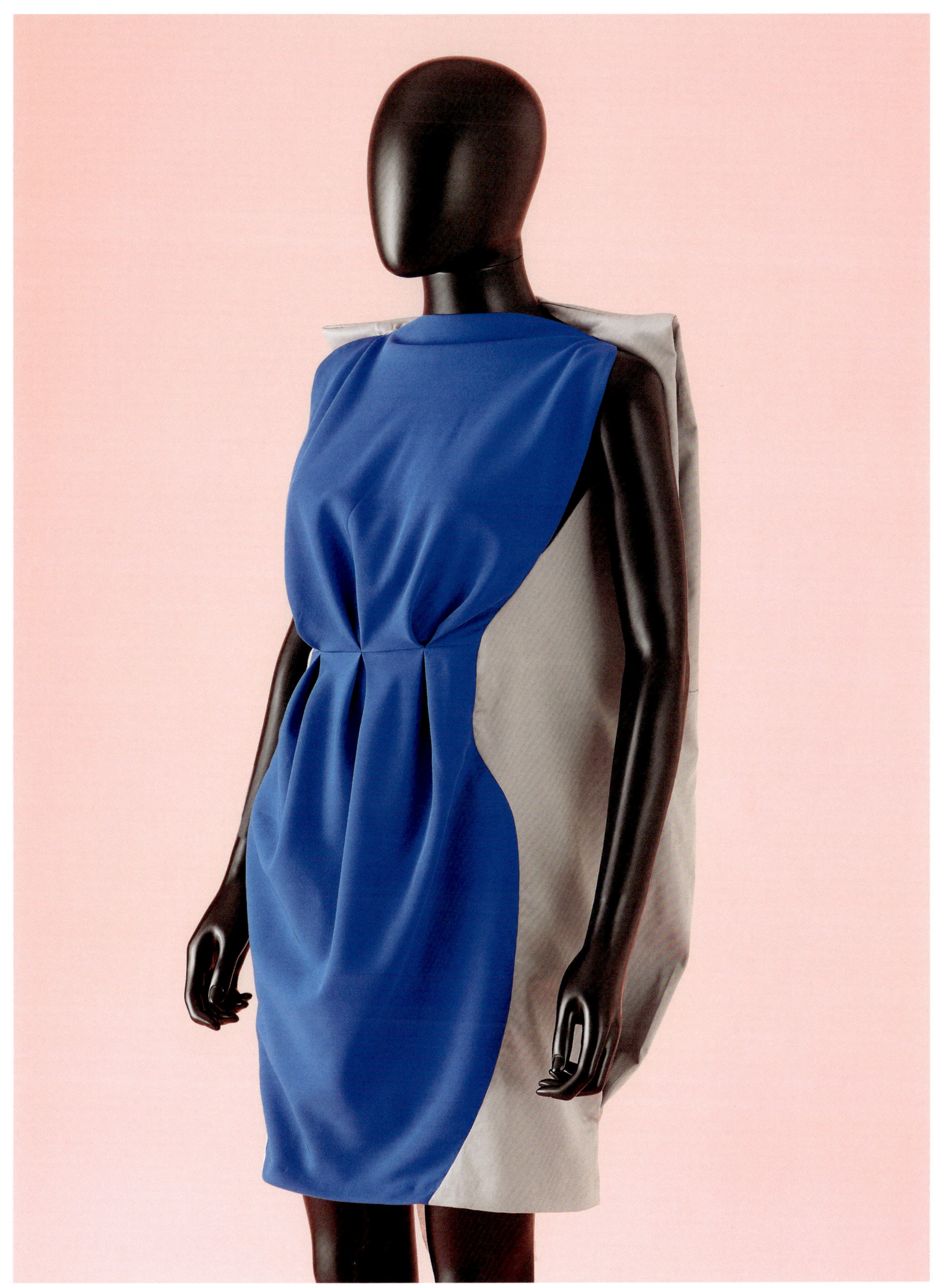

Formes dress

Papiers Découpés top

Matisse's *Papiers Découpés* poster features a circular background on which sit three birds of different sizes. I removed the birds from the circle, then used it to enrobe the body, fitting it to the figure with gathers and darts to create a top. I then sewed the birds back into their original positions and used them to form asymmetric sleeves and a hemline embellishment.

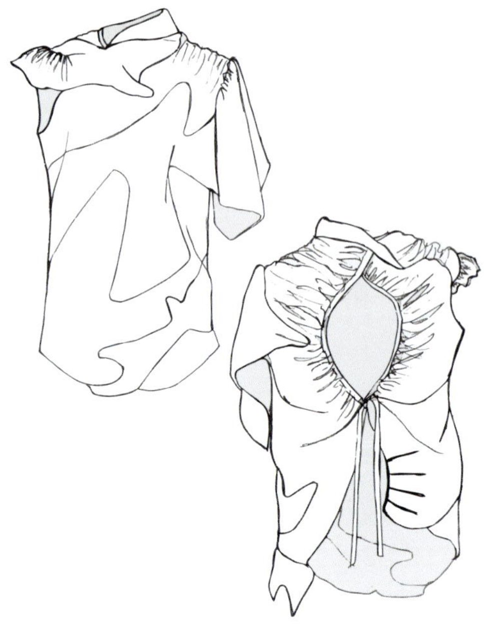

SIZING

The example here is a size 12 (US 8).
Measurements:
Bust: 98cm (38⅝in)
Waist: 90cm (35⅜in)
Hips: 102cm (40⅛in)
Length: 79cm (31⅛in)

To create additional sizes, grade the pattern (see p. 10).

FABRIC SUGGESTIONS

All colours: Viscose georgette, silk georgette, drape jersey, cotton jersey with minimal stretch.

COLOUR REFERENCES

Peach #FAA795
Blue #242B83
Coral #E23C22
Green #17402E

1

Examine the artwork shapes.

Peach = **A1** and **A2**
Blue = **B**
Coral = **C**
Green = **D**

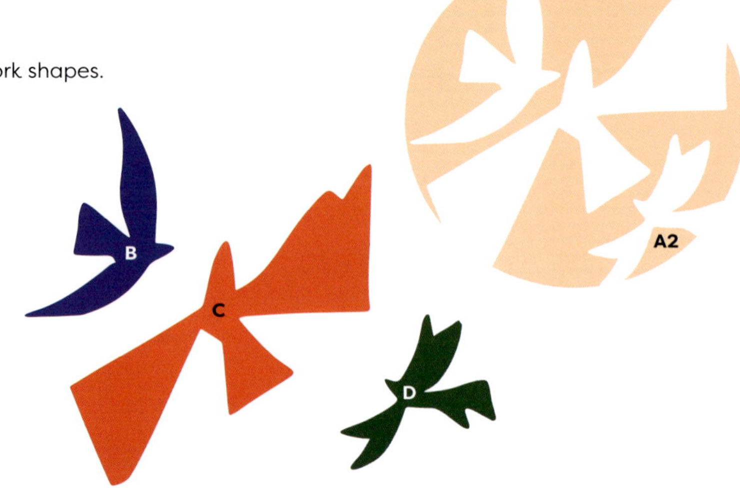

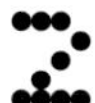

Plot the outlines of the shapes onto plain pattern paper. Place 5cm (2in) squared paper underneath the pattern paper as a guide.

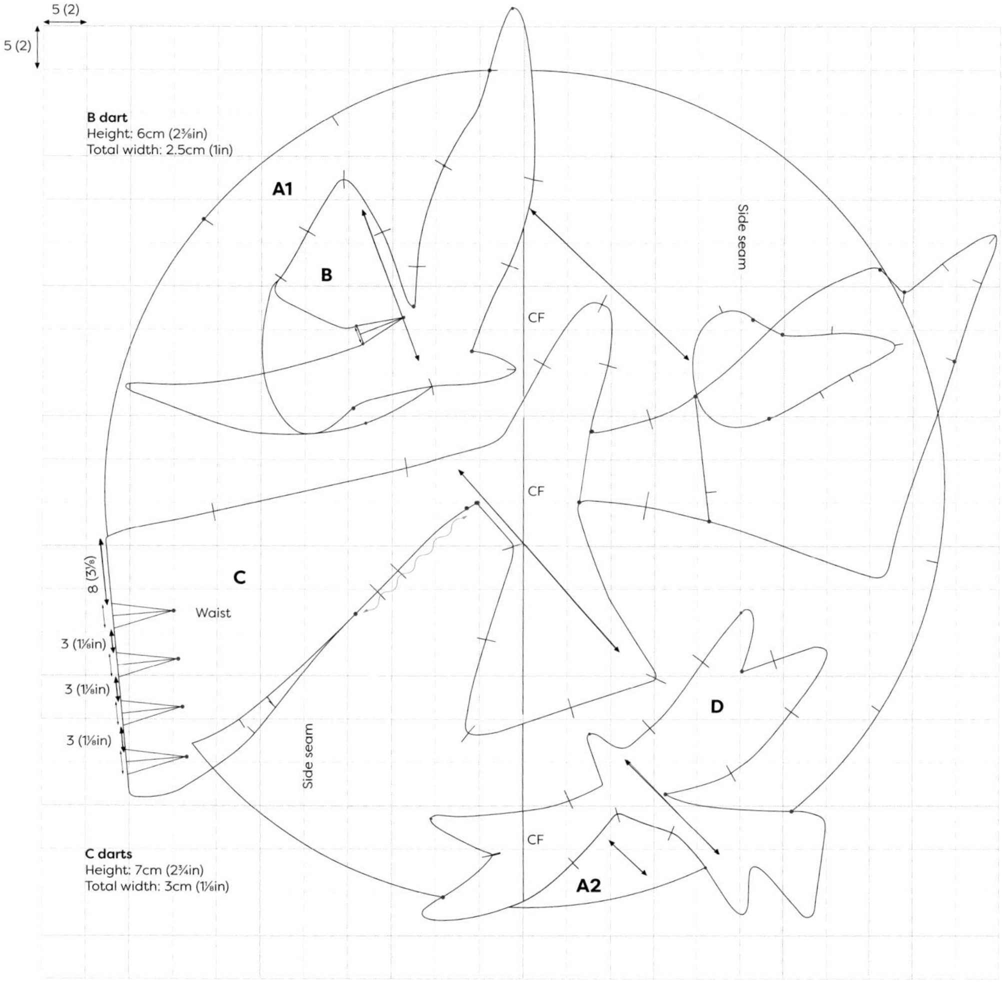

5 (2)
5 (2)

B dart
Height: 6cm (2⅜in)
Total width: 2.5cm (1in)

A1
B
Side seam
CF
CF
C
8 (3⅛)
Waist
3 (1⅛in)
3 (1⅛in)
3 (1⅛in)
Side seam
D
CF
A2

C darts
Height: 7cm (2¾in)
Total width: 3cm (1⅛in)

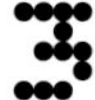

Trace the right section of C and flip it horizontally to create a facing (C1).

Mark grainlines, side seams, waist lines, drill holes and notches on all pattern pieces.

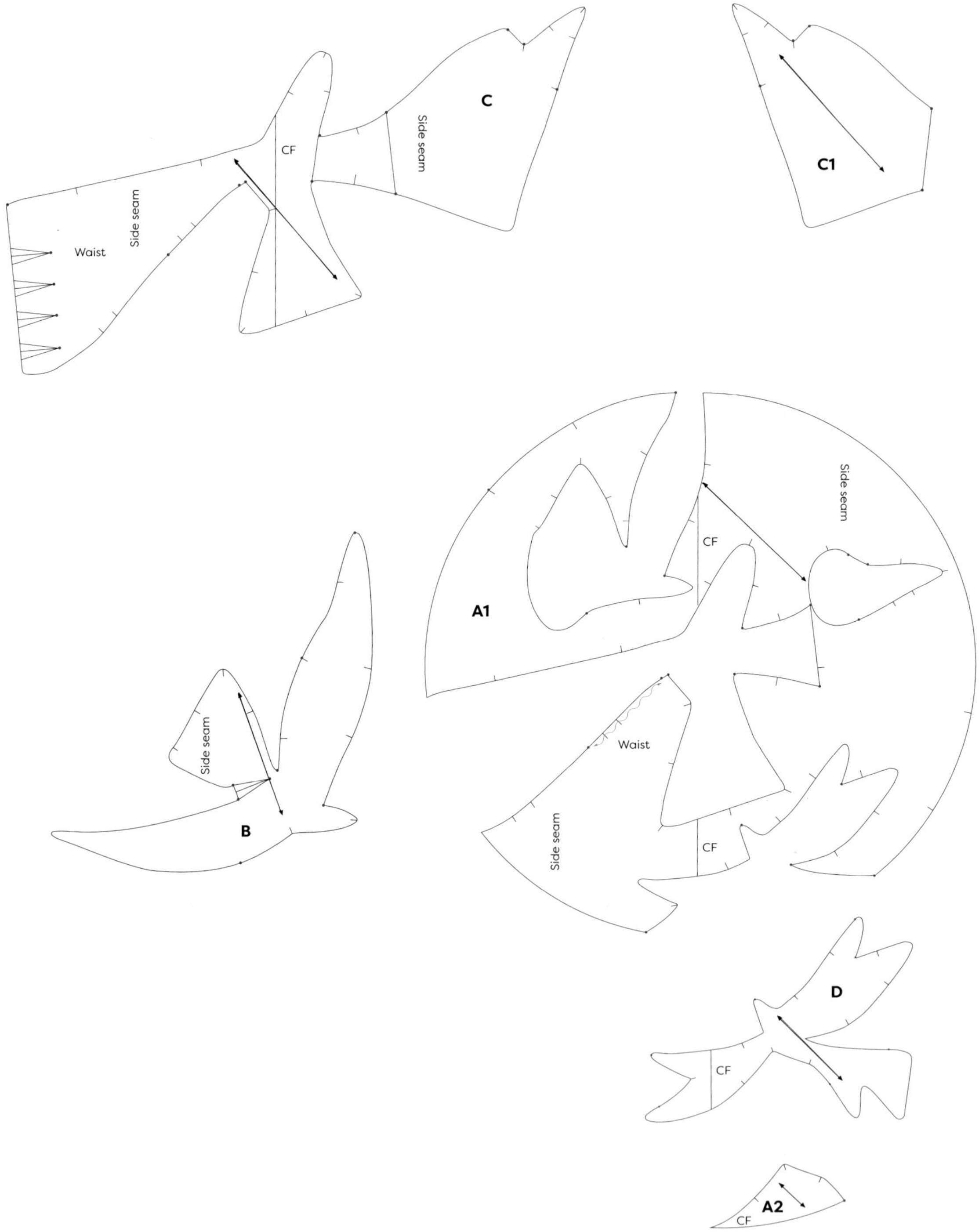

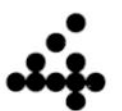

Draw a 1cm (⅜in) seam allowance around each piece. Cut out the pattern pieces in lightweight calico (muslin).

A1 x 1 RSU
A2 x 1 RSU
B x 1 pair
C x 1 RSU
C1 (Facing) x 1 RSU
D x 1 RSU

Using a tracing wheel and carbon paper, transfer grainlines, CF, darts, drill holes and notches onto BOTH sides of the fabric.

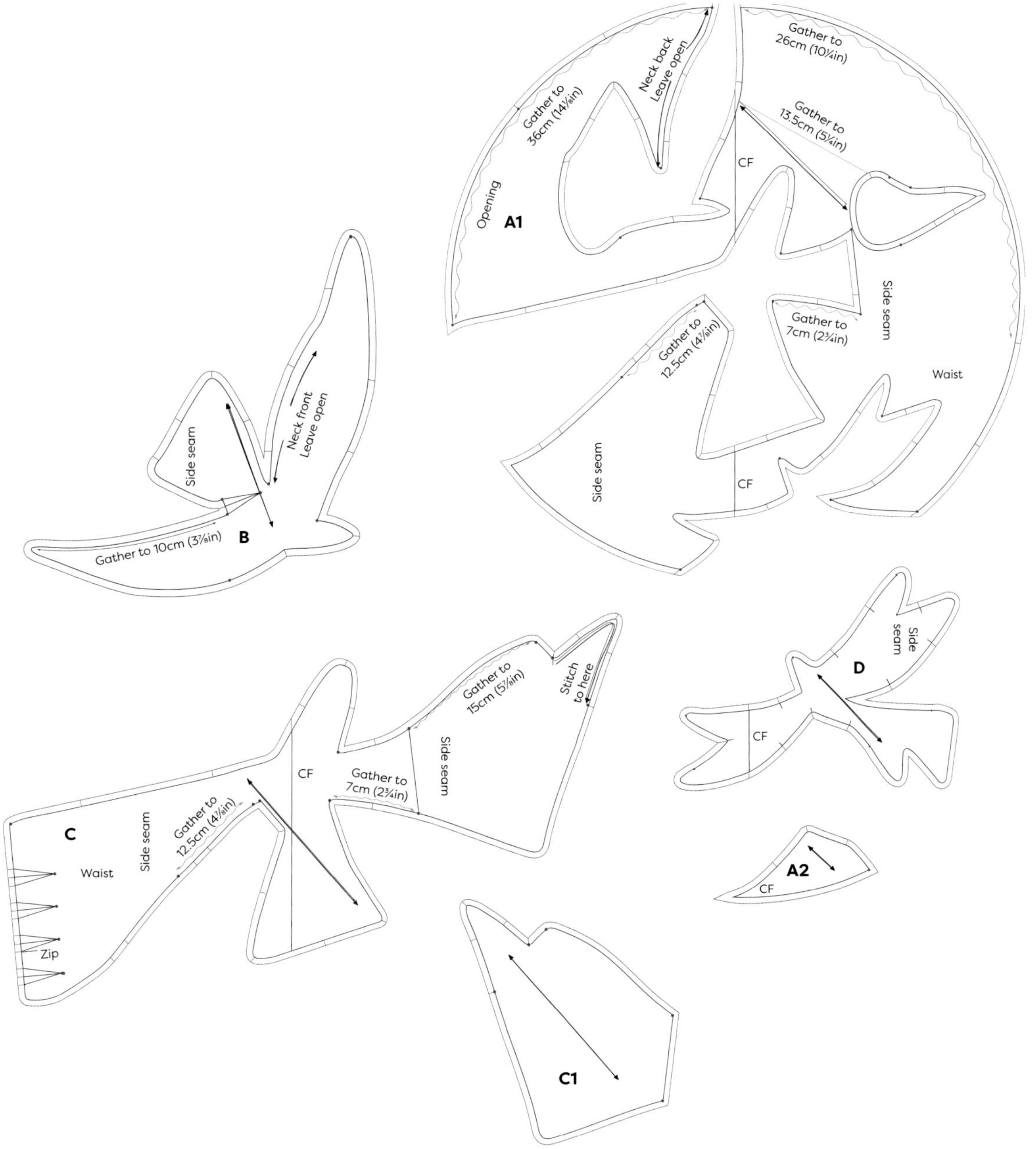

DRAPING THE SHAPES

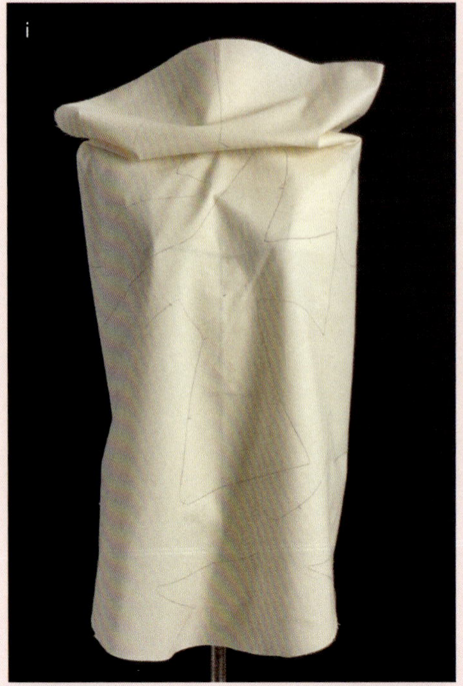
i

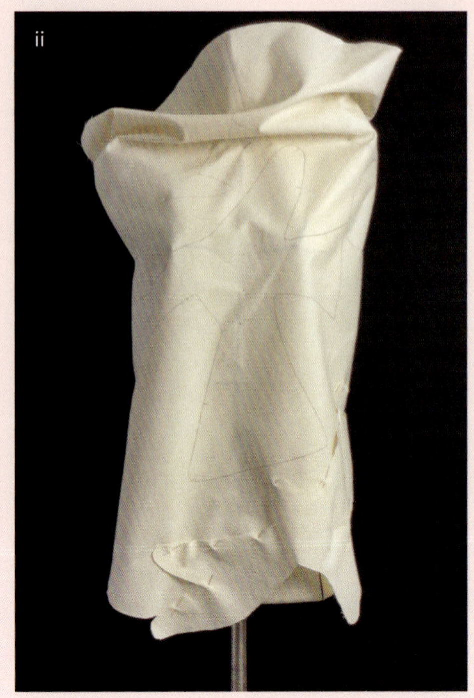
ii

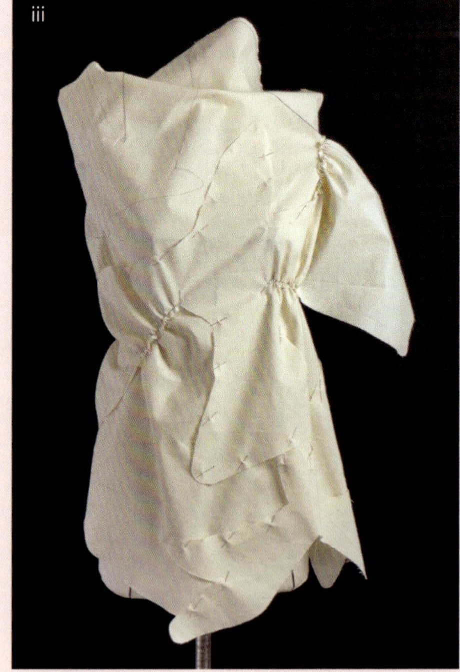
iii

Prepare A1 as a circle following step 2 of the pattern-cutting instructions (p. 95), but do not remove the bird shapes.

(i) Mark the outlines of the birds on A1. Sew a running stitch on the areas marked 'Gather' (see step 4, p. 97). Drape A1 on the dress form.

(ii) Cut out the green bird (D) from A1, leaving a 1cm (⅜in) seam allowance on A1 around the outline of D. Attach section A2 to D.

(iii) Cut out the coral bird (C), leaving a 1cm (⅜in) seam allowance on A1 around the edge of C. Gather the two front sections on A1 and lay C on top of A1. Gather the two areas under the wings of C to fit the corresponding gathers on A1. Gather the top of C to form the shoulder.

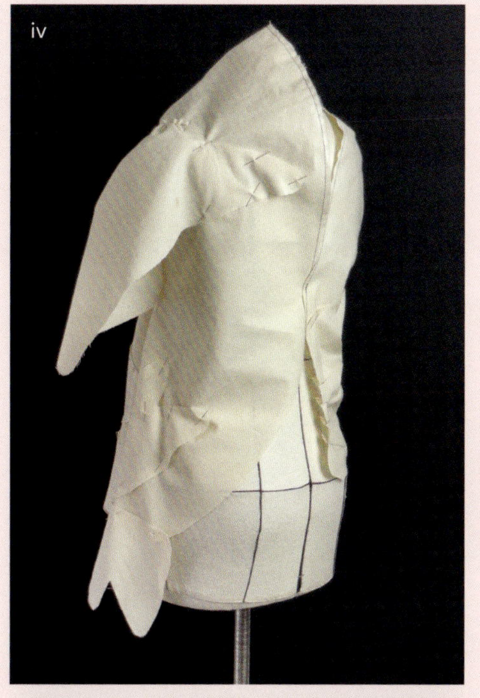

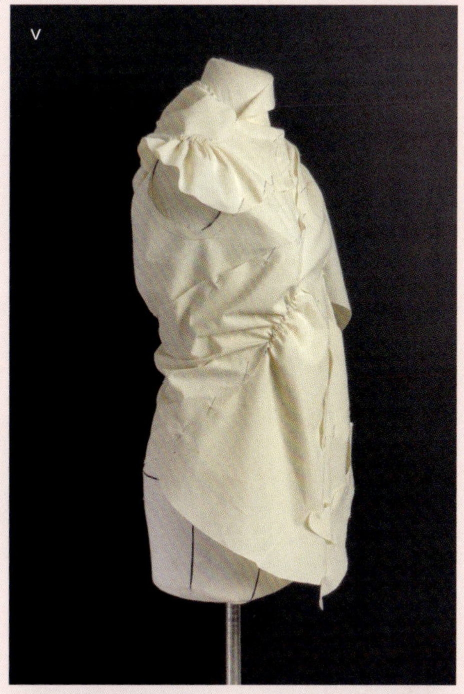

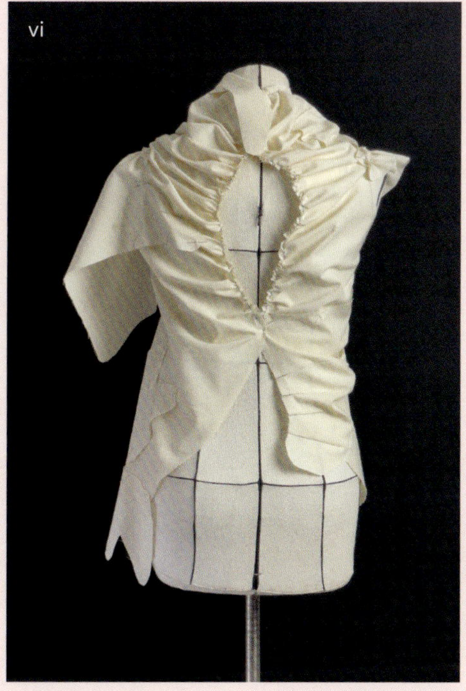

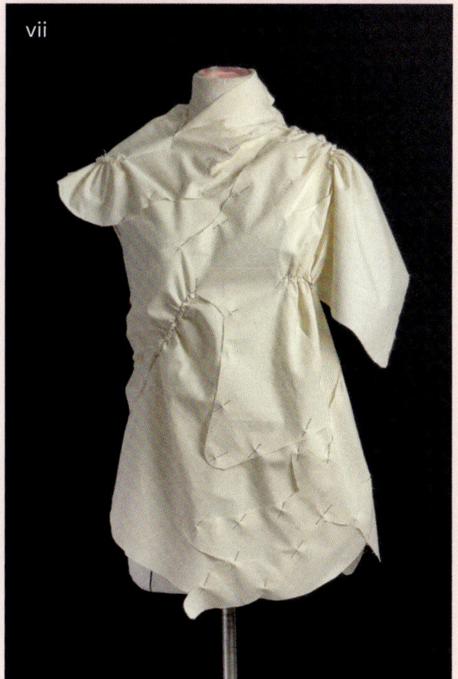

(iv) Attach C to the left back of A1. Sew the darts on the back right side of A1.

(v) Cut out the blue bird (B), leaving a 1cm (⅜in) seam allowance on A1 around the edge of B. Gather the marked section on B and attach it to the shoulder of A1.

(vi) Gather the back of the top.

(vii) The finished drape.

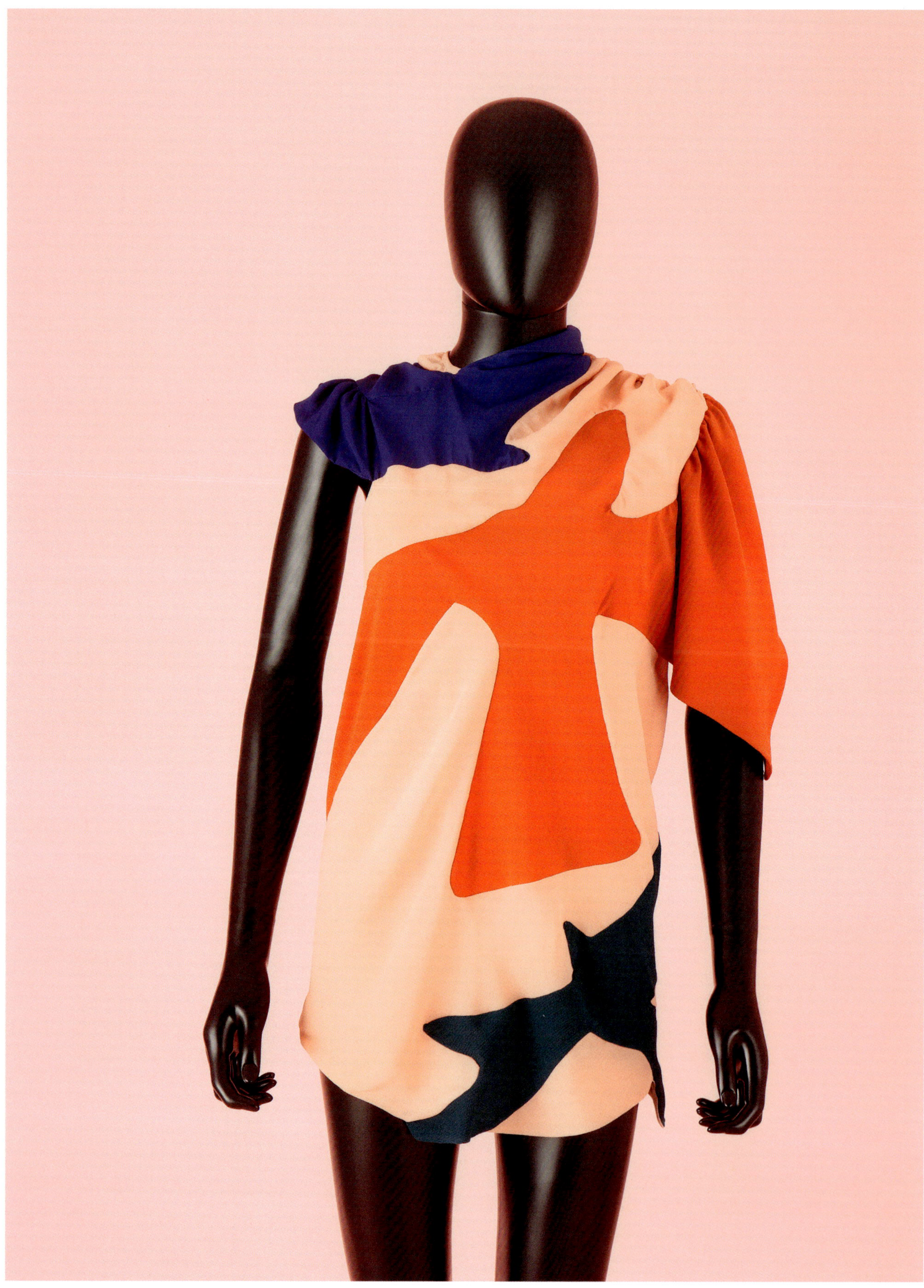

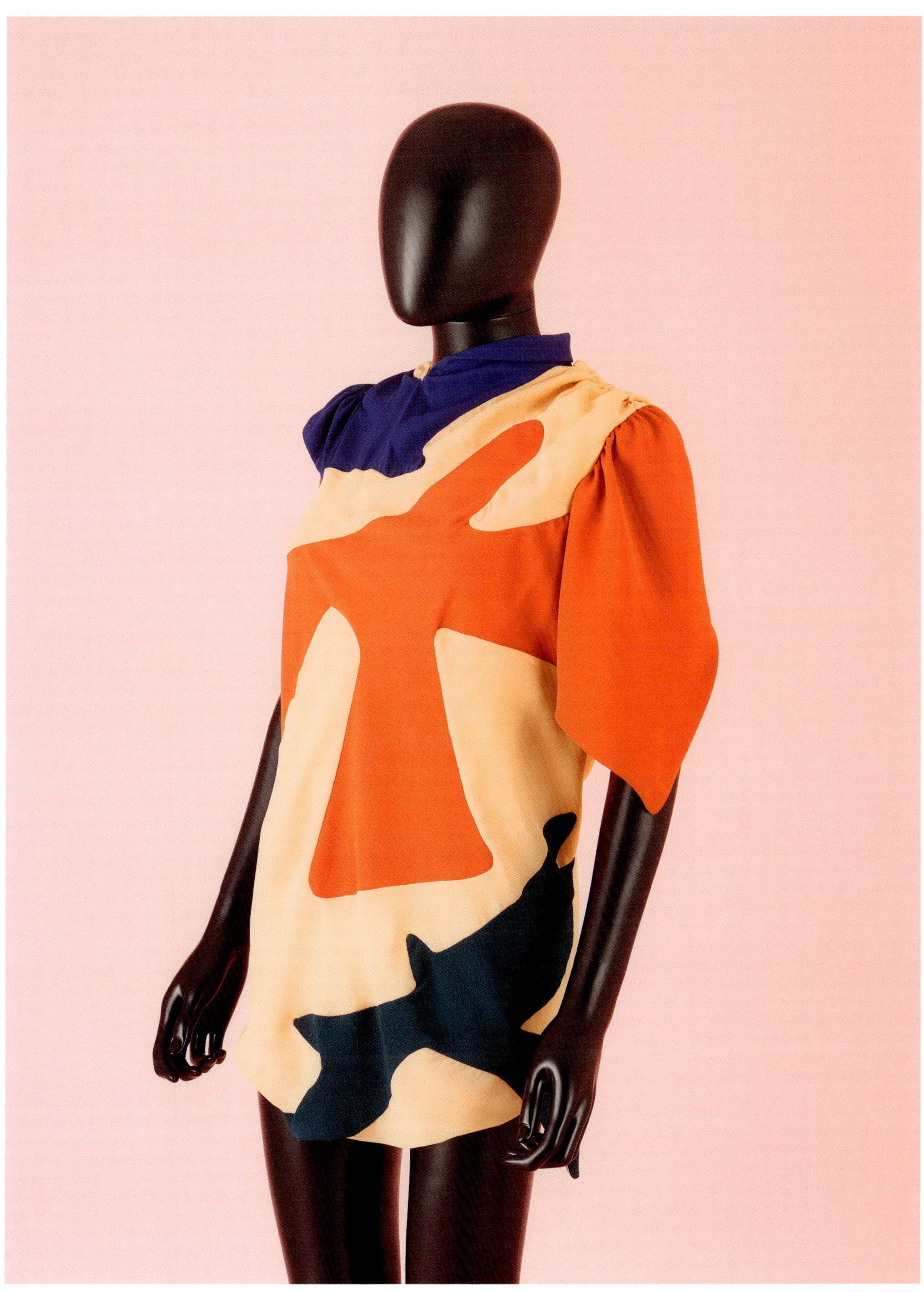

Papiers Découpés top

SERGE POLIAKOFF

Serge Poliakoff's (b. 1900, Moscow; d. 1969) early works were painted in the academic style. A visit to London in the mid-1930s led him to discover the abstract art of Egyptian sarcophagi, which would influence his later works. The painting style of Wassily Kandinsky, Sonia and Robert Delaunay, and Otto Freundlich – whom he met a little later – also inspired him. After settling in Paris, Poliakoff specialized in Tachisme, a French abstract painting movement of the 1940s and 1950s, often considered a reaction to Cubism and a European form of Abstract Expressionism.

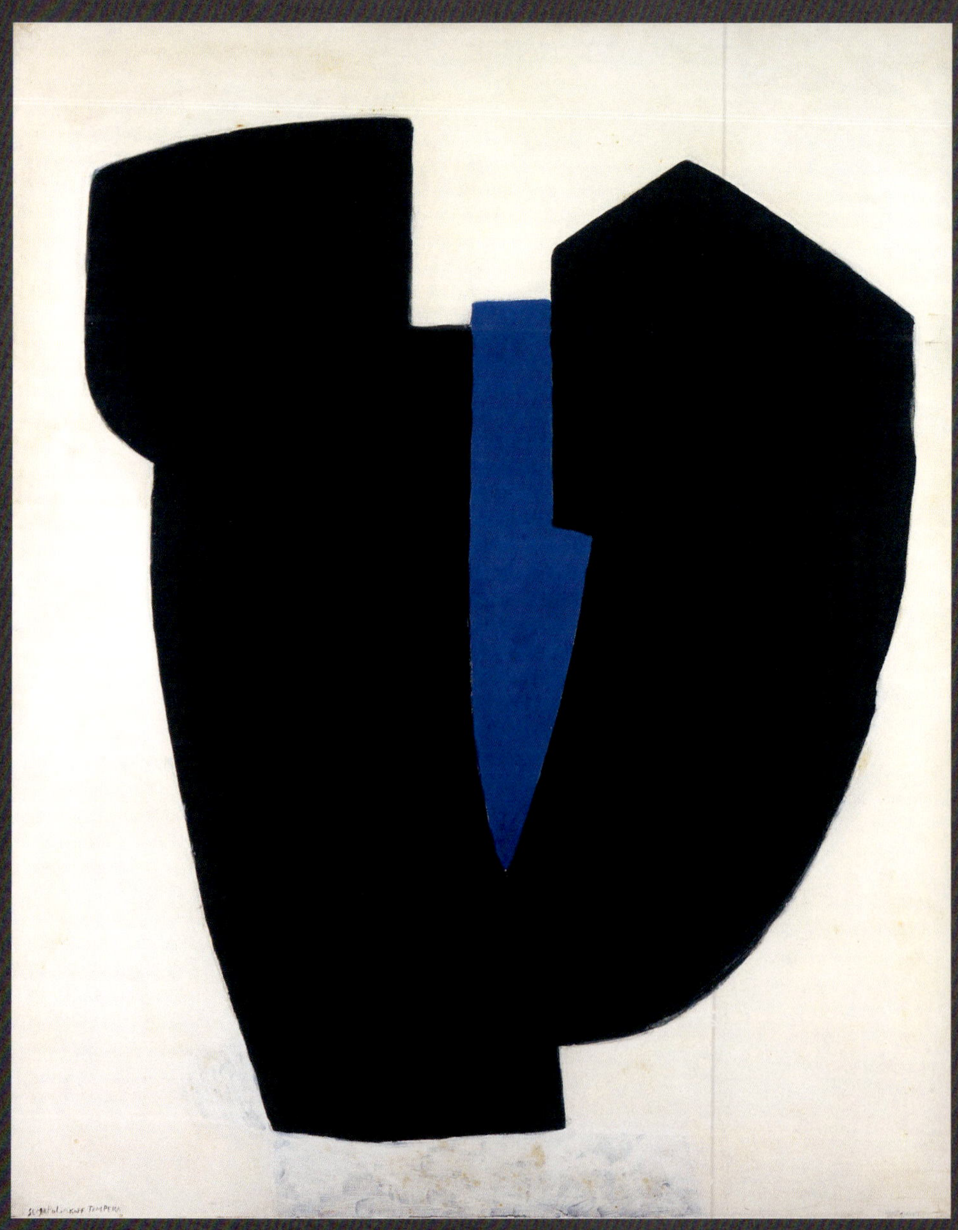

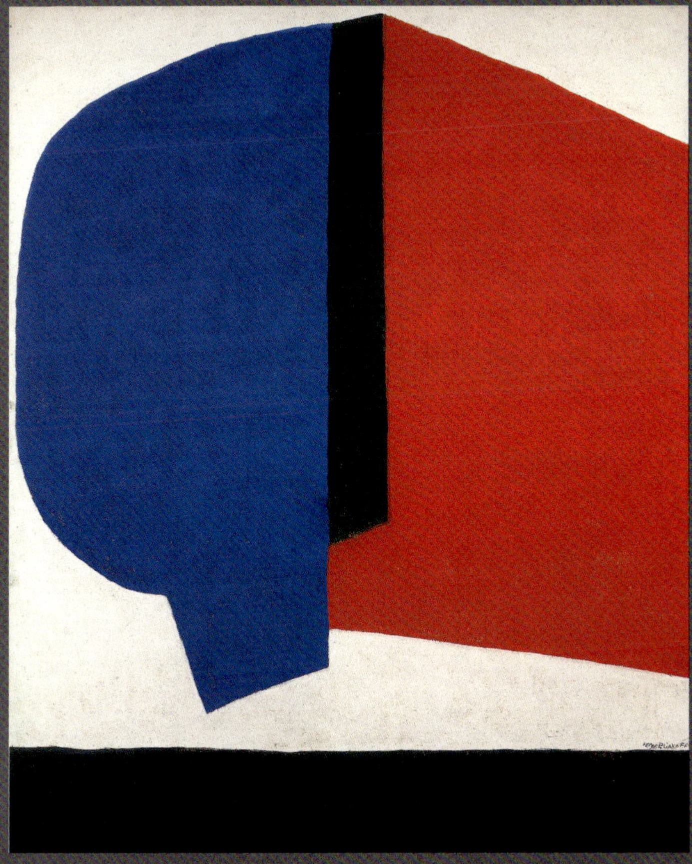

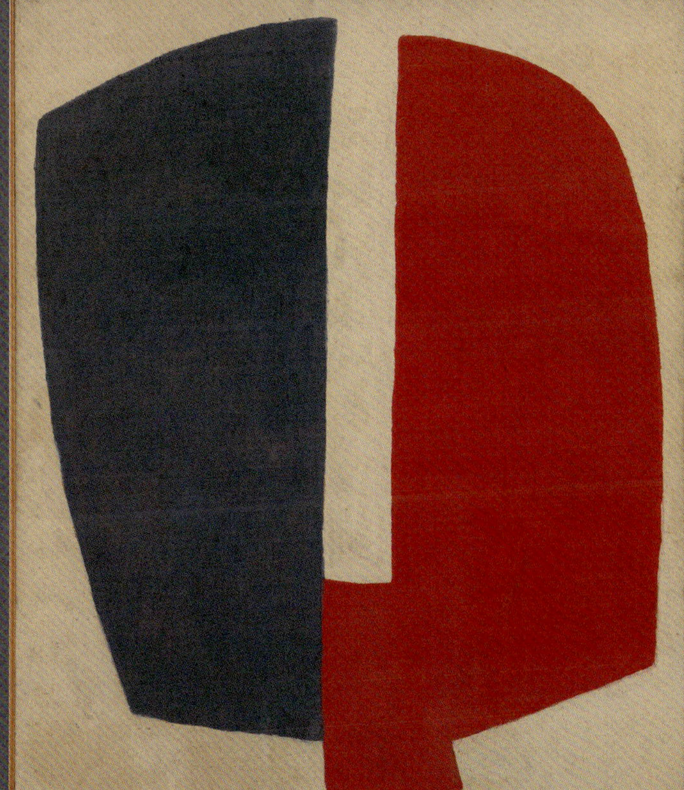

Left:
Composition Abstraite, 1968,
tempera on canvas, 162 × 130cm
(63¾ × 51⅛in)

Top right:
Composition Abstraite, 1968,
tempera on canvas, 162 × 130cm
(63¾ × 51⅛in)

Bottom right:
Composition Abstraite, 1968,
oil on canvas, 162 × 130cm
(63¾ × 51⅛in)

Composition Abstraite tunic

For more designs based on this artwork, scan the QR code

This tunic is a literal translation of the defined, Hard-Edge, cobalt-blue and black shapes of Poliakoff's *Composition Abstraite* (p. 102). Two darts at the neck give the tunic a gently contoured fit, and a hem opening on the lower-left curved section allows ease of movement. I've made the garment in two different fabrics: duchesse satin for a cocoon-style structured look and jersey for a softer, draped finish. If you use jersey, the hem should fit tighter on the hips. Play with the width of the hem by adjusting the height of the stitching on section A2.

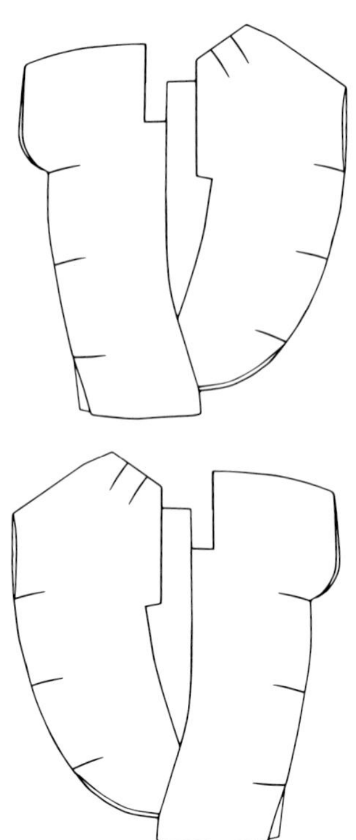

SIZING

The example here is size B (14–18; US 10–16).

Measurements:

Bust: 128cm (50⅜in)

Hips: 116cm (45⅝in)

Length from shoulder: 90cm (35⅜in)

To create additional sizes, grade the pattern (see *Pattern Cutting Deconstructed*, p. 10).

FABRIC SUGGESTIONS

Black and blue: Duchess satin, silk dupion, taffeta or any medium-weight fabric with a crisp finish (structured look).

Drape jersey, sweat-shirting, or any drapey fabric with minimal stretch (softer look).

COLOUR REFERENCES

Black #000000

Blue #3952A4

1

Examine the artwork shapes.

Black = **A1** and **A2**
Blue = **B**

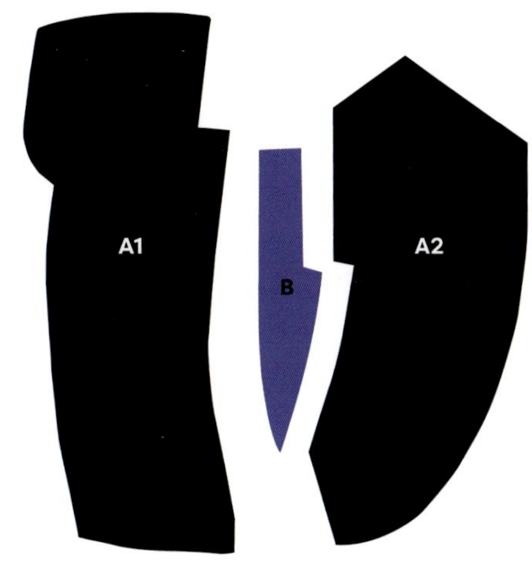

2

Plot the outlines of the shapes onto plain pattern paper. Place 5cm (2in) squared paper underneath the pattern paper as a guide.

If you're making the tunic in jersey, disregard the darts on the side seams.

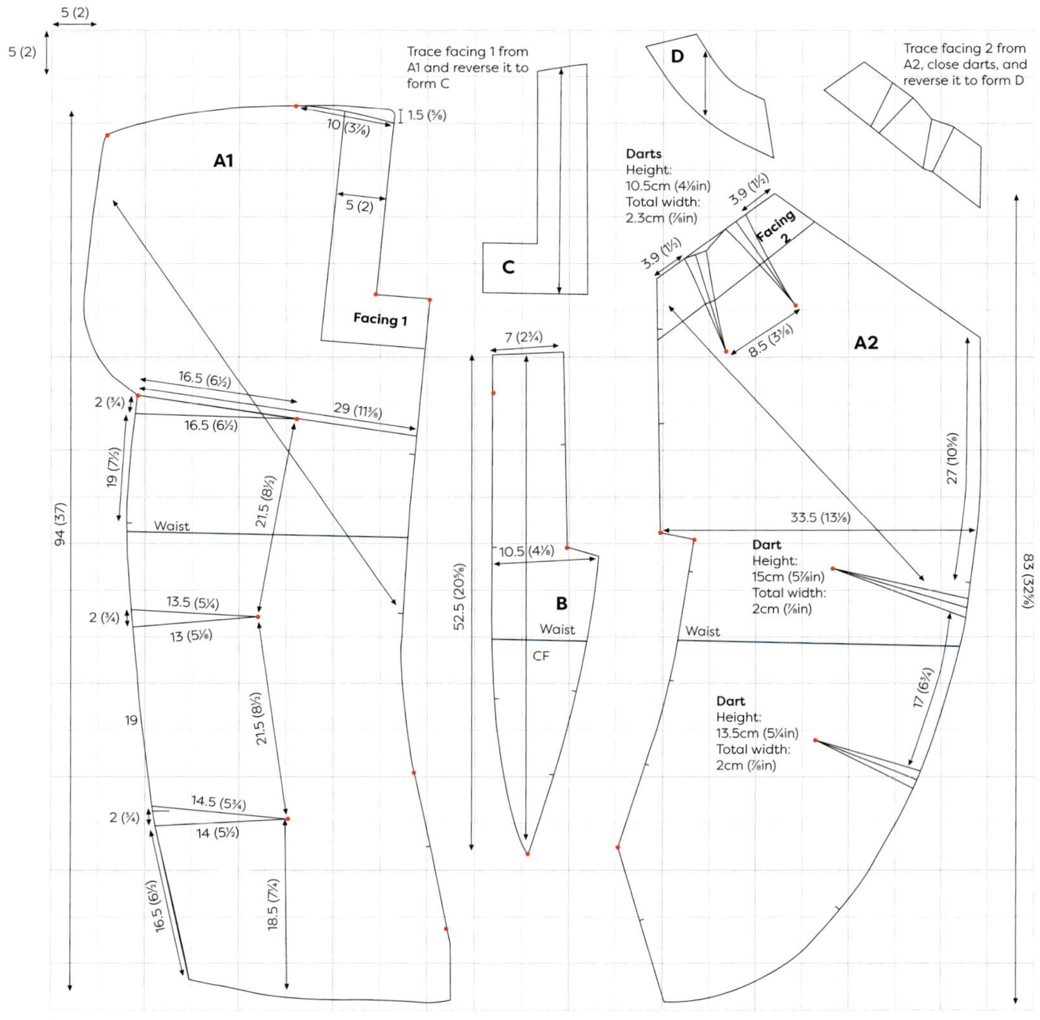

Trace facing 1 from A1 and reverse it to form C

Trace facing 2 from A2, close darts, and reverse it to form D

Darts
Height:
10.5cm (4⅛in)
Total width:
2.3cm (⅞in)

Dart
Height:
15cm (5⅞in)
Total width:
2cm (¾in)

Dart
Height:
13.5cm (5¼in)
Total width:
2cm (¾in)

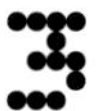

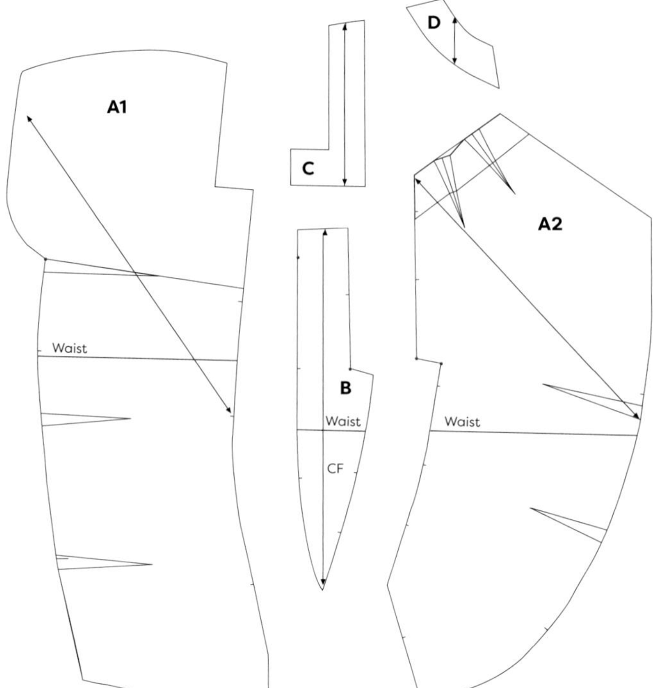

Mark bias and straight grainlines, CF, darts, drill holes and notches on the pattern pieces.

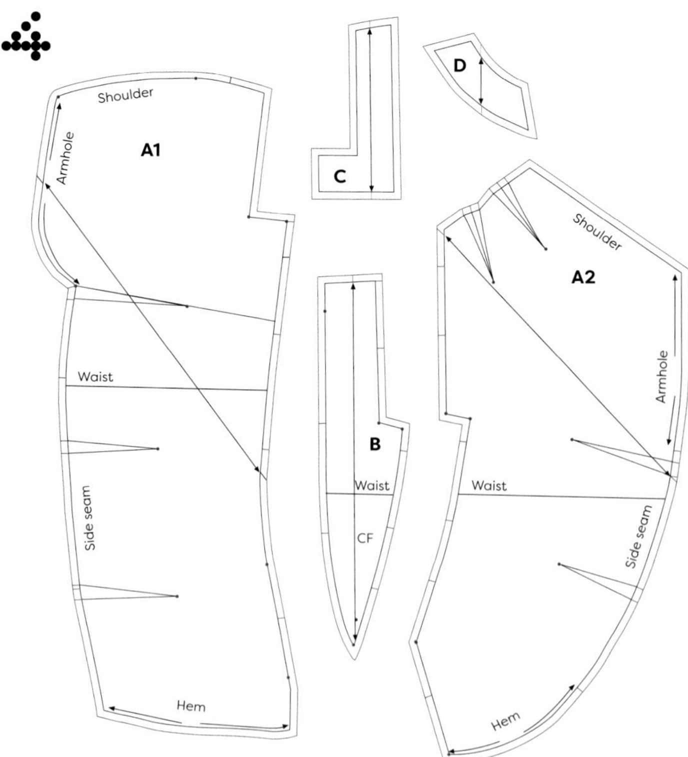

Add a 1cm (⅜in) seam allowance to each pattern piece.

Cut out the pieces in calico (muslin) for a structured look, or in jersey for a softer look.

A1 (Front and back) x 1 pair
A2 (Front and back) x 1 pair
B (Inset) x 1 pair
C (Facing 1) x 1 RSU
D (Facing 2) x 1 RSU

Using a tracing wheel and carbon paper, transfer grainlines, CF, darts, drill holes and notches onto BOTH sides of the fabric.

DRAPING THE SHAPES

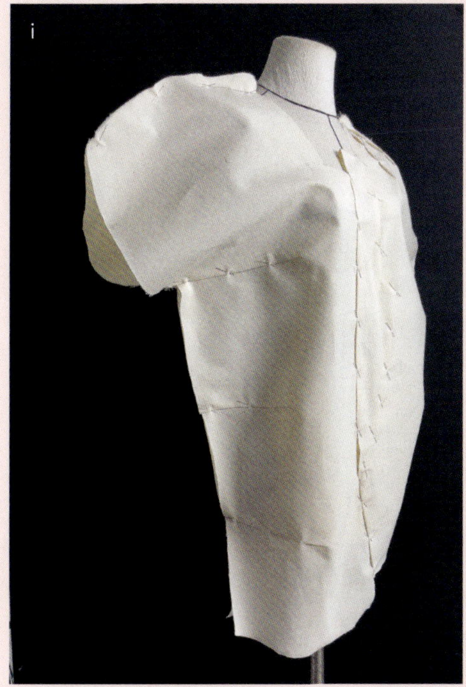
i

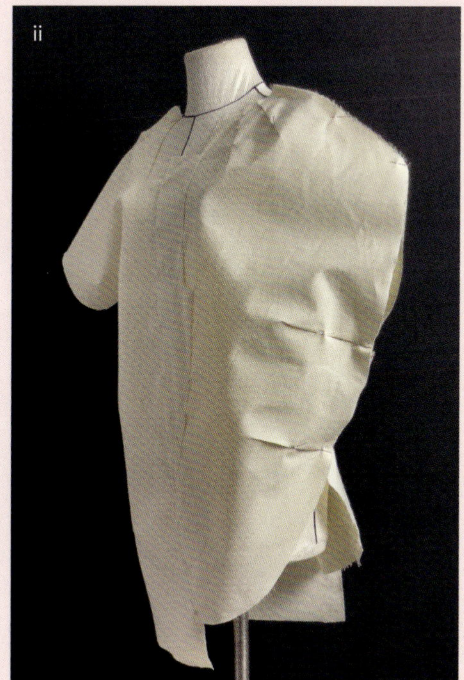
ii

Prepare the shapes following steps 2–4 of the pattern-cutting instructions (pp. 105–6).

Here the tunic is draped in calico (muslin). You could also try jersey, which will create a softer silhouette.

(i) Attach the inset (B) to A1 and A2 and pin to the dress form. Make the darts on the right sides (A1), front and back.
Pin the side seams together. Pin the shoulder line.

(ii) On the left side (A2), pin the darts along the neckline, front and back, and on the side. Pin the front and back together.

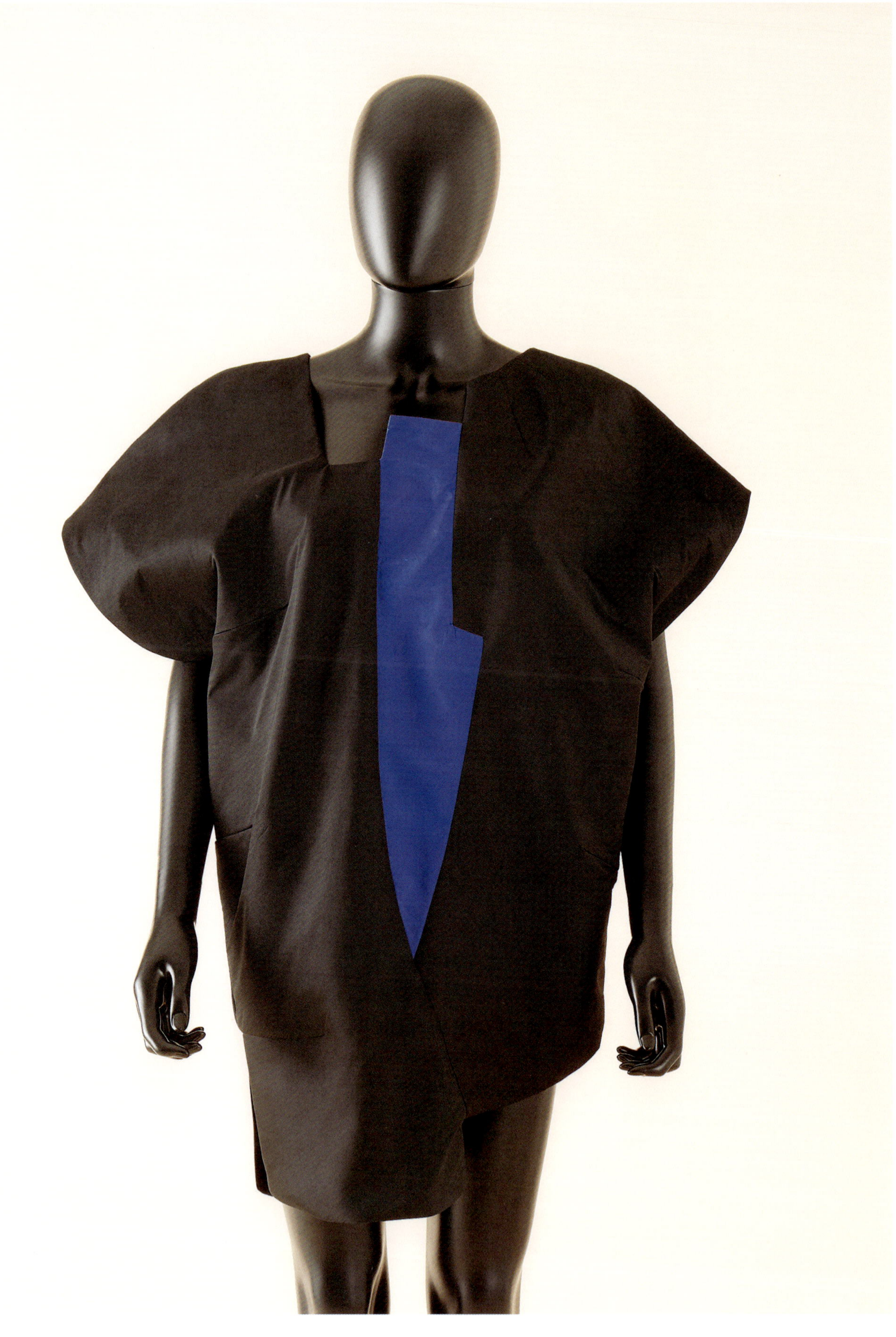

Poliakoff

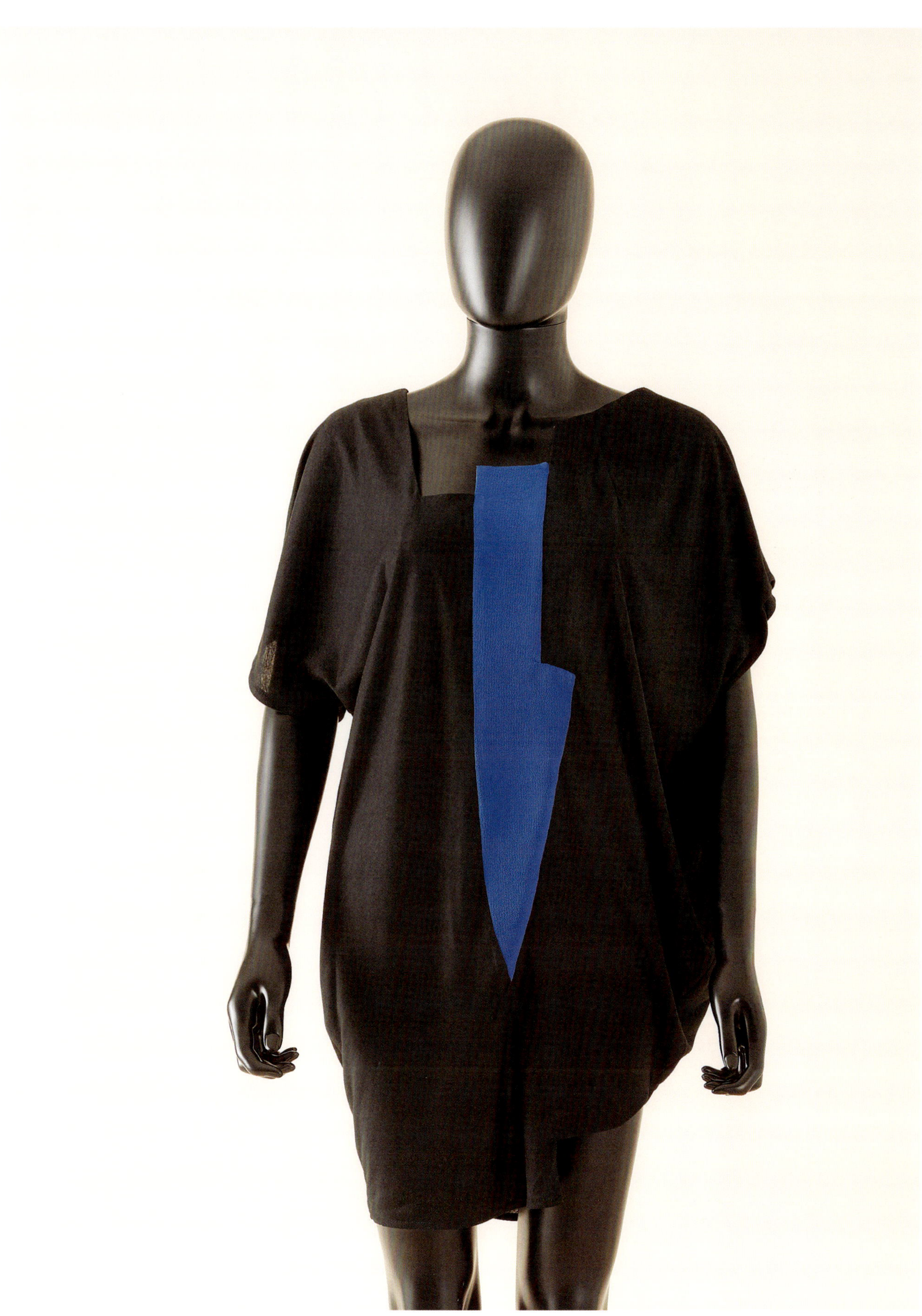

Composition Abstraite tunic

Composition Abstraite dress and jacket

Poliakoff's *Composition Abstraite* (p. 103 top) conjured up for me an image of a dress and jacket with a 1960s aesthetic. The cream rectangle and bottom black strip were developed into an A-line sleeveless dress, the blue section of the painting formed the back and sleeves of a voluminous jacket, and the red became two geometric panels folded across the front for a bold pop of colour. The black vertical strip became a collar. The jacket is cut on the bias to maximize the draped effect.

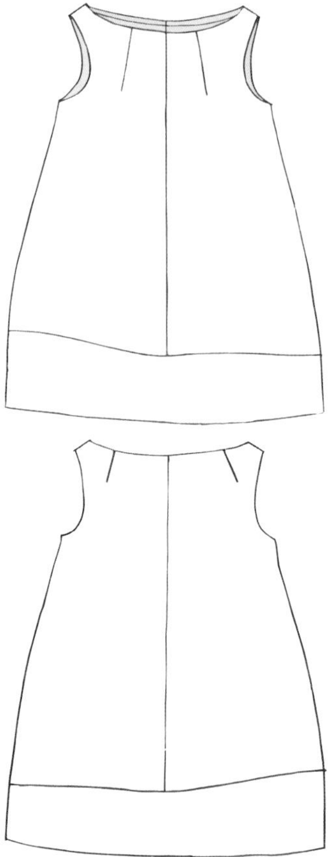

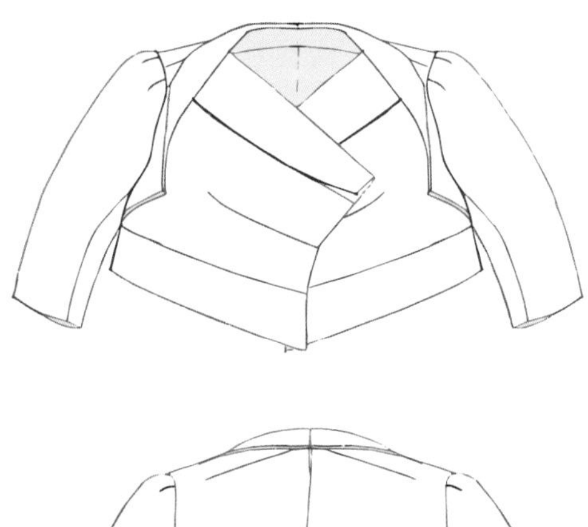

SIZING

The example here is a size 10 (US 6).

Measurements:

Dress

Bust: 94cm (37in)

Waist: 104cm (41in)

Hips: 114cm (44⅞in)

Length: 79cm (31⅛in)

Jacket

Bust: 100cm (39⅜in)

Length: 45cm (17¾in)

Sleeve length: 45cm (17¾in)

To create additional sizes, grade the pattern (see p. 10).

FABRIC SUGGESTIONS

All colours: Double-wool crepe, suiting, heavy wool jersey, sweat-shirting, linen, cotton drill.

For the sample I used deadstock double-wool crepe.

The dress and jacket were backed with tarlatan in order to hold their shape.

COLOUR REFERENCES

Cream #FBE9D1

Blue #2A3072

Black #000000

Red #DC1E26

1 Examine the artwork shapes.

Cream = **A**

Blue = **B**

Black = **C** and **E**

Red = **D**

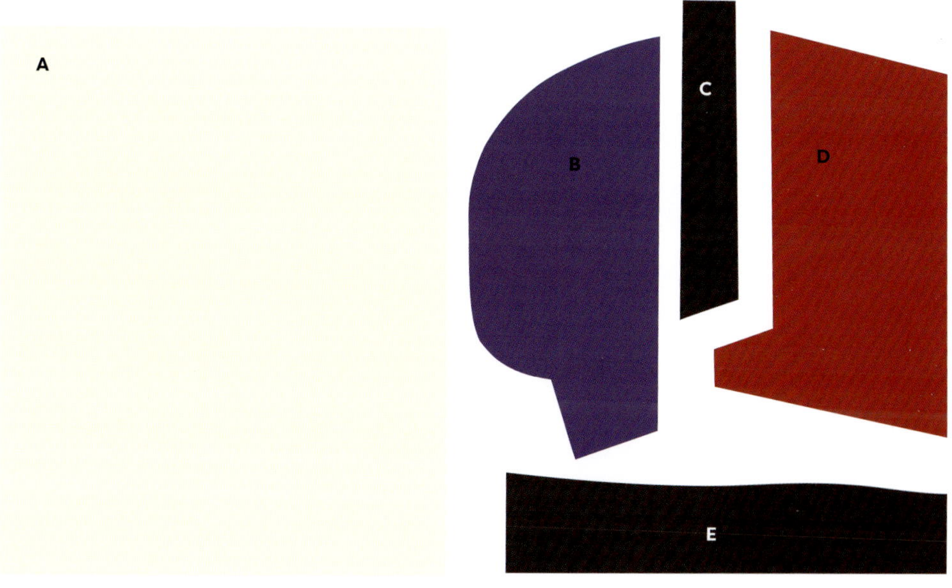

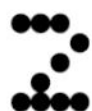

Plot the outlines of the shapes onto plain pattern paper. Place 5cm (2in) squared paper underneath the pattern paper as a guide.

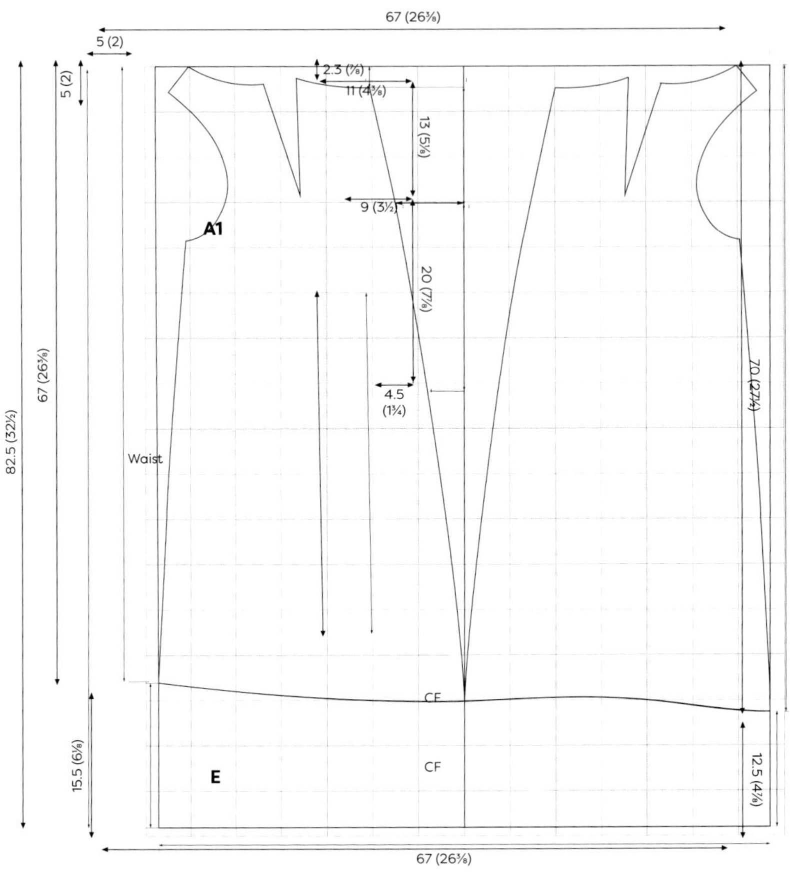

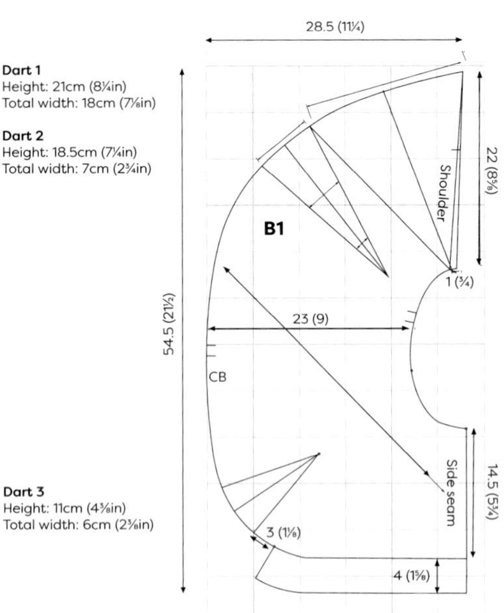

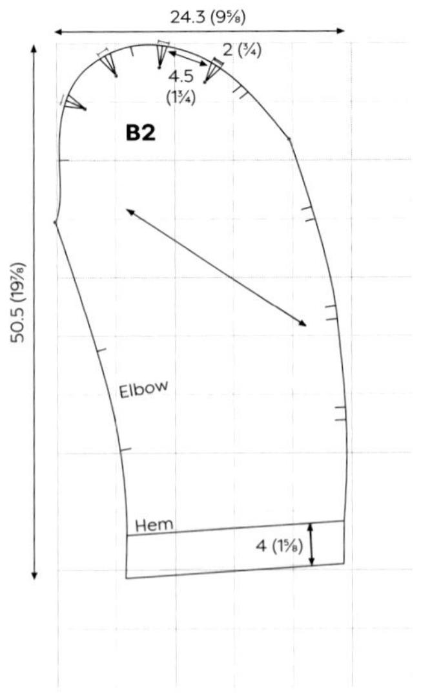

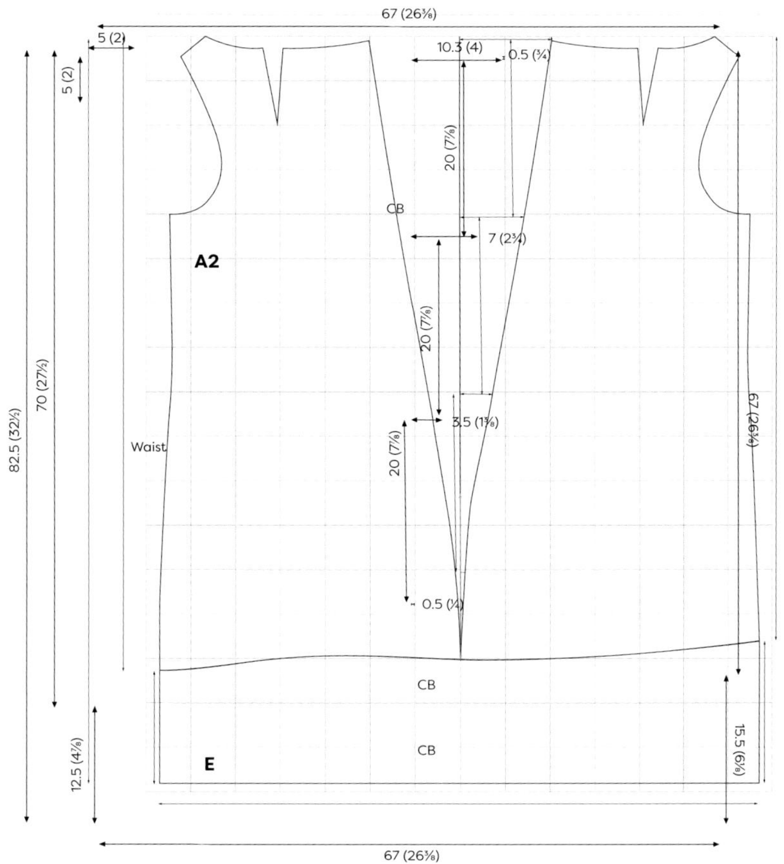
67 (26⅜)
5 (2)
10.3 (4)
0.5 (¾)
5 (2)
20 (7⅞)
CB
7 (2¾)
A2
20 (7⅞)
82.5 (32½)
70 (27½)
3.5 (1⅜)
67 (26⅜)
Waist
20 (7⅞)
0.5 (¼)
CB
CB
E
12.5 (4⅞)
15.5 (6⅛)
67 (26⅜)

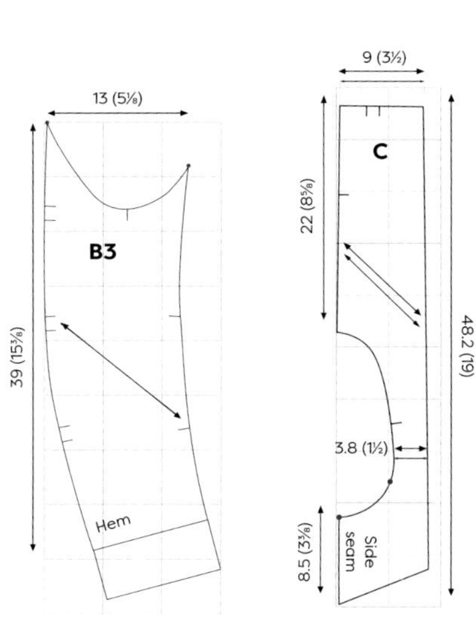
13 (5⅛)
9 (3½)
C
B3
22 (8⅝)
39 (15⅜)
48.2 (19)
3.8 (1½)
Hem
8.5 (3⅜)
Side seam

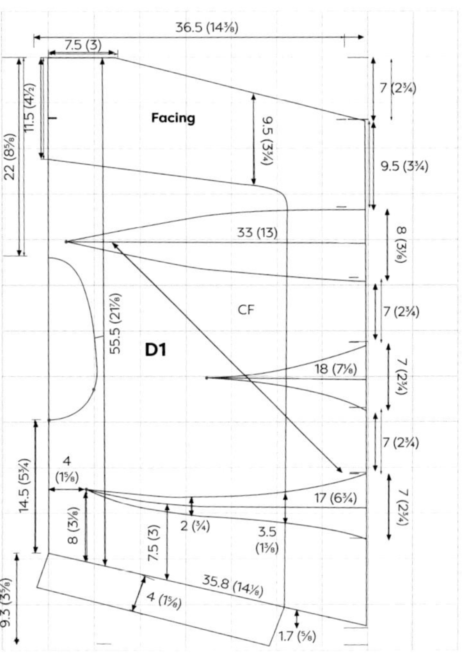
36.5 (14⅜)
7.5 (3)
7 (2¾)
Facing
11.5 (4½)
22 (8⅝)
9.5 (3¾)
9.5 (3¾)
33 (13)
8 (3⅛)
CF
7 (2¾)
55.5 (21⅞)
D1
18 (7⅛)
7 (2¾)
7 (2¾)
4 (1⅝)
14.5 (5¾)
17 (6¾)
7 (2¾)
2 (¾)
3.5 (1⅜)
8 (3⅛)
7.5 (3)
35.8 (14⅛)
4 (1⅝)
9.3 (3⅝)
1.7 (⅝)

Trace the jacket facing from the jacket front (D1) and close the darts to form D2.

Mark grainlines, CF and CB, darts, drill holes and notches on all pattern pieces.

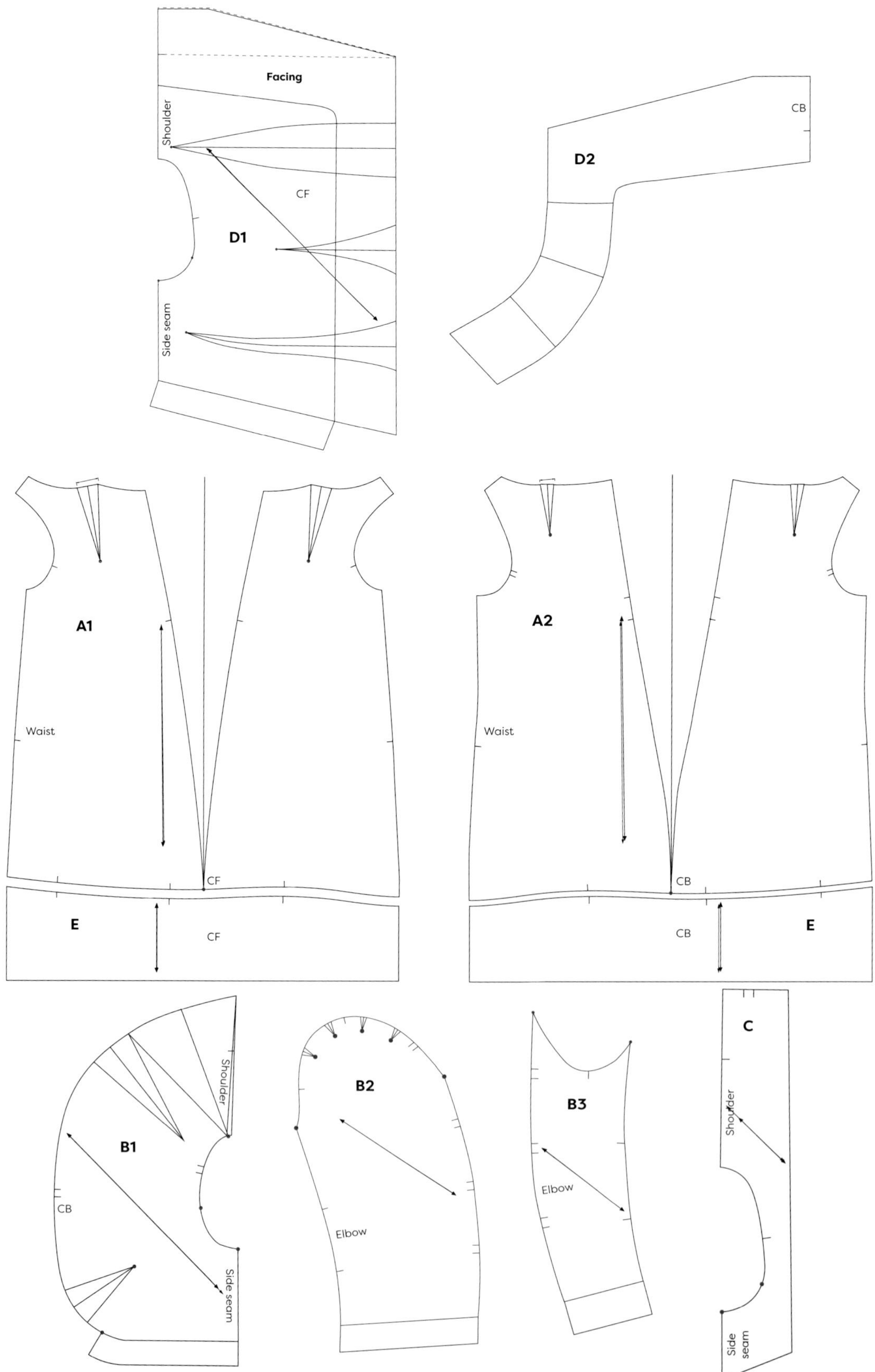

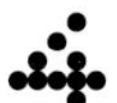

Add a 1cm (⅜in) seam allowance to each pattern piece. Add a 4cm (1⅝in) hem allowance to the dress hem (E). Note that the jacket front and back (B1, D1) and sleeves (B2, B3) already have hem allowances.

Cut out the pattern pieces in calico (muslin) and use a tracing wheel and carbon paper to transfer grainlines, CF and CB, darts, drill holes and notches onto BOTH sides of the fabric.

A1 (Dress front) x 1 RSU
A2 (Dress back) x 1 RSU
B1 (Jacket back) x 1 pair
B2 (Jacket upper sleeve) x 1 pair
B3 (Jacket under sleeve) x 1 pair
C (Jacket side panel/collar) x 2 pairs
D1 (Jacket front) x 1 pair
D2 (Jacket facing) x 1 pair
E (Dress hem) x 1 pair

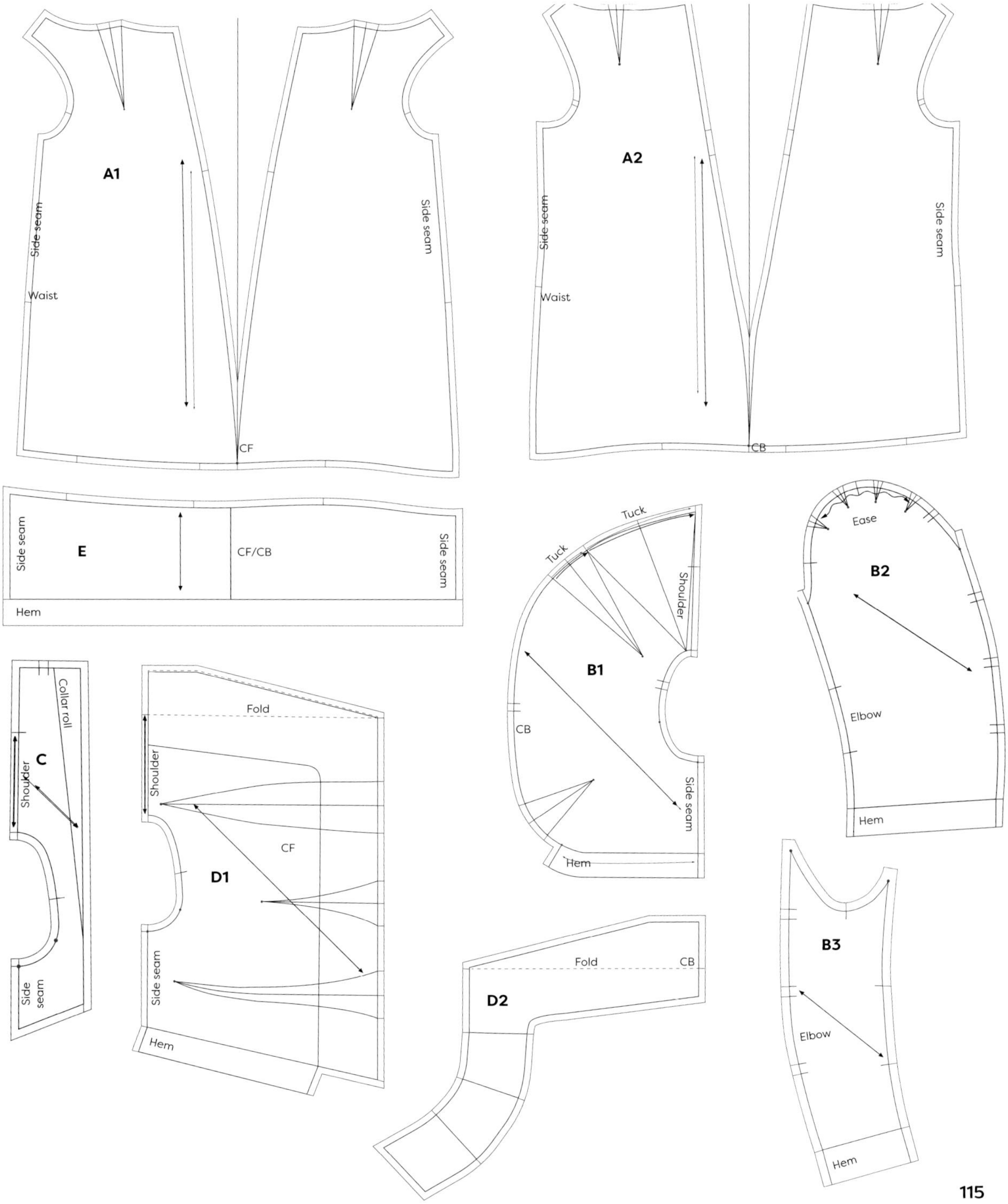

DRAPING THE SHAPES

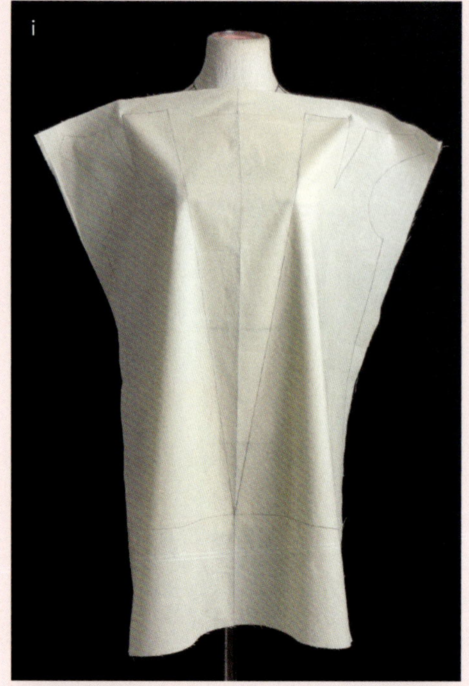
i

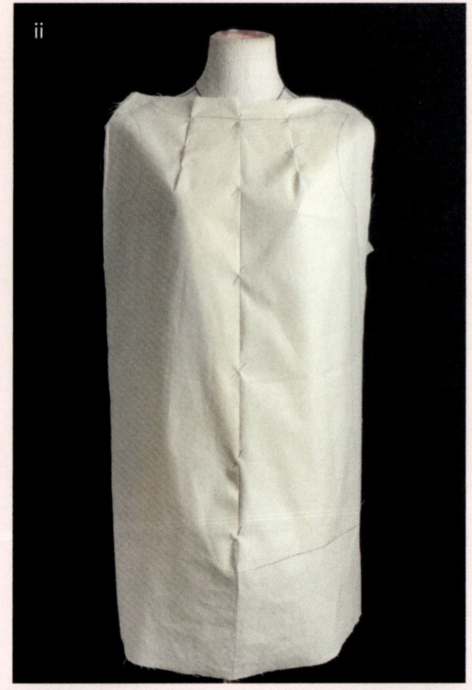
ii

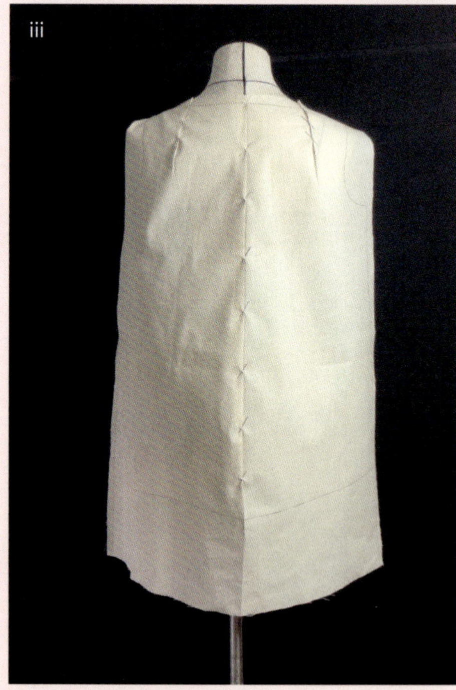
iii

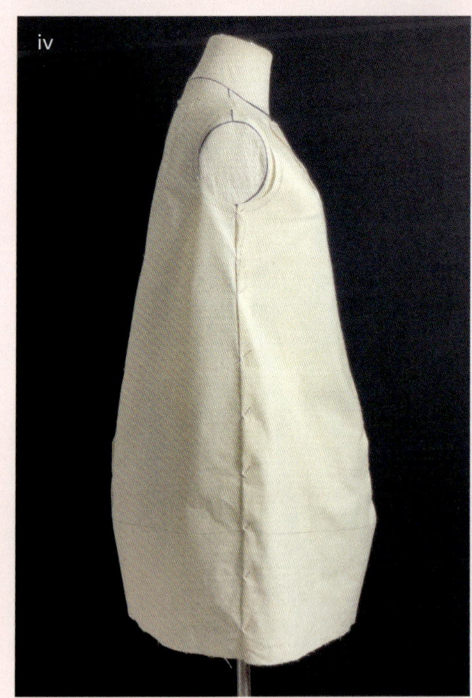
iv

Dress

Prepare A1 and A2 following the pattern-cutting instructions in step 2 (pp. 112–13). Cut them out with armholes and necklines intact, and including the dress hems (E).

(i) Drape A1 on the dress form.

(ii) Add the two darts to the neckline of A1. Pin the CF seam.

(iii) Join the two back sections of A2 together and drape them on the dress form. Add the two darts to the neckline of A2.

(iv) Cut out the armholes and the neckline.

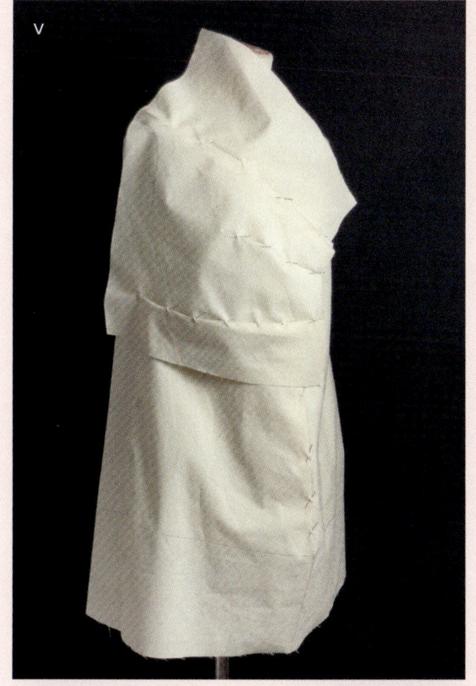

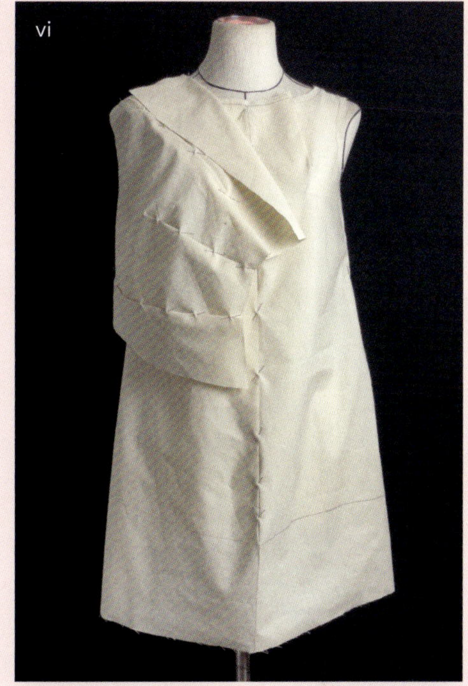

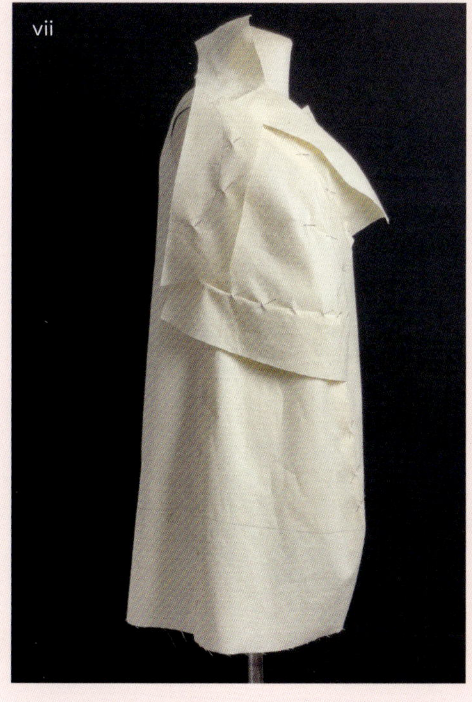

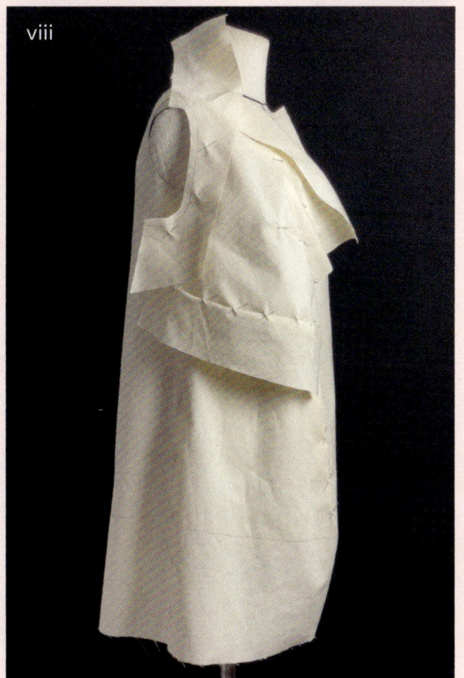

Jacket
Prepare D1, C, and B1, B2 and B3 following the pattern-cutting instructions in step 2 (pp. 112–13). Cut out D1 and C with the armholes intact.

(v) Make the three darts on the jacket front (D1). Mark the armhole. Drape the piece on the dress form.

(vi) Fold the lapel back and pin it into place.

(vii) Mark the armholes on the jacket side panel (C) and place it on top of D1, matching the armholes.

(viii) Cut out the armholes on C and D1.

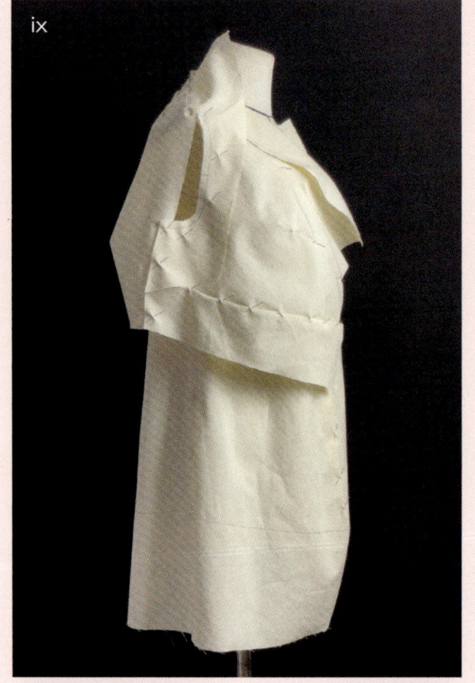

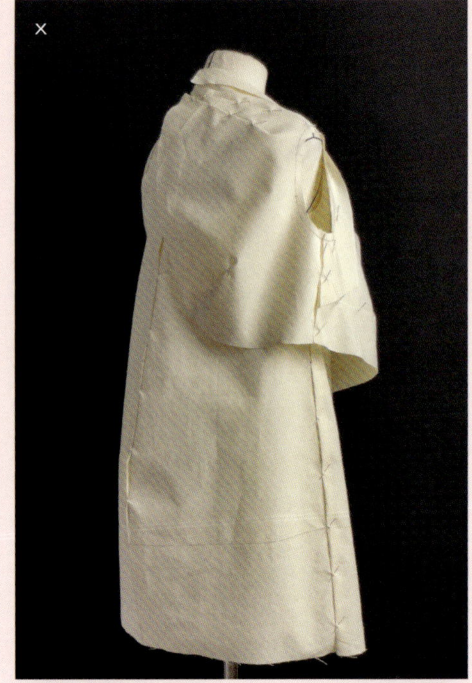

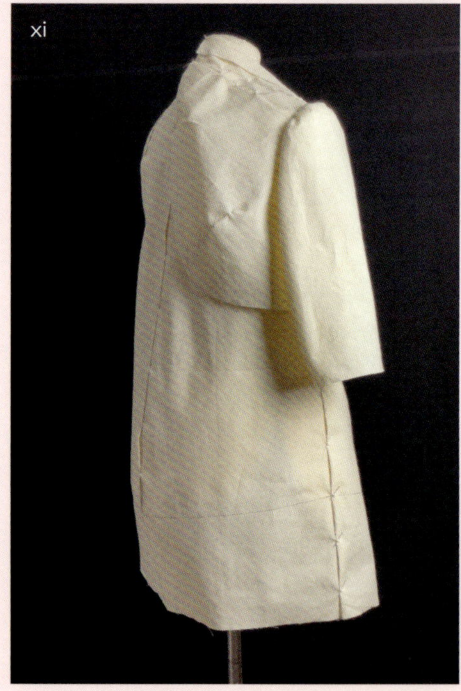

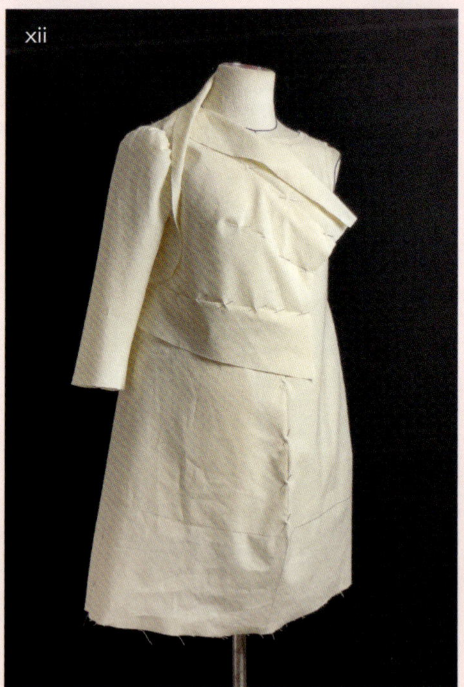

(ix) Mark the armholes on the jacket back (B1). Make the three darts and drape the piece onto D1, securing at the shoulder and side seam.

(x) Cut out the armhole on C.

(xi) Make the four darts on the head of the upper sleeve (B2). Join the upper and under sleeves (B2 and B3) together. Make an ease stitch on the sleeve head. Attach the sleeve to the jacket.

(xii) The finished drape.

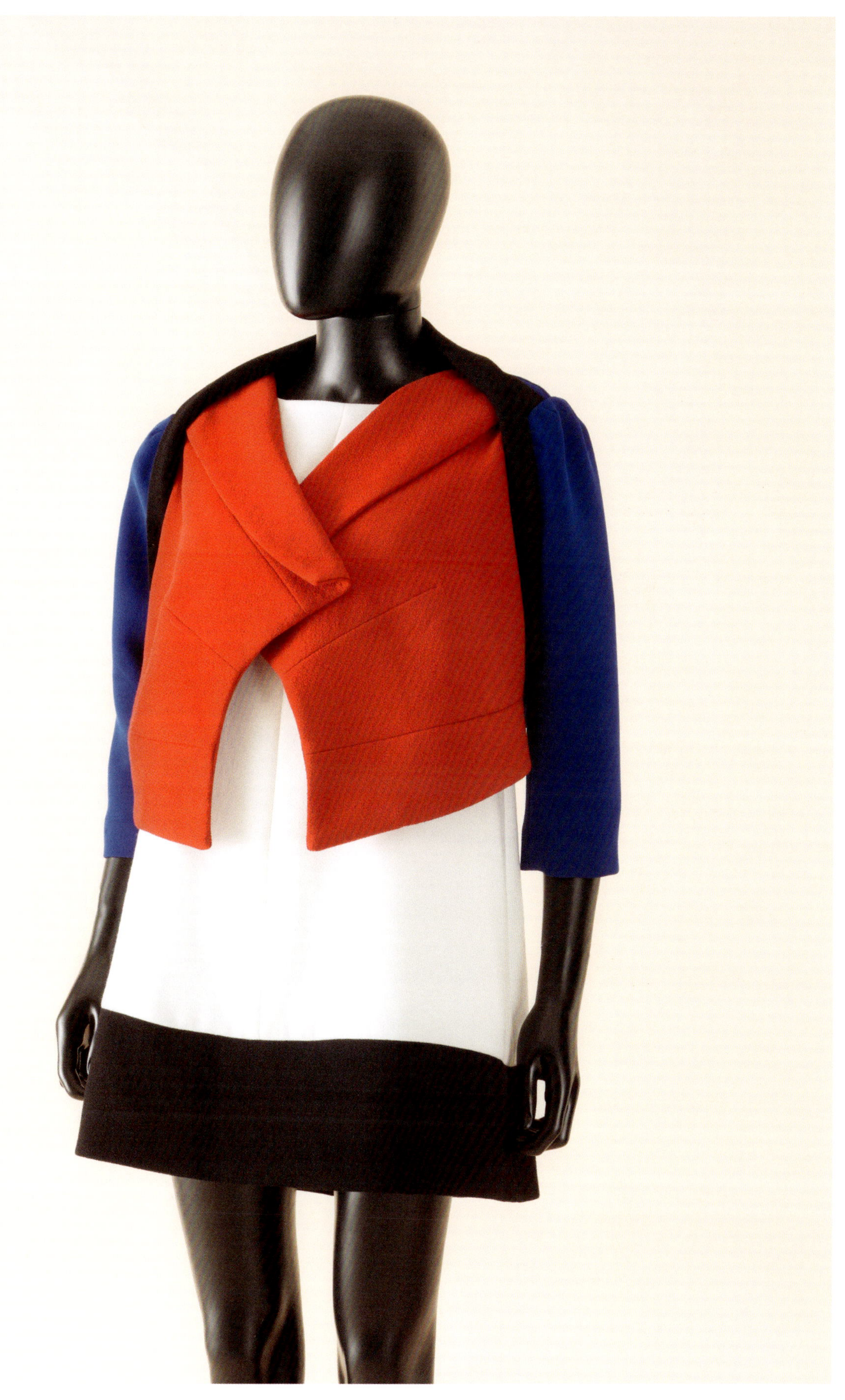

Composition Abstraite dress and jacket

Composition Abstraite minidress

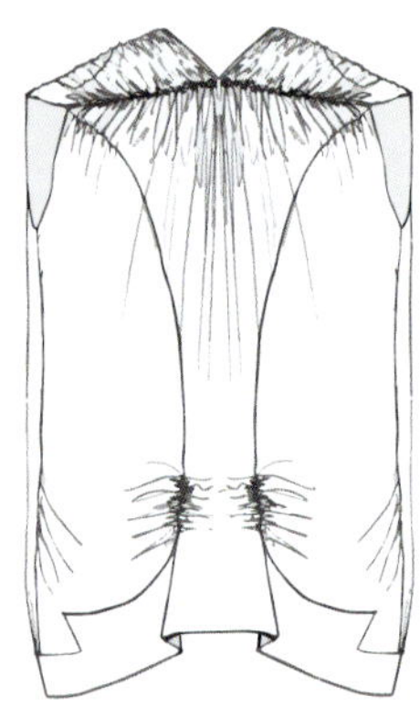

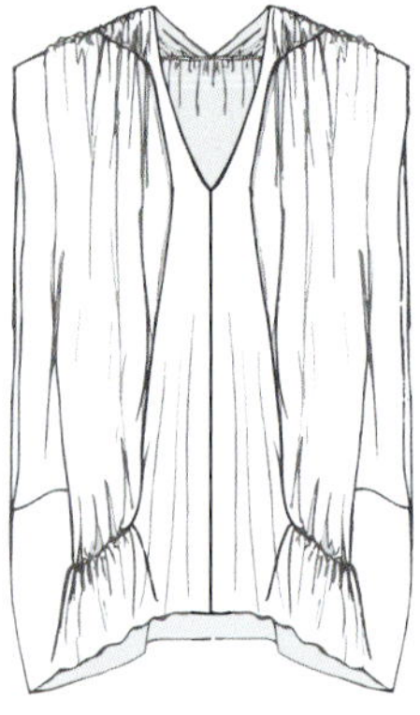

I was struck by the dynamism of the solid blocks of colour in Poliakoff's *Composition Abstraite* (p. 103 bottom). I initially intended to disregard the cream background and use only the two abstract shapes in blue and red. However, during development, the background became an integral part of the garment, acting as a frame to contain the blue and red sections. The garment features gathers that form soft drapes throughout, enhanced by a viscose jersey with minimum stretch; the blue and
red sections are cut on the bias to maximize the draped effect. The final minidress can be worn back-to-front.

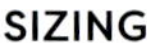

SIZING

The example here is a size B (12–16; US 8–12).

Measurements:
Width: 68cm (26¾in)
Height: 85cm (33½in)
Length: 82cm (32¼in)

To create additional sizes, grade the pattern (see p. 10).

FABRIC SUGGESTIONS

All colours: Viscose jersey, or any drapey fabric with minimal stretch.

COLOUR REFERENCES

Custard: #E6D8AC
Blue: #2A3B3F
Red: #BE2628

1

Examine the artwork shapes.

Custard = **A**
Blue = **B**
Red = **C**

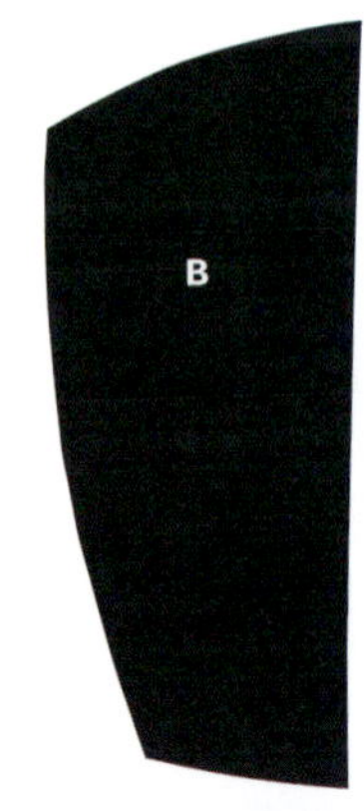

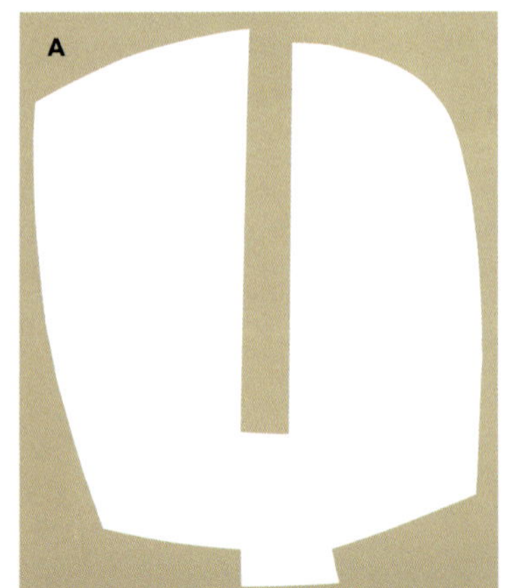

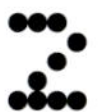

Plot the outlines of the shapes onto plain pattern paper. Place 5cm (2in) squared paper underneath the pattern paper as a guide.

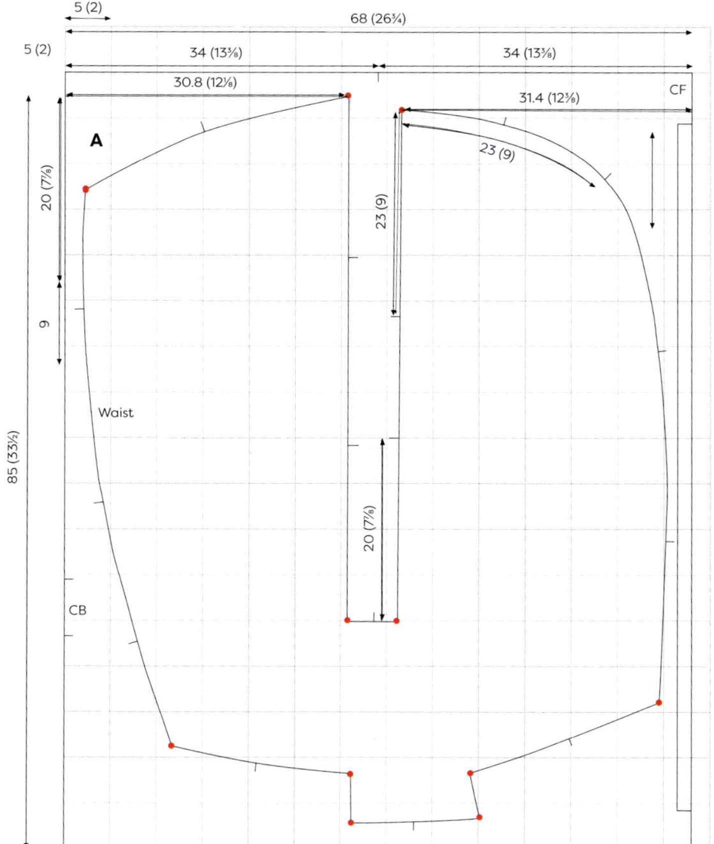

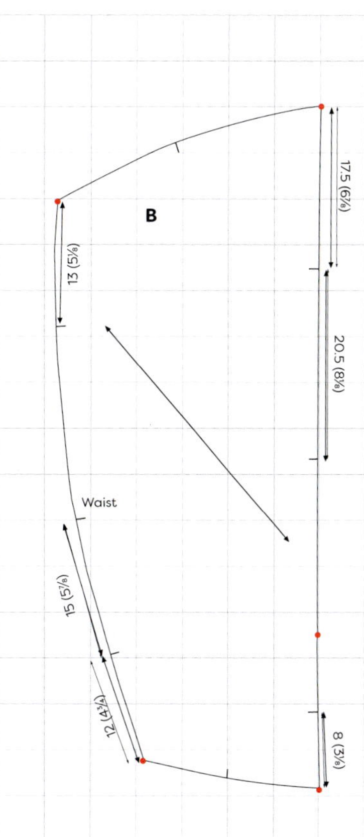

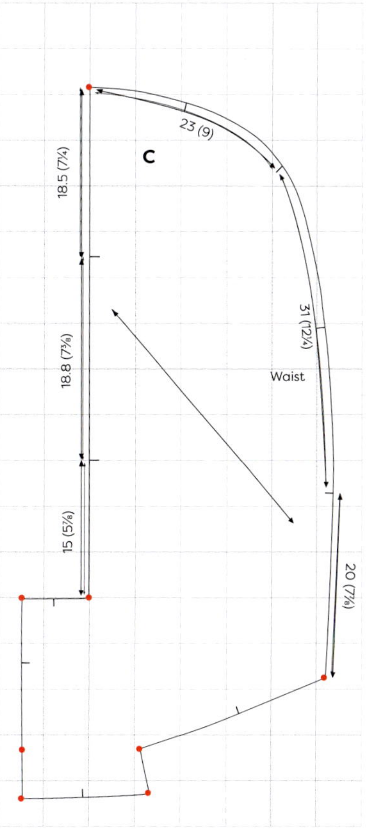

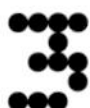

Mark grainlines, CF and CB, drill holes and notches on all pattern pieces.

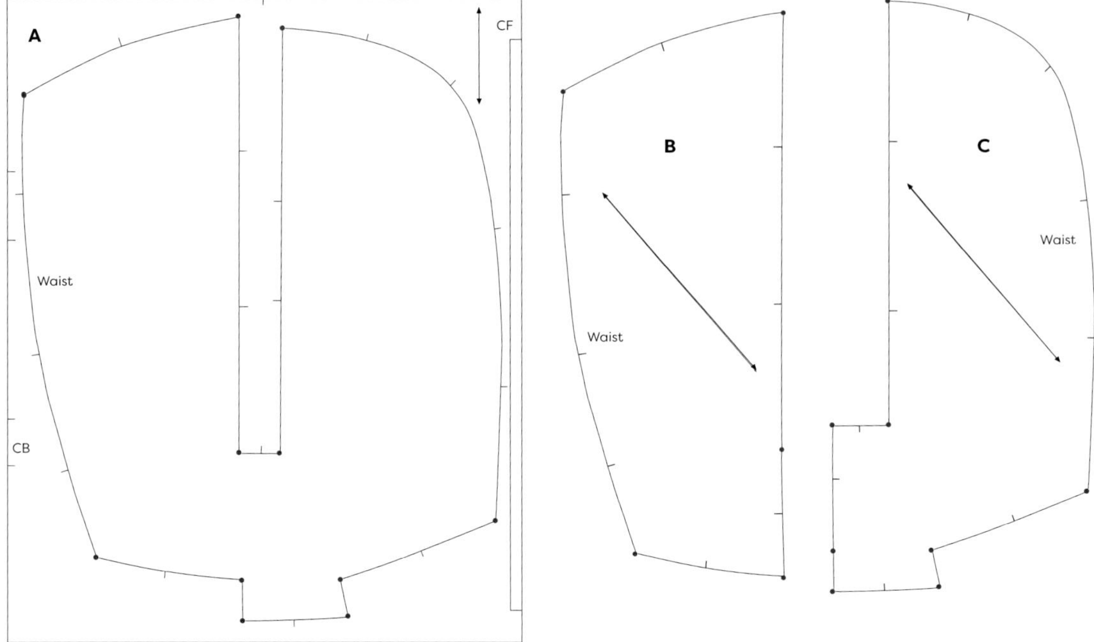

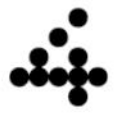

Add a 1cm (⅜in) seam allowance to each pattern piece. Add a 4cm (1⅝in) hem allowance to A.

Cut out the pattern pieces in jersey. Using a tracing wheel and carbon paper, transfer grainlines, CF and CB, drill holes and notches onto BOTH sides of the fabric.

A x 1 on fold

B x 1 pair

C x 1 pair

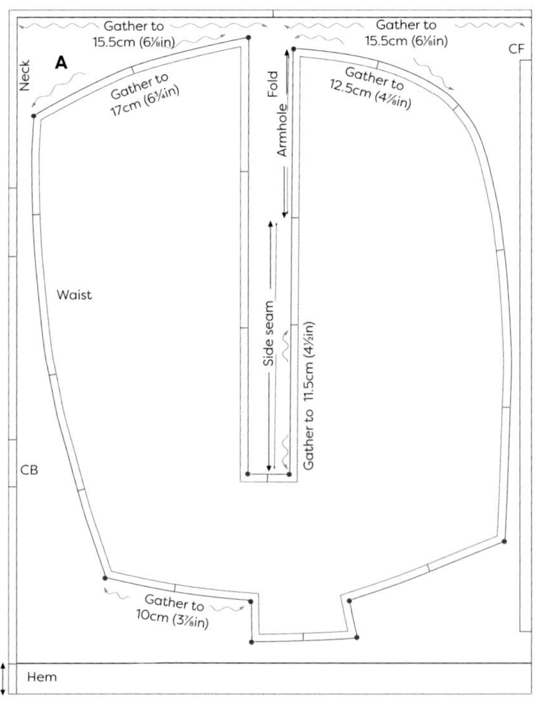

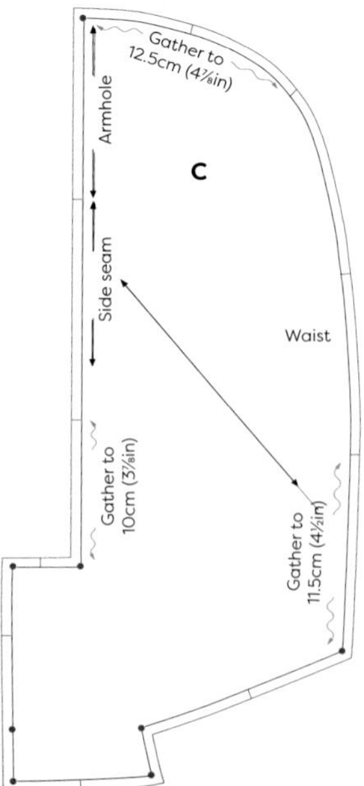

DRAPING THE SHAPES

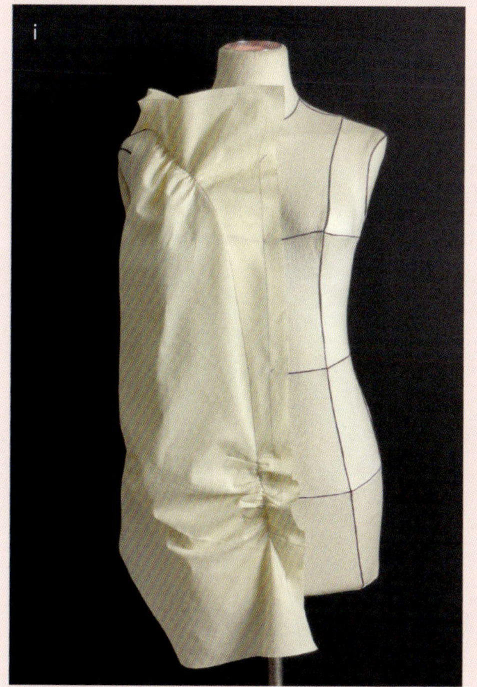
i

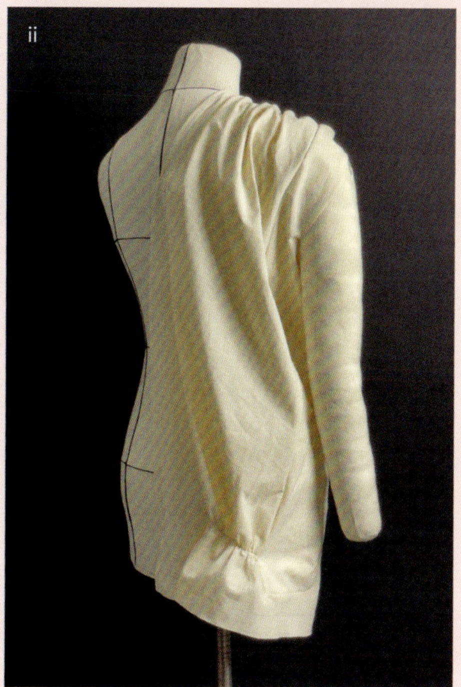
ii

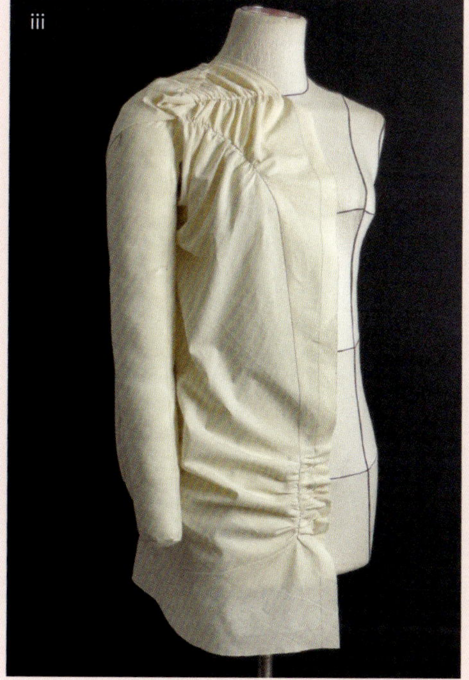
iii

Prepare the shapes following steps 2–4 of the pattern-cutting instructions (pp. 121–22).

As this design is symmetrical, it can be draped on one half of the dress form.

(i) Gather the marked sections on A (except for those along the top edge) and C. Attach C to the front of A.

(ii) Gather the marked sections on B and attach to the back of A.

(iii) Gather the top edge of A. Fold A in half where marked and stitch together.

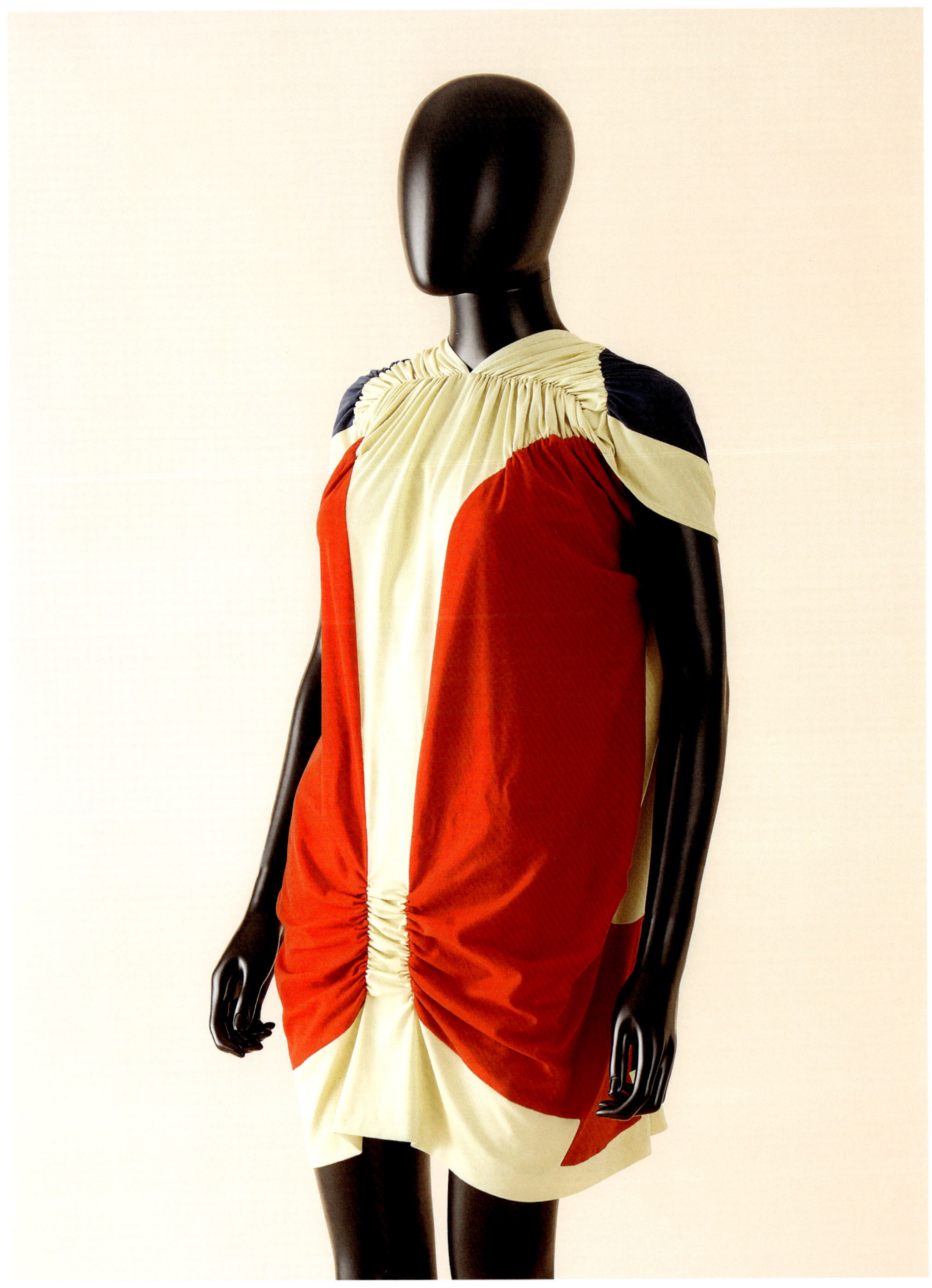

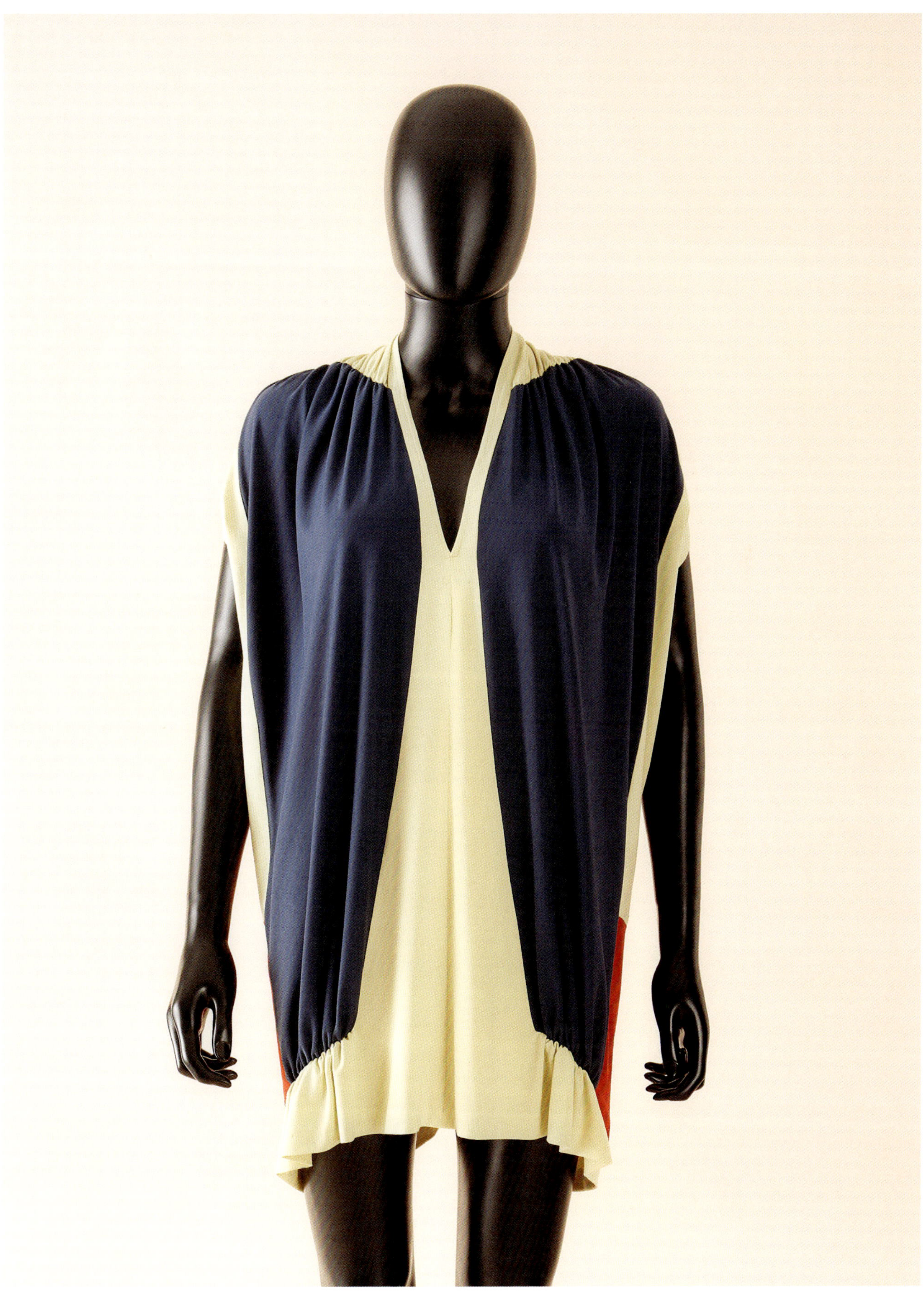

Composition Abstraite minidress

MICHAEL WALL

Michael Wall (b. 1992, Norwich, Norfolk, UK) is a London-based artist whose work in painting, sculpture and digital media addresses scale, form and colour. Wall's work is profoundly influenced by Kazimir Malevich, who founded Suprematism, an artistic movement focused on geometric forms, which Malevich felt expressed 'pure feeling'.

Pink Natural IV, 2017, powdered pigments and paint on paper.

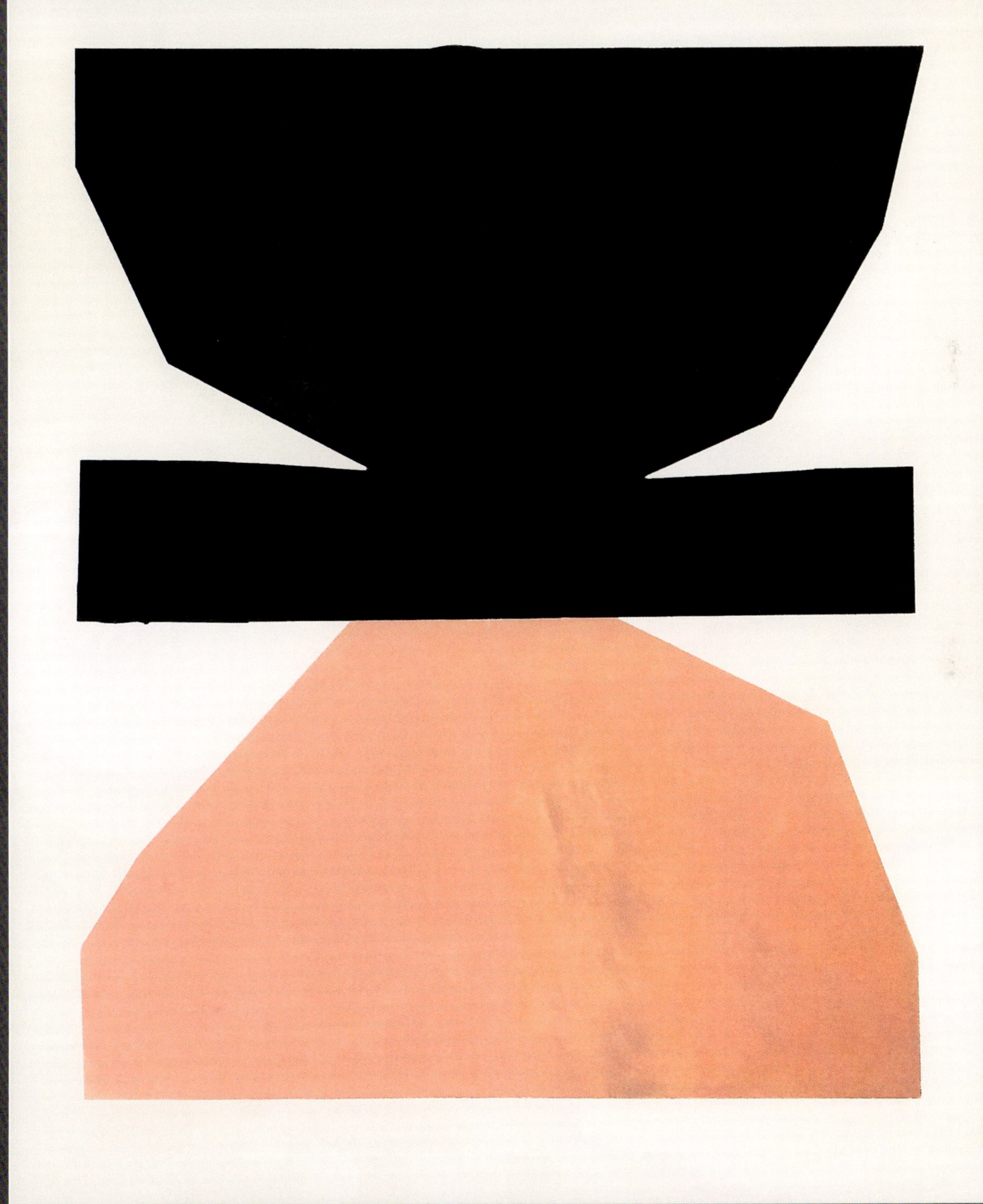

Pink Natural IV bodice

One of my favourite colour combinations is pink and black, so I was immediately drawn to Wall's *Pink Natural IV*. The dynamic geometric shapes led me to envision a bustier-style bodice with a structured peplum, reminiscent of an 18th-century court dress. The top is fitted under the bust but sits away from the figure at the waist and hips.

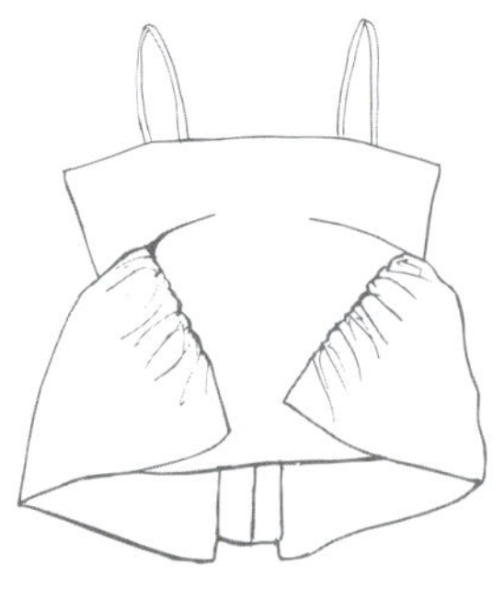

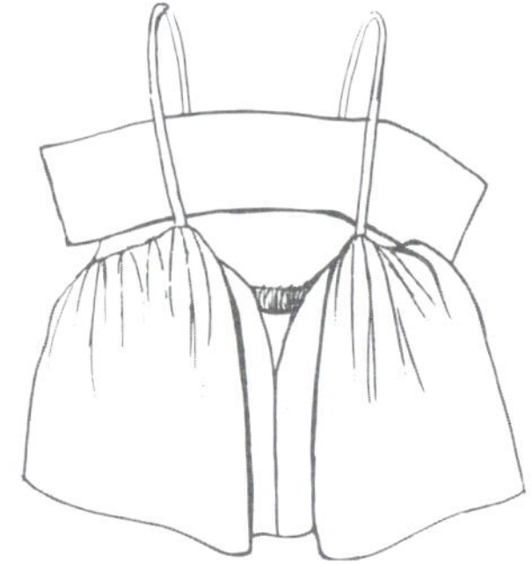

SIZING

The example here is a size 10 (US 6).

Measurements:

Under bust: 82cm (32¼in)

Length: 42cm (16½in)

Grosgrain ribbon: Two pieces, each 22 × 2.5cm (8⅝ × 1in)

To create additional sizes, grade the pattern (see p. 10).

FABRIC SUGGESTIONS

Black: Medium-weight woven fabrics, such as double wool crepe or viscose; heavy wool jersey double-knit.

Pink: Viscose or silk duchesse satin, organdie, heavy satin-backed crepe.

For the sample I used deadstock double wool crepe and viscose satin backed with tarlatan.

COLOUR REFERENCES

Black #000000

Pink #CC8687

Examine the artwork shapes.

Black = **A**

Pink = **B1** and **B2**

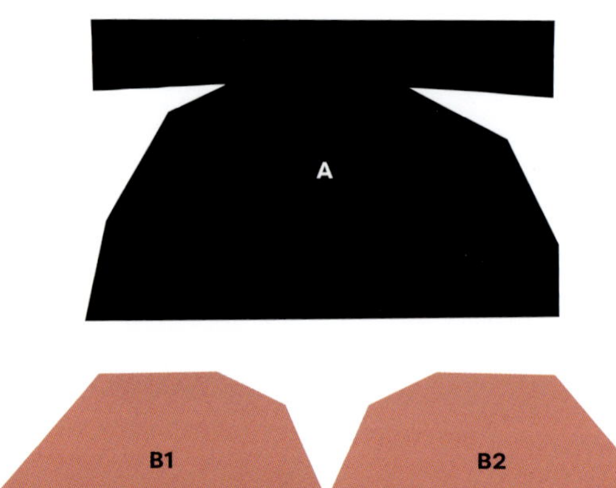

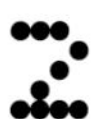

Plot the outlines of the shapes onto plain pattern paper. Place 5cm (2in) squared paper underneath the pattern paper as a guide. To create the facing (C), trace the top rectangular part of section A and reverse it.

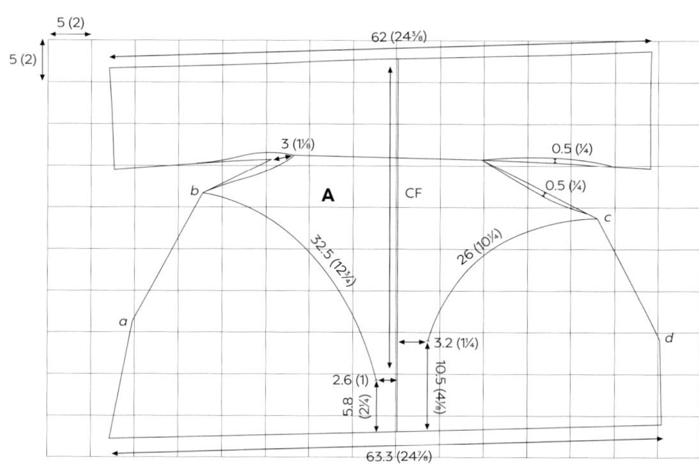

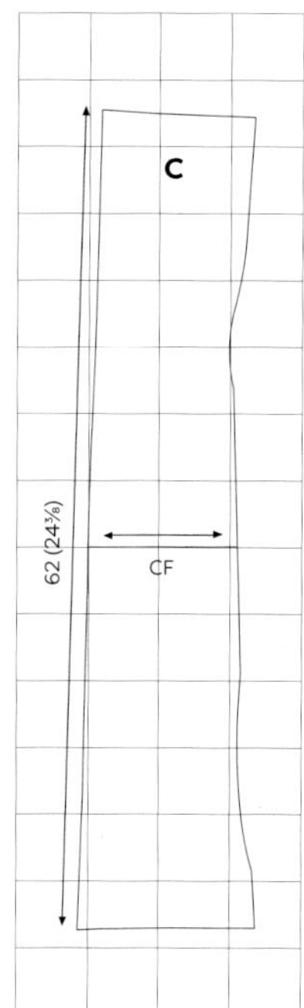

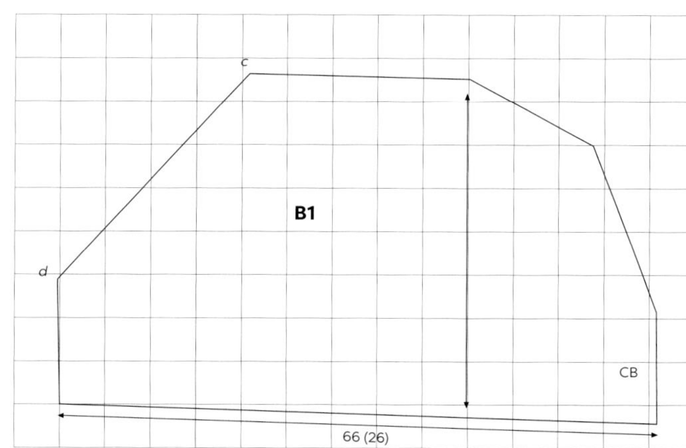

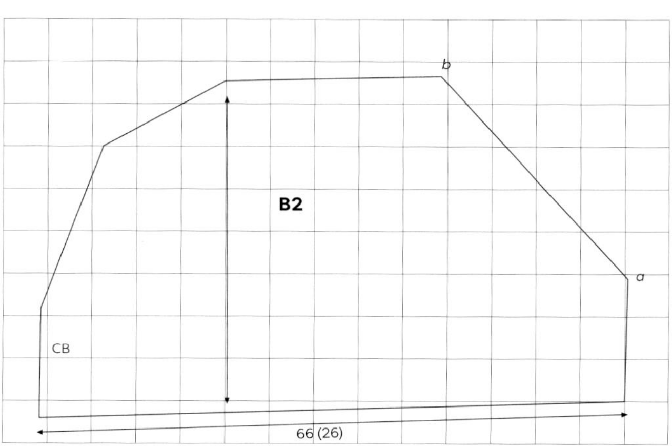

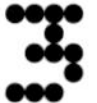

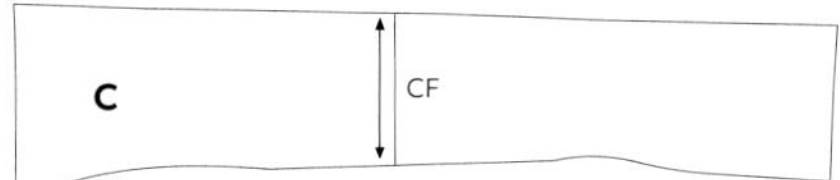

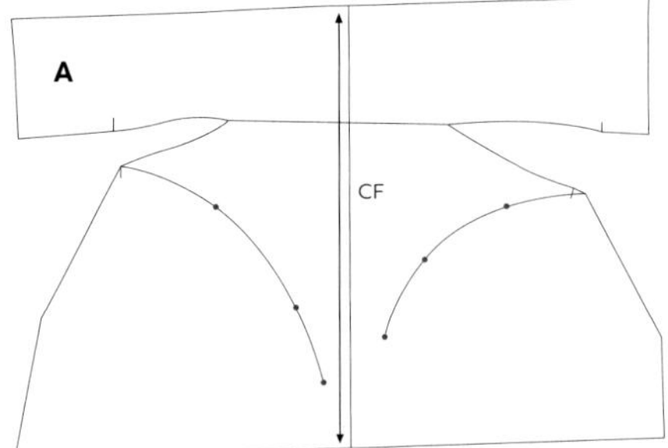

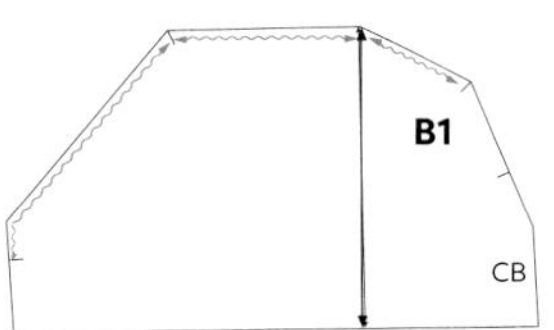

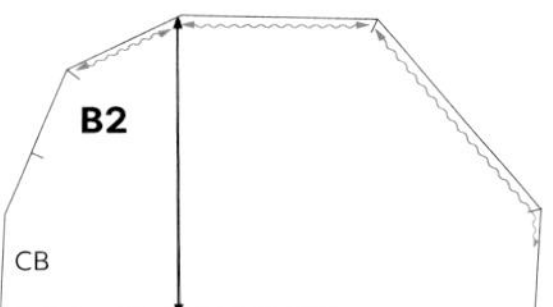

On A, soften the angles of the bust darts, following the grid diagram. Mark CF and CB and grainlines on all pattern pieces. Mark the arcs on A. Mark the darts on B1 and B2. Mark grainlines, CF and CB, drill holes and notches on all pieces.

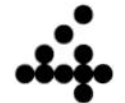

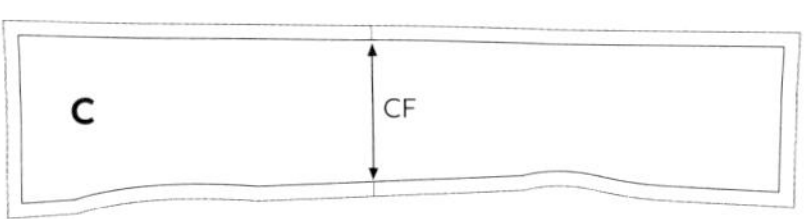

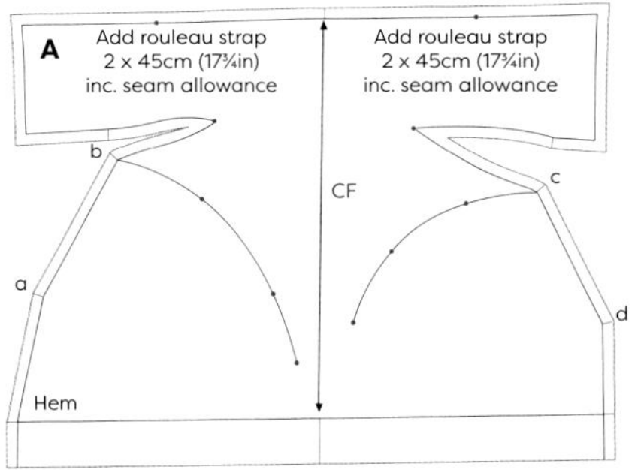

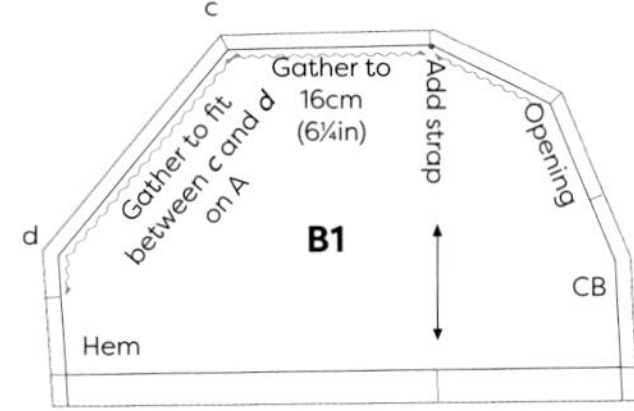

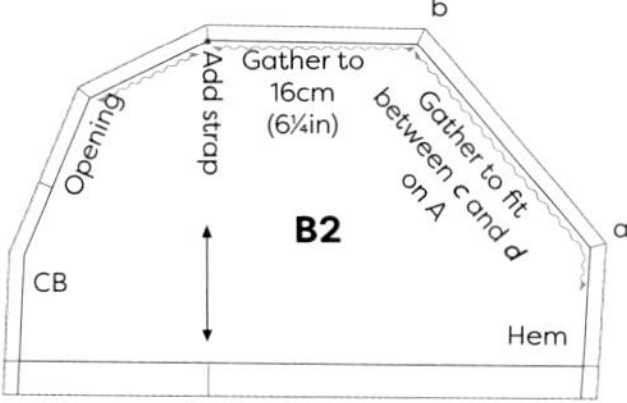

Add a 1cm (¼in) seam allowance around each pattern piece. Add a 4cm (1⅝in) hem allowance to A, B1 and B2. Cut out the pieces in calico (muslin):

A (Front) x 1 RSU
B1 (Back left) x 1 RSU
B2 (Back right) x 1 RSU
C (Front facing) x 1

Using a tracing wheel and carbon paper, transfer grainlines, CF and CB, darts, arcs, drill holes and notches onto BOTH sides of the fabric.

DRAPING THE SHAPES

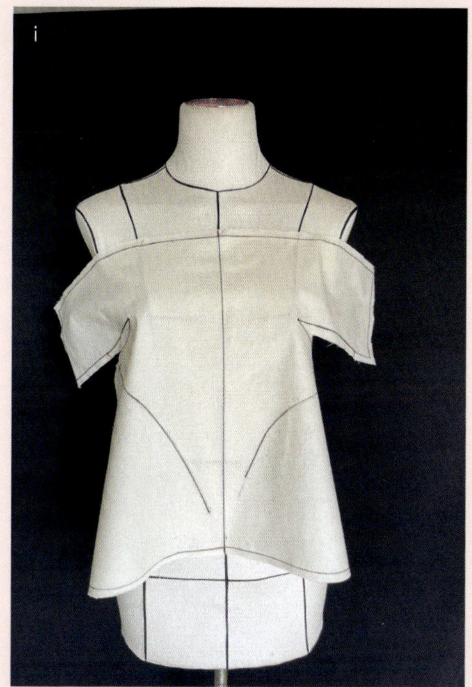
i

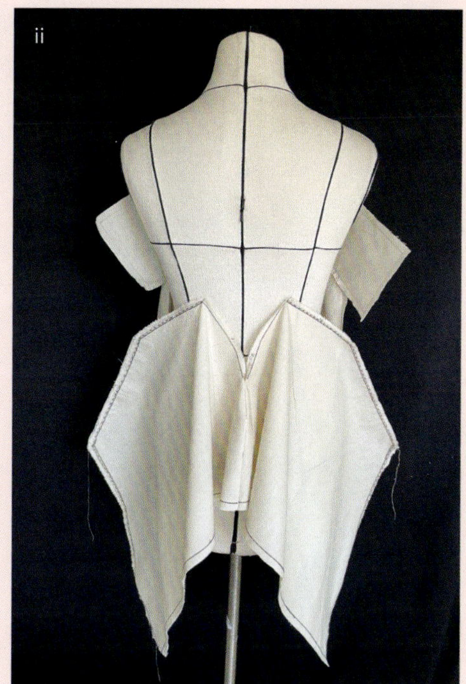
ii

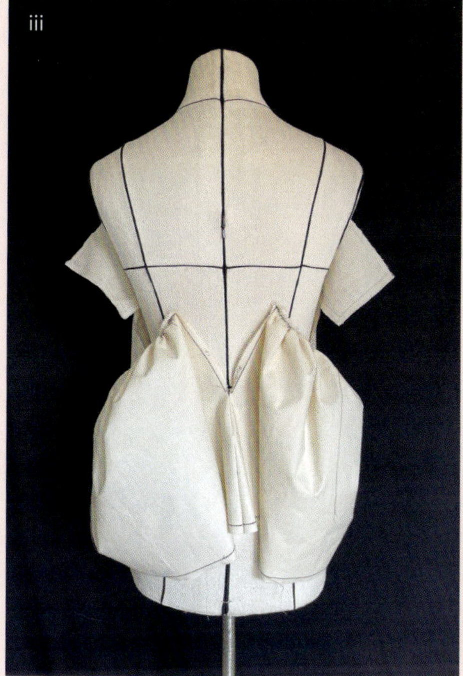
iii

Prepare the shapes following steps 2–4 of the pattern-cutting instructions (pp. 129–30).

(i) Pin the front (A) onto the dress form, aligning the CF and setting the bust darts into position. Close the darts.

(ii) On the back sections (B1 and B2), stitch two rows of gathering stitches within the seam allowance. Join B1 and B2 together along the CB. Pin the joined B section onto the dress form 10.5cm (4⅛in) above the waistline and 6.5cm (2½in) out from the CB (position 1).

(iii) Gather the back sections to fit between the side seam and position 1.

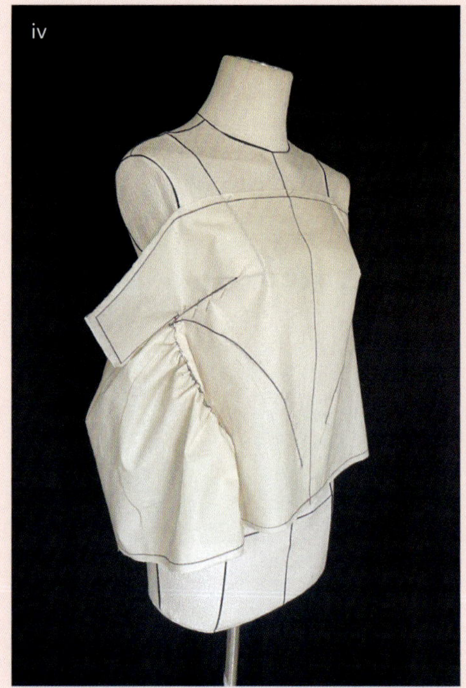

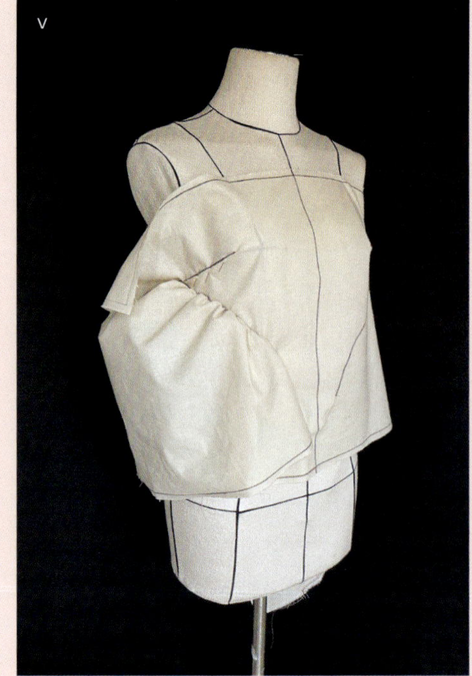

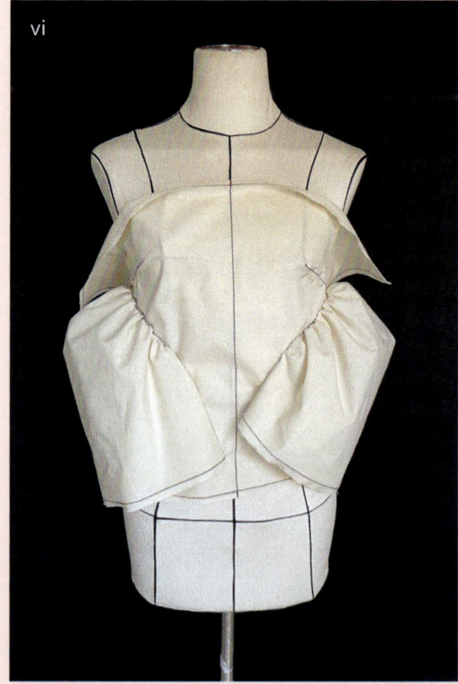

(iv, v) Attach the gathered section on the back right of B to the front right of A, easing the gathering to fit. Pin to the curve.

(vi) Attach the gathered section on the back left of B to the front left of A, easing the gathering to fit. Pin to the curve to complete the drape. Add straps following the pattern instructions.

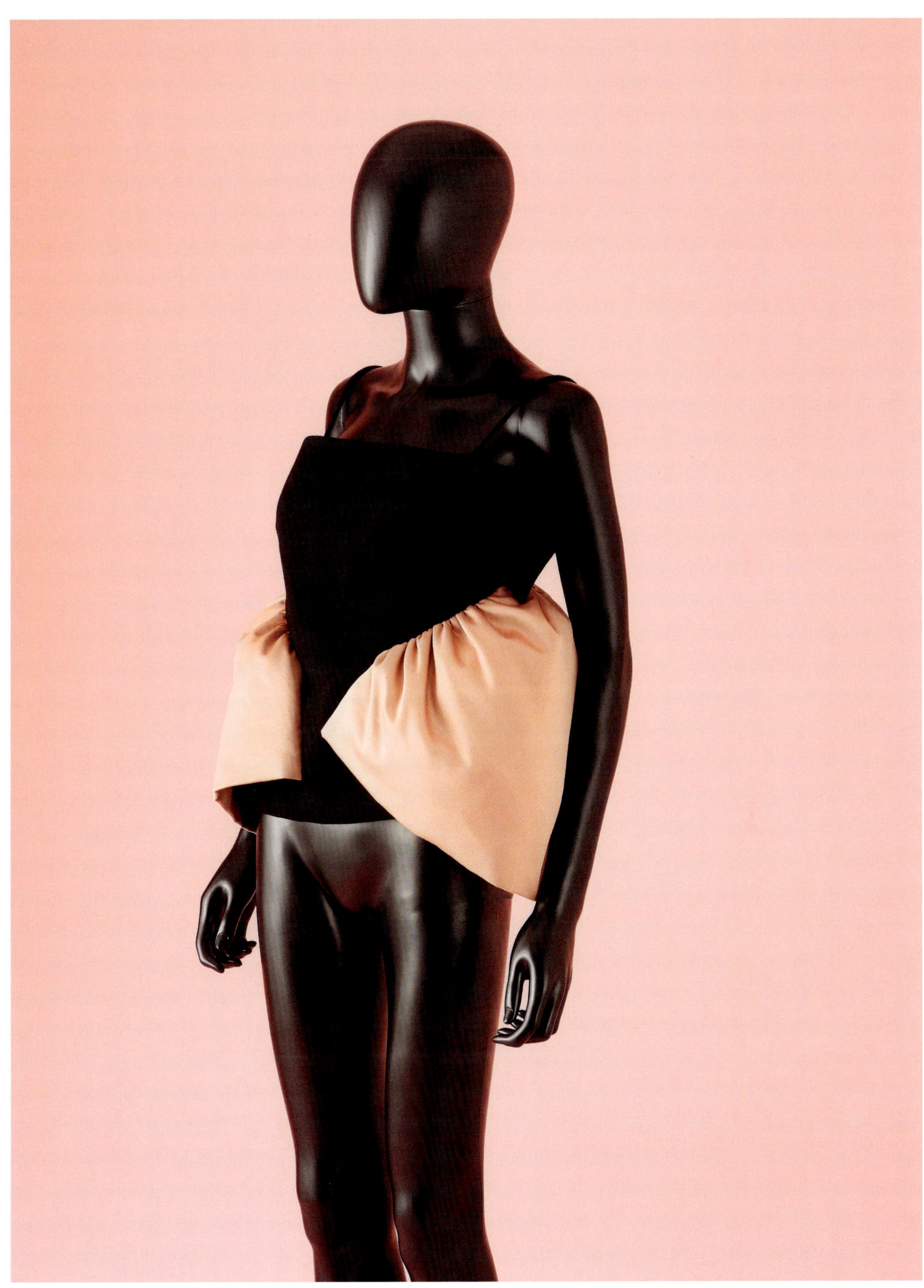

Pink Natural IV bodice

ACKNOWLEDGEMENTS

Thank you to the following suppliers for their generous discounts on purchased fabrics and services used for developing the projects:

Julie at **Harris Tweed Scotland** (harristweedscotland.co.uk), for supplying the tweed for the Lubaina Himid *Carpet* jacket: theharristweedstore.co.uk/collections/all-plain-pieces-by-the-metre-half-quarter.

Nick Parkin at **Parkin** (www.parkinfabrics.co.uk), for supplying the tarlatan I used to develop my initial drapes: www.parkinfabrics.co.uk/products/tarlatan-150cm.

Doug Davies at **The Silk Bureau Limited** (www.silkbureau.co.uk), for printing the artwork pattern for the June Harwood Untitled 1974 top. Patterns can be uploaded to The Silk Bureau's on-demand textile printing service at www.silkbureau.co.uk/submit-an-order.

The team at **Woolcrest Fabric** (woolcrestfabric.com), for supplying deadstock fabric.

Ciment Pleating (www.cimentpleating.com) crystal-pleated the fabric for the Ronan Bouroullec *Drawing 10* and *Drawing 11* dresses through their pleating service: www.cimentpleating.com/services.

The viscose jersey stretch knit for the Serge Poliakoff *Composition Abstraite* (3) minidress was sourced through **Minerva** (www.minerva.com).

Sewable pattern material is available from the **Pattern Cutting Deconstructed** online store (www.patterncuttingdeconstructed.com/store/products/pcd-trace-sew-sewable-pattern-material.

Special thanks to my editors, Sophie and Jodi, for their enthusiasm and support for my idea that only resolved itself as I worked through each project.

Thanks to my family and friends for their encouragement.

Love to Ren, my god-grandson, who was seven years old when I started this book. He made me laugh as we chatted about how important it is to cry and not bottle up emotions. Our conversation continued with me excitedly sharing news of my book deal and explaining how I now had to test everything to ensure my ideas translated into viable projects. With the wisdom only a child could have, he asked, 'Would you cry if things didn't work out?' My answer was an emphatic yes. But I reassured him – and myself – that I would keep going until I got it right. I hope I've done just that.

CREDITS

All final garment photography by Simon Pask.
All draping photography by Monisola Omotoso.

Introduction, p. 7 (left): Alamy/Antiquarian Images; **p. 7 (right):** Alamy/Alain Gil Gonzalez/ABACAPRESS.COM; **p. 8:** Getty Images/Victor VIRGILE/Gamma-Rapho; **p. 9:** Monisola Omotoso

Ronan Bouroullec, pp. 14–15: © Ronan et Erwan Bouroullec

June Harwood, pp. 26–27: © The June Harwood Charitable Trust

Carmen Herrera, pp. 44–45: *Yesterday* © Estate of Carmen Herrera; Courtesy Lisson Gallery. *Equation* © Estate of Carmen Herrera; Courtesy Lisson Gallery. *Blanco y Verde* © Estate of Carmen Herrera; Courtesy Lisson Gallery. Image Courtesy The Ella Fontanals-Cisneros Collection

Lubaina Himid, pp. 64–65: © Lubaina Himid

Henri Matisse, p. 76–77: *Le Coeur* and *Formes,* images: Bridgeman Images/Philadelphia Museum of Art, Pennsylvania, PA, USA. *Papiers Découpés,* image: Berggrüen et Cie

Serge Poliakoff, pp. 102–3: © Poliakoff Estate. Courtesy Timothy Taylor Gallery, London. © ADAGP, Paris and DACS, London 2024

Michael Wall, pp. 126–27: ©Michael Wall (https://mmmwww.co.uk)

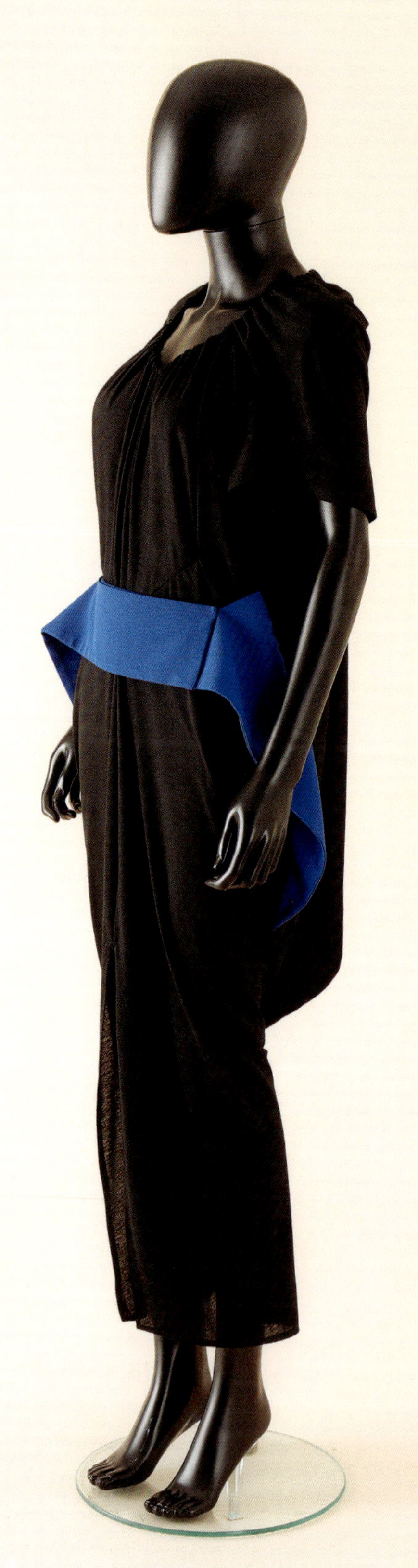